ILEX FOUNDATION SERIES 4

THE RHETORIC OF BIOGRAPHY

Also in the Ilex Foundation Series

Dreaming across Boundaries:
The Interpretation of Dreams in Islamic Lands

Strī:
Women in Epic Mahābhārata

Persian Literature and Judeo-Persian Culture:
Collected Writings of Sorour S. Soroudi

THE RHETORIC OF BIOGRAPHY

NARRATING LIVES IN PERSIANATE SOCIETIES

Edited by
L. Marlow

Ilex Foundation
Boston, Massachusetts
and
Center for Hellenic Studies
Trustees for Harvard University
Washington, D. C.

Distributed by Harvard University Press
Cambridge, Massachusetts, and London, England

The Rhetoric of Biography: Narrating Lives in Persianate Societies
Edited by L. Marlow

Published by Ilex Foundation, Boston, Massachusetts and the Center for Hellenic Studies, Trustees for Harvard University, Washington, D.C.

Distributed by Harvard University Press, Cambridge, Massachusetts and London, England

Production editor: Christopher Dadian
Cover design: Joni Godlove
Printed in the United States of America

Cover images are from a nineteenth-century *qalamdān* in the collection of Olga M. Davidson

Library of Congress Cataloging-in-Publication Data
The rhetoric of biography : narrating lives in Persianate societies / edited by L. Marlow.
p. cm. -- (The Ilex Foundation series ; 4)
Includes bibliographical references and index.
ISBN 978-0-674-06066-1 (pbk. : alk. paper)
1. Persian prose literature--History and criticism. 2. Iran--Biography--History and criticism. 3. Autobiography--Persian authors. I. Marlow, Louise.
PK6413.R54 2011
891'.5509--dc22
[B]

2010052568

CONTENTS

Introduction

Of the six articles gathered in this collection, four originated as papers delivered at the Fifth Biennial Conference on Iranian Studies held in Bethesda, Maryland in May 2004. At that conference, Michael Cooperson, Stephen Dale, Olga Merck Davidson and Mohammad Jafar Mahallati participated in a panel devoted to the production of biographies and autobiographies in Iran or written in the Persian language. Devin Stewart and Maria Szuppe kindly agreed to contribute articles of their own at a later date. Some of the essays that comprise the present volume have evolved considerably in the years that have passed since the convening of the conference. The emphasis on cultural production in Iran and the larger Persianate world has been retained, however, and of the three languages (Arabic, Persian and Turkish) used in the materials in the collection, it is Persian that is predominant.

The volume's central purposes are to highlight, through a series of case studies, the scope, range and significance of the biographical and autobiographical literatures that have been composed in Persian, or that have arisen in a Persianate cultural milieu, and to explore the particular place and functions of biography and autobiography in Persianate societies. The rich biographical literature in Arabic, epitomised by the distinctive genre of the "biographical dictionary," has enjoyed extensive study,[1] and Arabic autobiographical writings, once unacknowledged or ignored, have also received considerable attention over the past decade and a half.[2] It is hoped that the collection of the current articles into a single volume will not only augment the still relatively limited scholarly literature devoted to Persian auto/biographical writings but also facilitate larger, more comparative studies, including considerations of the connections of the Persian literature with its counterparts in Arabic and Turkish.

The present collection has been assembled in accordance with Arnaldo Momigliano's observation of the fluidity among biography, autobiography and history, expressed in an interlinking of the historical events of the external world with the internal and subjective life of individuals, such that

1. On the distinctive quality of the (Arabic) biographical dictionary, see Rosenthal 1968, 100-6; Khalidi 1973; Young 1990, 168–9; al-Qadi 1995. Recent years have seen the publication of many studies related to this abundant material; for a small number of examples, see bibliography.

2. Reynolds 1997, 2001.

"[a]utobiography referred back to biography, and biography to history."[3] Scholars of Arabic literature have long recognised the many intersections between biography and historiography: Franz Rosenthal's pioneering *A History of Muslim Historiography* (Second Revised Edition, Leiden: E. J. Brill, 1968) treated biography as sub-division of historiography; more recently Chase Robinson has proposed a generic typology according to which biography, prosopography and chronography comprise the three principal ways of organising historical narrative.[4] Wadad al-Qadi has presented biographical dictionaries as media for an "alternative" history of the Muslim community, in which scholars availed themselves of the freer, more flexible form of the biographical dictionary rather than the more circumscribed chronicle.[5] Specialists in the Arabic biographical literature have also drawn attention to its close relationship to *adab*.[6] Until relatively recently, Persian historiography and biography, especially for the early centuries of literary production in the language, had received considerably less sustained scholarly attention than their Arabic counterparts. In the past decade and a half, however, Julie Scott Meisami's landmark *Persian Historiography to the End of the Twelfth Century* (Edinburgh: Edinburgh University Press, 1999), together with the publications of several contributors to the current volume, have rectified this deficiency in significant measure, especially as far as historiography is concerned.[7]

The volume is inevitably far from comprehensive in its coverage of Persian biographical and autobiographical writings. Particularly regrettable, perhaps, is the lack of a contribution devoted to Persian hagiography.[8] Collectively, however, the articles are suggestive of the abundant and varied nature of Persianate auto/biographical writings, which differ widely in presentation, arrangement and subject.[9] Some contributions examine well-known works; others explore examples or aspects of auto/biographical

3. Momigliano 1985, 91; see further Momigliano 1971, 1–7, 12, 39–42, 101–4; Bowersock 1991, esp. 29–30.

4. Rosenthal 1968, 99–106; Robinson 2003, 55–79. See also W. al-Qadi 1998, I: 150.

5. Al-Qadi 2006.

6. Fähndrich 1973; Khalidi 1994.

7. See further Daniel 2004, Melville 2004, Szuppe 2004, Quinn 2004, and the works there cited.

8. Recent research into the literary representations in Persianate societies of the lives of saints and holy persons has generated a stimulating body of scholarship. A small number of relevant publications, many adopting the perspective of comparative hagiography, is included in the bibliography appended to this introduction; see especially Aigle 1995, 2000, Gajano 1997, and Paul 2003.

9. For example, as Grotzfeld has demonstrated for the Arabic biographical tradition, many collections of biographies were devoted to persons of standing in a particular profession, city or region, but people of lesser social status also attracted attention (Grotzfeld 1995); for similar trends in Persian, see the contribution of Maria Szuppe to the present volume.

writing that have received little or no previous attention. In their approach, the essays are concerned with the literary dimensions of biographical and autobiographical writings, and with the historical and cultural contexts that produced specific compositions. The contributing authors move beyond a utilitarian treatment of biographical writings principally as sources of factual information (or "data banks")[10] to consider the forms, functions, qualities and meanings of the literature in its own terms. Individual essays explore considerations of the public and private realms, the exemplary, cautionary or didactic functions of portraying lives, and what Momigliano referred to as the "experimentation on the borders of reality and fiction."[11] If only incidentally, the collection's constituent articles also address notions of "individuality," "personality" and "the self."[12] Certain essays constitute studies in the history of mentalities, and more than one contribution draws particular attention to the roles of women, both as subjects of biographies and as memoirists in their own right.[13]

As a group, the essays gathered in this collection indicate that, contrary to the presuppositions of an earlier era of scholarship, biographical and autobiographical writings were not restricted to European literatures but were well represented in the literatures of Muslim-majority societies from an early date. The articles suggest the extent, range and richness of biographical and autobiographical genres in the pre-modern and early modern Persian (as well as Arabic and Turkish) literary traditions. It is acknowledged that for readers of the modern literatures in European languages, the terms "biography" and "autobiography" evoke specific expectations, not all of which would have been shared by, or perhaps even recognisable to, the first audiences for the writings studied in the present volume (or, indeed, their pre-modern counterparts in European societies). Given that overly specific definitions of "biography" and "autobiography" have sometimes complicated or even precluded the recognition of biographical and autobiographical writings in non-European languages, however, the present volume avoids rigid classificatory formulations, including the drawing of fixed boundaries between the realms of biography and autobiography.[14]

10. Robinson 2003, 71. Notable approaches to the study of (primarily Arabic) biographical dictionaries include those deployed in Bulliet 1970, 1979; Malti-Douglas 1977, 1980; and Fähndrich 1973, 1977. See also Young 1990, 176–7; Robinson 2003; Hurvitz 1997, 43–4, n. 8.

11. Momigliano 1971, 65.

12. For treatments of these issues with primary reference to Arabic writings, see especially Leder 1990, Schippers 1995, Reynolds 2001.

13. For treatments of the roles in women in Arabic biographical sources, see Roded 1994, Köhler 1997. For examples in Persian or Persianate contexts, see Hambly 1998, and especially Szuppe 1998.

14. "Since any biography is inevitably selective we cannot separate biography from autobiography which is the account of a life written by the man who is living it" (Momigliano 1971, 11).

It has been noted that biographical writings often include autobiographical passages, and that classical Arabic lacks a designation for "autobiography" as opposed to "biography," although this absence should not be taken to imply that autobiographies did not constitute an established genre.[15] As the contributions to the present volume demonstrate, the Arabic, Persian and Turkish biographical and autobiographical genres, like their European counterparts, are characterised by memories of and reflections on the past; as Karl Weintraub has written, "The meaning of the past is intelligible and meaningful in terms of the present understanding.... Facts are thus placed into relationships retroactively in which they did not stand when they were first experienced."[16]

As a whole, the present volume treats the literary production of a broad but culturally interlinked geographical area. Although, as already noted, a majority of the articles are devoted to biographical and autobiographical writings in Persian, some of them address compositions in Arabic and Chaghatay Turkish, and several essays illustrate the relationships among two or more of the three literatures in specific historical contexts. In cultural settings where many educated persons were at least bilingual if not multilingual, the role of Arabic remained important, especially (though by no means inevitably) in religious and scientific contexts. Olga Davidson's article, devoted to the vita of Ferdowsī, reflects the period in which, in the context of a multilingual environment where Arabic had served as a literary, if not a spoken, lingua franca, new forms of literary Persian were emerging and developing. The contribution of Devin Stewart explores an Arabic biographical dictionary produced in seventeenth-century Iran, and demonstrates the continuing significance of the Arabic language in the scholarly culture of a predominantly Persian-speaking environment. Persian also developed into and functioned widely as a literary lingua franca in wider Iranian and Persianate cultural settings. As Stephen Dale indicates, the Mughal Emperor Bābur (1483–1530) wrote in Chaghatay Turkish, but his work was closely fashioned on Persian models and was rapidly made available in that language; Bābur's family members followed his example with compositions in Persian of their own. The biographical works explored by Maria Szuppe, also written in Persian, reflect the Turkic-Persianate environment of Central Asia. Indeed, several of the essays collected in this volume attest to the interconnections among various languages, and the passage of literary materials from one linguistic context to another. Most notably, the

15. Kilpatrick 1998, I: 111. On the appearance of and usage of terms for "biography" and "autobiography" in classical, late antique and European contexts, see Momigliano 1971, 12, 14–15, 23–42; Cox 1983; cf. Robinson 2003, 71.

16. Weintraub 1975, 826.

example studied by Michael Cooperson involves multiple transpositions, across cultural and linguistic boundaries and, even more dramatically, from one medium to another, from classical Arabic historiographical sources to modern Iranian television.

Olga Merck Davidson's article studies the traditional biographical narratives that arose in connection with the figure of Ferdowsī, and the role of these narratives in shaping (and reflecting) the reception history of his great epic, the *Shāhnāma*. Davidson's principal materials for this study are the varied prefaces, composed in prose, appended to manuscript copies of the poem. She explores these prefaces, and in particular the two most frequently encountered examples, the "Older" Preface and the Baysonghorī Preface, less as sources for historical information than as compositions with a distinct narrative logic and meaning of their own. Most notably, Davidson brings to light not only the positive reception of the epic but also a corresponding negative reception. Concerned less with the historical accuracy or veracity of the biographical accounts contained in the prefaces than with the poetic agenda that they seek to convey, she demonstrates the ways in which the prefaces served to contexualise the poet and his poem. Davidson's article presents a case study of the processes by which myth supercedes history, or historicity, in such "lives of poets" traditions.

Mohammad Jafar Mahallati's discussion of the *Tārīkh-i jahān-goshā* treats the celebrated work of Mongol historiography less as a source for the history of the period than as an incidental work of autobiography, in which the author, Aṭā-Malek Jovaynī, reveals himself. The article is concerned with Jovaynī not only as an observer of but also as an actor in the historical events that he recounts. Mahallati draws attention to Jovaynī's ambiguous position: he identifies with the plight of the conquered peoples, yet serves the Mongol administration; in his writing, he is beholden to and yet critical of his overlords. The article illustrates Jovaynī's careful balancing of perspectives, and his employment of a range of literary devices designed to convey and conceal meanings for the benefit of various constituencies among his audience. Mahallati demonstrates how Jovaynī's unsettled position recapitulates an already well-established model of the rewards and perils of administrative service, a trajectory that leads in this case, as in many others, towards the statesman-historian's unfortunate end.

With reference to a broad set of Persian materials devoted to "lives of poets," **Maria Szuppe** explores collections (*tadhkeras*) of poets' biographies composed in post-Timurid Central Asia. Drawing extensively on unpublished manuscript sources, Szuppe's essay documents a change in mentality in the sixteenth to nineteenth centuries, during which period readers developed a strong interest in actual places, real people and their quotidian lives, as opposed to normative depictions of these subjects. From the late fifteenth-century collection of Dawlatshāh onwards, Persianate *tadhkeras* of poets include large amounts of contemporary material, and display an emphasis on the lives and verses of contemporary figures, many of them occasional rather than professional poets. Szuppe illustrates the degree to which poetic activity and poets' gatherings permeated all levels of society; the collections of the period indicate that poets, calligraphers and other literati originated not only from the upper administrative, military and religious classes, but also from the middle and even lower sections of post-Timurid society. Whereas the "life of Ferdowsī" traditions studied by Davidson reflect the "canonisation" of a version of the poet's life in conjunction with the growing stature of his unparalleled poem, Szuppe's compilers of poets' lives preserved the poetic utterances of figures whose names — let alone verses — would otherwise almost certainly have been lost.

Stephen Dale's article explores the relationships among the autobiographical compositions of four members of the Mughal ruling family of India: Bābur, the founder of the dynasty; his cousin Ḥaydar Mīrzā Dughlāt; his daughter Gulbadan Begim; and his great-grandson, the emperor Jahāngīr (1569–1628). Two of these individuals became rulers; one, a woman, was a devotee of the Chishti organisation of Sufis. As Dale indicates, the four royal individuals' writings are distinctive, yet in several places they allude to, draw on or amplify the works of their predecessors. Long recognised for their historical as well as their literary significance, these autobiographical writings serve to humanise these prominent figures from the past. The four compositions differ considerably in form, and indeed in language, and they were written with different purposes and audiences in mind. The earliest, Bābur's *Vaqāʾiʿ*, was written in Turki or Chaghatay Turkish, for purposes that the author does not specify; parts of it may have derived from a personal diary. The remaining three works were composed in Persian, ranging from the simple and unadorned style of Gulbadan Begim to the sophisticated works of Ḥaydar Mīrzā and Jahāngīr, both of whom, like Bābur, conformed to established standards of literary excellence by including plentiful citations of poetry. All four of these autobiographical works include the authors' retrospective reflections on the episodes and experiences of their lives.

Devin Stewart's article addresses the lives of women in Safavid Iran through a study of the entries concerned with women's lives in Mīrzā ʿAbdallāh al-Iṣfahānī's *Riyāḍ al-ʿulamāʾ*, a large biographical collection composed in Arabic in the late seventeenth century. Stewart's work explores in greater detail the important, if inconspicuous, place of women in the premodern biographical literature, and demonstrates the valuable resource that this literature provides for studies of the lives of women. Stewart's article augments and complements the growing number of such studies by its attention to the *Riyāḍ al-ʿulamāʾ*, a hitherto neglected collection that illuminates the roles of women in a Twelver Shiite scholarly context. It serves as a corrective to perceptions of pre-modern women, in predominantly Muslim societies as elsewhere, as having been deprived of agency, uneducated, invisible and lacking in status and power. In the course of his analysis, Stewart addresses several aspects of the roles of biographies, and of biographical dictionaries, in their historical contexts, and highlights especially their role in the construction of the authority of particular groups. In this context, he argues, the very inclusion of women in biographical collections indicates that the authors of such collections were ready to regard and present women as figures endowed with authority, and to confer on them the status implied by their belonging to the group with which the particular collection was concerned. Stewart's article includes a fully annotated translation of the section of the *Riyāḍ al-ʿulamāʾ* devoted to the biographies of women.

Michael Cooperson's article explores the translation of historical and hagiographical treatments of the relationship between the Caliph al-Maʾmūn and the Imam ʿAlī al-Riḍā (Emam Reza) to Iranian television. Cooperson analyses a recent serialisation of the historical events involving the two figures between the years 193–202/809–18, and explores the ways in which the television series draws on, recapitulates, modifies, synthesizes or ignores a variety of historical sources. The events, of high ideological significance in subsequent history, are presented differently in different historical sources, and a televised serialisation necessarily involves choices among the variant narratives contained in historical materials. Cooperson explores the adjustments and even inventions that are inescapable when written materials are translated to an audio-visual medium, as well as certain specific characteristics of the Iranian production. His article attests to the highly effective, indeed moving, results of the creative biographical process.

Presented together, the six articles demonstrate some of the range of Persian auto/biographical texts, and some of the historical and cultural conditions that affected their composition and reception. The essays also illuminate the roles played by the major languages in use in Iran and other Persianate societies, Arabic, Persian and Turkish, and the interplay among them. It is hoped that the articles assembled in this volume will supplement the scholarly literature on Persian biographical and autobiographical forms and stimulate further research.

Out of respect for each contributor's preferences, transliteration of Persian is consistent within articles but not necessarily across them; it is hoped that the reader will not find such occasional inconsistencies overly distracting. The editor is grateful to her colleagues at the Ilex Foundation, especially

Christopher Dadian, Olga Merck Davidson, Niloo Fotouhi and Gregory Nagy, for their unfailing support and many forms of assistance in the preparation of this collection.

L. M.

Bibliography

Abbott, N. (1957), *Studies in Arabic Literary Papyri I: Historical Texts*, Chicago: University of Chicago Press.

Abiad, M. (1979 [1980]), "Origine et développement des dictionnaires biographiques arabes," *Bulletin d'études orientales* 31: 7–15.

Aigle, D. (ed.) (1995), *Saints orientaux*, Paris: De Boccard.

—— (ed.) (2000), *Miracle et karāma. Hagiographies médiévales comparées*, Turnhout: Brepols.

Auchterlonie, Paul (1987), *Arabic Biographical Dictionaries: A Summary Guide and Bibliography*, Durham: Middle East Libraries Committee.

Bowersock, G. W. (1991), "Momigliano's Quest for the Person," *History and Theory* 30: 27–36.

Bulliet, R. W. (1970), "A Quantitative Approach to Medieval Muslim Biographical Dictionaries," *Journal of the Economic and Social History of the Orient* 13: 195–211.

—— (1979), *Conversion to Islam in the Medieval Period*, Cambridge: Harvard University Press.

Cooperson, Michael (2000), *Classical Arabic Biography: The Heirs of the Prophets in the Age of al-Maʾmūn*, Cambridge: Cambridge University Press.

—— (2005), *Al-Maʾmūn*, Oxford: Oneworld.

Cox, Patricia (1983), *Biography in Late Antiquity: A Quest for the Holy Man*, Berkeley: University of California Press.

Dale, S. (2004), *The Garden of the Eight Paradises: Babur and the Culture of Empire in Central Asia, Afghanistan and India (1483-1530)*, Leiden: E. J. Brill.

Daniel, Elton (2004), "Historiography iii: Early Islamic Period," *EIr* VII: 330–48.

Edwards, M. J. and S. Swain (1997), *Portraits: Biographical Representation in the Greek and Latin Literature of the Roman Empire*, Oxford: Clarendon Press.

El-Hibri, T. (1995), "The Regicide of the Caliph al-Amīn and the Challenge of Representation in Medieval Islamic Historiography," *Arabica* 42: 334–64.

Fähndrich, H. (1973), "The *Wafayāt al-aʿyān* of Ibn Khallikān: A New Approach," *Journal of the American Oriental Society* 93: 432–45.

—— (1977), "Compromising the Caliph: Analysis of Several Versions of an Anecdote about Abū Dulāma and al-Manṣūr," *Journal of Arabic Literature* VIII: 36–47.

Gajano, Sofia Boesch (ed.) (1997), *Santità, culti, agiografia: Temi e prospettive: Atti del I Convegno di studio dell'Associazione italiana per lo studio della santità, dei culti e dell'agiografia, Roma, 24–26 ottobre 1996*, Rome: Viella, 1997.

Gibb, H. A. R. (1962) "Islamic Biographical Literature," in: *Historians of the Middle East*, ed. B. Lewis and P. M. Holt, London: Oxford University Press, 54–8.

Gilliot, Cl. (2000), "Ṭabaḳāt," *EI2* X: 7–10.

Grotzfeld, H. (1995), "Social Mobility Seen from a Worm's-eye View. Low Class People's Careers Seen by Lower Middle Class Biographers," *Actas XVI Congreso UEAI*, Salamanca, 229–36.

Hafsi, I. (1976, 1977), "Recherches sur le genre ṭabaqāt dans la littérature arabe," *Arabica* 23: 227–65; 24: 1–41, 150–86.

Hamad, B. (1998), "History and Biography," *Arabica* 45: 215–32.

Hambly, Gavin R. G. (ed.) (1998), *Women in the Medieval Islamic World: Power, Patronage, and Piety*, New York: St. Martin's Press.

Humphreys, R. S. (1991), *Islamic History: A Framework for Inquiry*, Revised Edition, Princeton: Princeton University Press.

Hurvitz, Nimrod (1997), "Biographies and Mild Asceticism: A Study of Islamic Moral Imagination," *Studia Islamica* 85: 41–65.

Khalidi, T. (1973), "Islamic Biographical Dictionaries: A Preliminary Assessment," *The Muslim World* 63: 53–65.

—— (1994), *Arabic Historical Thought in the Classical Period*, Cambridge: Cambridge University Press.

Kilpatrick, H. (1991), "Autobiography and Classical Arabic Literature," *Journal of Arabic Literature* 22: 1–20.

—— (1998), "Autobiography, medieval," *Encyclopedia of Arabic Literature*, ed. J. S. Meisami and P. Starkey, London and New York: Routledge, I: 111–12.

Köhler, B. (1997), "Die Frauen in al-Wāqidīs *Kitāb al-Maġāzī*', *Zeitschrift der Deutschen Morgenländischen Gesellschaft* 147: 303–53.

Leder, Stefan (1990), "Features of the Novel in Early Historiography: The Downfall of Xālid al-Qasrī," *Oriens* 32: 72–96.

Lichtenstadter, Ilse (1945), "Arabic and Islamic Historiography," *The Moslem World* 35: 126–32.

Malti-Douglas, Fedwa (1977), "Controversy and Its Effects in the Biographical Tradition of al-Khaṭīb al-Baghdādī," *Studia Islamica* 46: 115–31.

—— (1980), "Dreams, the Blind, and the Semiotics of the Biographical Notice," *Studia Islamica* 51: 137–62.

Meisami, J. S. (1995), "Exemplary Lives, Exemplary Deaths: The Execution of Ḥasanak," *Actas XVI Congreso UEAI*, Salamanca, 357–64.

—— (1999), *Persian Historiography to the End of the Twelfth Century*, Edinburgh: Edinburgh University Press.

Melville, Charles (2004), "Historiography iv: Mongol Period," *EIr* VII: 348–56.

Miracles, prodiges et merveilles au Moyen Âge: XXVe Congrès de la Société des historiens médiévistes de l'enseignement supérieur, Orléans, juin 1994, Paris: Publications de la Sorbonne, 1995.

Momigliano, A. (1971), *The Development of Greek Biography*, Cambridge, Massachusetts: Harvard University Press.

—— (1985), "Marcel Mauss and the Quest for the Person in Greek Biography and Autobiography," in: *The Category of the Person: Anthropology, Philosophy, History*, ed. M. Carrithers, S. Collins and S. Lukes, Cambridge: Cambridge University Press.

Paul, Jürgen (2003), "Hagiographic Literature," *EIr* XI: 536–9.

Peacock, A. C. S. (2007), *Mediaeval Islamic Historiography and Political Legitimacy: Balʿamī's* Tārīkhnāma, London and New York: Routledge.

al-Qadi, W. (1995), "Biographical Dictionaries: Inner Structure and Cultural Significance," in: *The Book in the Islamic World*, ed. G. Atiyeh, Albany: State University of New York Press, 93–122.

—— (1998), "Biography, medieval," *Encyclopedia of Arabic Literature*, ed. J. S. Meisami and P. Starkey, London and New York: Routledge, I: 150–52.

—— (2006), "Biographical Dictionaries as the Scholars' Alternative History of the Muslim Community", in: *Organizing Knowledge: Encyclopaedic Activities in the Pre-Eighteenth Century Islamic World*, ed. G. Endress, Leiden and Boston: E. J. Brill, 23–75.

Quinn, Sholeh (2004), "Historiography vi: Safavid Period," *EIr* VII: 363–7.

Reynolds, Dwight F. (ed.) (1997), *Arabic Autobiography*, Special Issue, *Edebiyât* NS 7/2.

—— (ed.) (2001), *Interpreting the Self: Autobiography in the Arabic Literary Tradition*, Berkeley: University of California Press.

Robinson, Ch. F. (2003), *Islamic Historiography*, Cambridge: Cambridge University Press.

Roded, Ruth (1994), *Women in Islamic Biographical Collections: From Ibn Saʿd to Who's Who*, Boulder, Colorado: Lynne Rienner Publishers.

Rosenthal, Franz (1937), "Die arabische Autobiographie," *Studia Arabica* I: 1–40.

—— (1968), *A History of Muslim Historiography*, Second Revised Edition, Leiden: E. J. Brill.

Schippers, Arie (1995), "Autobiography in Medieval Arabic Literature," *Actas XVI Congreso UEAI*, Salamanca, 482–7.

Szuppe, M. (1998), "The 'Jewels of Wonder': Learned Ladies and Princess Politicians in the Provinces of Early Ṣafavid Iran," in: *Women in the Medieval Islamic World*, ed. G. R. G. Hambly, New York: St. Martin's Press, 325–45.

—— (2004), "Historiography v: Timurid Period," *EIr* VII: 356–63.

Young, M. J. L. (1990), "Arabic Biographical Writing," in: *Religion, Learning and Science in the ʿAbbasid Period*, ed. M. J. L. Young, J. D. Latham and R. B. Serjeant, *The Cambridge History of Arabic Literature*, Cambridge: Cambridge University Press, 168–87.

The Testing of the *Shāhnāma* in the "Life of Ferdowsī" Narratives[1]

Olga M. Davidson

It is well known that manuscripts of Ferdowsī's *Shāhnāma* begin not with the poet's monumental work itself but with an introduction in prose. The content of the introductory section differs from one manuscript to another, and the various prefaces that have been preserved fall into four main versions.[2] The present article is concerned with these prose prefaces as vehicles for conveying narratives of what I have referred to as the "Life of Ferdowsī." What I mean by using this expression is a set of narratives about the life and times of Ferdowsī that are based on poetic traditions that are recognized as typical of Ferdowsī. These narratives, in my view, represent a traditional Iranian literary form, a prose tradition that complements the poetic tradition that culminated in the *Shāhnāma* of Ferdowsī.[3] Furthermore, despite their prosaic exterior, the Life of Ferdowsī narratives contain poetic agenda, which are evident in certain stylized visualizations, or tropes, referring to the making of poetry.

The Life of Ferdowsī narratives reflected in the diverse prefaces to the *Shāhnāma*, and supplemented by additional versions attested in other prose works, can be read as sources of historical information regarding the reception of Ferdowsī's poetry. The present article explores two of the major Life of Ferdowsī narratives: those recorded in the so-called "Older Preface" to the *Shāhnāma*, dated to the middle of the fourth/tenth century, and those contained in the Bāysonghorī Preface, dated 829/1426 and appended to the recension of the *Shāhnāma* commissioned by Prince Bāysonghor (d. 837/1433), son of the Timurid ruler Shāhrukh (r. 811–50/1409–47) and a celebrated artist and patron of the arts.[4] Both of these prefaces feature nar-

1. An earlier version of this paper was presented on the happy occasion of a celebration of the life and works of Jerome W. Clinton, organized by his students in June 2002. Parts of the article have appeared in a similar form in my "Some Iranian Poetic Tropes as Reflected in the 'Life of Ferdowsi' Traditions" (Davidson 2001).

2. Riyahi 1993.

3. Davidson 2001.

4. Bāysonghor took possession of Tabriz in 823/1420 and was appointed governor of Astarabad in 835/1431, but never ascended the throne. On the two prefaces I will explore in

ratives designed to explain important historical phases in the reception of the *Shāhnāma*.

As I have demonstrated in my previous work, both the Older and the Bāysonghorī Prefaces depict in vivid fashion the positive aspect of the *Shāhnāma*'s reception. This positive reception is conveyed in narratives in which Persian elites represent the idealized notion of a Persian Empire.[5] In addition, the Bāysonghorī Preface highlights a corresponding negative aspect in the *Shāhnāma*'s reception. It is this latter aspect, conveyed by means of a narrative concerning the Caliph Omar (ʿUmar b. al-Khaṭṭāb, r. 11–13/634–4), a non-Persian, that forms the focus of the present study.

Before proceeding with an analysis of the narrative concerning Omar, it is necessary to examine in detail the Life of Ferdowsī narratives featured in both the Older and the Bāysonghorī Prefaces. As I have argued previously, the Older Preface and the Bāysonghorī Preface serve to contextualize on the one hand the poet Ferdowsī himself and on the other, the poetry in its historicized setting. In the Life of Ferdowsī traditions, the poet is contextualized through the narration of his life and times. These narratives address above all the question of how this one man, known by the poetic name of Ferdowsī, came to compose a poem of such length and grandeur, concerned with the entirety of Iranian civilization and conceptualized as a Book of Kings. The poetry is similarly contextualized through a narration of its impact, over time, on a wide variety of people in a broad range of historical settings.

A combination of diachronic and synchronic approaches serves to highlight an ongoing pattern of accommodation and coexistence between older and newer traditions in the evolving poetics of the *Shāhnāma*. This pattern is reflected in the likewise evolving rhetoric of the Life of Ferdowsī narratives. The older traditions represent the foundations of the pre-Islamic Persian Empire and draw on pre-Islamic worldviews, based especially on the ideology and religion of Zoroastrianism (a term used here in the broadest possible sense). In a previous study, I explored the ways in which the poetry of the *Shāhnāma* integrates, promotes and legitimizes poetic traditions associated with a Zoroastrian provenance.[6] The present study addresses the two aforementioned prose prefaces, the Older Preface and the Bāysonghorī Preface, from a similar combination of diachronic and synchronic perspectives.

---

this article, the "Older Preface" and the Bāysonghorī Preface, see Riyahi 1993: 170–80. The other two major prefaces to the *Shāhnāma* are: the preface to the Florence MS. of the *Shāhnāma*, dated 614/1217–18, supplemented by the preface to the Topkapi MS. (Riyahi 1993, 264–87), and the "third" or "intermediate" preface (see Riyahi 1993, 326–38).

5. See Davidson, 2001.

6. Davidson 1994, 42–53.

The Older Preface

The Older Preface (referred to hereafter as the OP) draws attention to the *Shāhnāma*'s Zoroastrian background, in terms of both patronage and general reception, even more explicitly than Ferdowsī's poem itself.[7] At the same time, the OP presents this Zoroastrian background in the context of a foreground made up of Islamic worldviews. According to the account related in the OP, a certain Ibn ʿAbd al-Razzāq, a local potentate of Ferdowsī's native city of Tus, commissioned a Book of Kings in concert with his administrator, Abū Manṣūr al-Maʿmarī (OP §6). The resulting work, finished in 346/957 (OP §7), was based on a "compilation" of older books (OP §6). The narrative relates that Ibn ʿAbd al-Razzāq had been inspired to commission this book after hearing the story of the genesis of the book *Kalīla and Dimna* (OP §6).

The OP's invocation of *Kalīla and Dimna* in this context is of particular interest. The sequence of events by which this celebrated collection of stories attained its most perfect form appears in the OP to prefigure the process by which the *Shāhnāma* reached its final and felicitous conclusion. According to the OP, King Anushirvan [r. 531–79] commissioned a translation of *Kalīla and Dimna* from the "Indian" language into Pahlavi (OP §4); the Caliph al-Maʾmūn [r. 198–218/813–33], through the agency of his administrator Ibn al-Muqaffaʿ,[8] ordered a translation of the collection from Pahlavi into Arabic (OP §4); the Samanid Amir Naṣr [II] b. Aḥmad [r. 301–31/914–43], through the agency of his secretary Balʿamī, commissioned a translation from Arabic into Persian prose (OP §5); and finally, Balʿamī's prose version was transposed into Persian verse by Rūdakī [d. ca. 329/940–1] (OP §5).[9] It is said of the Persian prose version that "the book fell into men's hands and every man turned its pages," and of the poetic version that from then on, *Kalīla and Dimna* "was on the tongues of the great and the lowly" (OP §5).[10]

From a synchronic point of view, the rhetoric and "poetics" of this narrative operate on an ascending scale of prestige. At its climax, the Persian prose version is capped by the Persian poetic version. As I have indicated in previous work, the same kind of rhetoric is at work in the "happy ending" built into the narrative about the genesis of the *Shāhnāma*. In the OP, just before the ending is reached, the Book of Kings (presumably at this point a translation of the original Pahlavi) has been turned into Persian prose (OP

7. In the following paraphrase, notations of paragraphs (§) refer to the divisions of the text of the OP in Minorsky's translation (Minorsky 1964).

8. Ibn al-Muqaffaʿ had, of course, been executed in approximately 142/759, well before the reign of al-Maʾmūn.

9. On Abū l-Fażl Balʿamī, see Bosworth 1989.

10. Translations from Minorsky 1964, 266.

§15–§16). Then, in a final and perfect culmination of the process of composition, the prose text is superseded by the poetic version. This time, it is Ferdowsī who converts the prose into poetry, and his patron is specified as Maḥmūd of Ghazna [r. 388–421/998–1030] (OP §16). In this narrative, there is no explicit time-gap between the compilation of the Persian prose version and its subsequent conversion into Persian poetry: "And after they had compiled it in prose, Sulṭān Maḥmūd, son of Subuk-tegin, ordered the sage Abū l-Qāsim Manṣūr Firdausī to turn it into the *darī* ('court') language in verse, and the circumstances of it will be mentioned at their proper place" (OP §16).[11]

According to one influential theory, associated above all with M. M. Qazvini and endorsed by V. Minorsky, this crucial part of the narrative, the conclusion, constitutes an "interpolation," and is, it is implied, of negligible importance.[12] In the readings of Qazvini and Minorsky, the rhetorical integrity of the OP is dismantled by means of editorial and interpretive excisions. The truncated text is then "archaeologized" as having had a completely different purpose from that which the OP itself announces as its raison d'être, namely to introduce the poetry of the *Shāhnāma*. Instead, it has been argued, the text was intended to introduce a hypothetical "prose *Shāhnāma*," which, although no longer extant, supposedly corresponded to the original text commissioned by Ibn ʿAbd al-Razzāq.[13]

The combining of synchronic and diachronic approaches provides a means of countering this theory. Viewed from a synchronic point of view, the narrative of the OP requires the predecessor-text of the poetic *Shāhnāma* to serve as a foil, marking the penultimate stage in the process that led to the perfection of the final product. Narrative precedents provide a clear model for the construction of such a foil: at least in terms of the rhetoric and "poetics" of the narrative, it is evident that the predecessor-text must have been written in prose, just as Balʿamī's prose Persian *Kalīla and Dimna* constituted the predecessor-text for the poetic Persian *Kalīla and Dimna* of Rūdakī. Similarly, in terms of the logic that takes shape in the narrative of the OP, the *Shāhnāma* must have existed in a prose version that functioned as a predecessor-text to the poetic *Shāhnāma* of Ferdowsī. Such a rhetorical crescendo, in which a prose *Shāhnāma* commissioned by Ibn ʿAbd al-Razzāq becomes a stepping-stone to a grander and more perfect work, articulates the point of view of a later era, marked by a poetic *Shāhnāma* commissioned by Maḥmūd of Ghazna.

11. The translation is Minorsky's (1964, 271).
12. Minorsky 1964, 271, n. 2.
13. For the most influential exposition of this theory, see Qazvini 1944 and Minorsky 1964, and the discussion in Davidson 2001.

The purpose of the preceding discussion is not to suggest that a prose *Shāhnāma* commissioned by Ibn ʿAbd al-Razzāq, the potentate of Tus, never existed. Rather, it is to demonstrate that the OP's account of the commissioning of such a prose *Shāhnāma* is inextricably tied to its narrative concerning the conversion of this prose into poetry by Ferdowsī, the poet of Tus. In other words, it is the narrative of the OP that rhetorically motivates the *Shāhnāma* of Ferdowsī, not the earlier "prose *Shāhnāma*" that serves as its foil.

It remains a possibility that the "prose *Shāhnāma*" mentioned in the narrative of the Older Preface not only existed but also provided a source for Ferdowsī. As I have argued previously, it is my conviction that Ferdowsī was not confined to any single textual source, and that he had free access to non-textual "sources" as well, most notably to contemporary oral traditions of the "Book of Kings" traditions. Moreover, the historicized narrative of the OP is strikingly parallel to Ferdowsī's own poeticized narrative concerning the genesis of the Book of Kings.[14]

The Bāysonghorī Preface

According to the narrative of the Bāysonghorī Preface (hereafter BP), it was King Anushirvan who commissioned a collection, drawn from all the provinces in his Empire, of popular stories concerning ancient kings (BP 368–9).[15] Furthermore, the narrative in the BP relates that the last king of the pre-Islamic Sasanian Empire, Yazdegerd [III, r. 632–51), commissioned the *dehqān* Dāneshvar to compile the Book of Kings (BP 369).

The BP, then, presents parallel accounts: two different generations of kings commission two different "prototypical" Books of Kings. Regardless of whether or not it possesses a historical foundation, the OP, like the BP, conforms to a narrative strategy that continually revalidates the Book of Kings by providing explanations of its "origins."[16] In the OP, it is not a king but a local potentate who commissions the Book of Kings, and this feature, in my view, should be regarded as a variant in its own right.[17] It might seem that the presentation in the OP, with its references to little-known personages rather than to such paradigmatic figures as the Sasanian monarchs, is more "historical" than that of the BP and other prefaces. The parallelism itself, however, indicates that the various narratives belong to the category of "myth" rather than "history."[18] In other words, it is important to recognize

14. Davidson 2000, 64–5.

15. References to the text of the BP are to the edition of Riyahi 1993.

16. Davidson 2001.

17. Ibid.

18. For a comparative study of the ways in which myth can trump history in "lives of poets" traditions, see Nagy 2004.

that it is not merely the historical details regarding Ibn ʿAbd al-Razzāq that drive the narrative of the OP.

The "historicized" specificity of the OP's narrative regarding the genesis of the Book of Kings contrasts with the universalism that characterizes the BP's narrative and also with the poeticized universalism of Ferdowsī's own narrative. In Ferdowsī's narrative of the formation of the Book of Kings, this universalism is achieved by generalizing on the basis of several different versions. In the BP, a similar universalism arises from the inclusion of the widest possible variety of different versions. Just as the "recension" of the *Shāhnāma* commissioned by Prince Bāysonghor is markedly inclusive in its synthesis of textual variants, the Preface to the Bāysonghorī Recension encompasses numerous narratological variants. The BP synthesizes the different versions of the story concerning the genesis of the Book of Kings as a way of explaining the genesis of the Bāysonghorī text itself.[19]

In contrast to the universalizing BP, the OP, as has been shown, particularizes one version of the account. The BP and the OP nevertheless share several characteristics, such as, most notably, the parallelism between the art of poetic composition and the "event" of turning prose into poetry. As I have demonstrated in detail in previous work, a juxtaposition of the narratives contained in the OP and the BP brings to light many parallels among the tropes employed in the two prefaces.[20] In the present article, I shall mention a few illustrative examples only.

An obvious point of contrast in the narratological material of the two prefaces lies in their relative length and complexity: the narrative of the OP is brief and straightforward, while that of the BP is extensive and involved. In the OP, the "event" of turning the prose of the Book of Kings into poetry can be paraphrased in a single narratological layer, whereas in the BP, the "event" can only be paraphrased in multiple layers, in which many figures unmentioned in the OP appear.

Among the figures who appear only in the BP is, as noted at the outset of this article, the Caliph Omar. In the BP's account, Omar rejects Ferdowsī's *Shāhnāma*, and his rejection functions as a critical event in the overall narrative about the reception of this masterpiece of Persian literature. The event of Omar's rejection is situated in a setting of open hostility toward the very existence of the kind of poetry that the *Shāhnāma* represents. In the narrative logic of the BP, as will be demonstrated below, the poetry of the *Shāhnāma* constitutes a threat to the Caliph's worldview.

It should be noted that while [Ibn] ʿAbd al-Razzāq and al-Maʿmarī appear

19. I intend to address the complex narratological structure of the BP in a future project.
20. Davidson 2001.

in the narratives of both the OP and the BP, in the latter text the two men share the credit for the composition of the prose *Shāhnāma* with Ya'qūb-i Layth the Saffarid [r. 253–65/867–79], who is said to have acquired the "original" Pahlavi version by sending an envoy to fetch it from India.[21] The version of the Book of Kings brought from India is said to have originated from the work compiled, in Pahlavi, by Dāneshvar at the behest of Yazdegerd. At the time of the Arab conquest of Iran, Dāneshvar's work was brought to the Caliph, who rejected it (BP 369–70). The Book then passed to Abyssinia, where it was greatly appreciated, and to India, from whence it was subsequently returned to Iran (BP 370). It was Ya'qūb who commissioned [Ibn] 'Abd al-Razzāq to have the Book of Kings translated into Persian prose, with the addition of materials covering the period from the reign of Khusrow Parviz [r. 590–628] to that of Yazdegerd; the resulting work thus covered the whole line of Iranian kings (BP 370). According to the BP, the new version was completed not in 346/957, as stated in the OP, but in 360/970, after collation with four other versions derived from the authority of four wise men. Patronage for the Book of Kings subsequently passed from the Saffarids to the Samanids, under whom the poet Daqīqī was commissioned to turn the prose of the Book into poetry. But the dynasty of the Samanids came to an end, and power was transferred to Maḥmūd of Ghazna. The life of the poet Daqīqī was likewise cut short, and the turning of prose to poetry was interrupted; Daqīqī completed only one or two thousand lines (BP 370). After an extended treatment of the efforts and exploits of the poets at Maḥmūd's court (BP 370–4), the narrative of the BP approaches its climax with the entry of Ferdowsī (BP 374–5). At this point, after pausing to offer a list of supplementary textual sources acquired by Maḥmūd to expand the repertoire of his Book of Kings (BP 375), the BP's narrative of the Life of Ferdowsī proceeds, and establishes him as the definitive poet of the Book of Kings (BP 375–418).[22]

Among the many contrasts between the OP and the BP, two points merit particular attention. First, it should be noted that in the OP, the trope of turning prose into poetry appears as an event that takes place in a single phase, whereas in the BP, the corresponding event involves several phases, many poets, and multiple sources. Secondly, India plays a contrasting but significant role in both prefaces. In the OP, Ibn 'Abd al-Razzāq was inspired to commission a new Book of Kings after hearing the story of Anushirvan's commissioning of an Iranian version of the Indic *Kalīla and Dimna* (OP §6). The linking of Anushirvan with India in this account is significant, since in

21. The name of [Ibn] 'Abd al-Razzāq appears in a different form in the BP (370).

22. For a fuller exposition of the narratological materials of the OP and the BP, see Davidson 2001, 9–10.

Iranian poetic traditions it is also Anushirvan who commissions the prototypical Book of Kings. In Ferdowsī's *Shāhnāma* itself, the poet draws an explicit parallel between his *Shāhnāma* and Rūdakī's *Kalīla and Dimna*: the uniqueness of both of these works of poetry, in the words of Ferdowsī, depends on the turning of prose into poetry.[23] In the BP, India again plays an important role in the regeneration of the Book of Kings: the Book of Kings was lost to Iran in the aftermath of the Arab conquest, but eventually re-entered Iran by way of India. The trope implies oral traditions according to which, after the Arab conquest of Iran, it is India that is conventionally imagined as the most authoritative provenance for books of such stature.

The preceding discussion provides necessary context for a consideration of the episode mentioned at the beginning of this article, namely, the BP's narrative concerning the Caliph Omar's rejection of the *Shāhnāma*. The account in the BP reads as follows:

> The performers of traditions (*rāviyān-i āthār*) and the reciters of information (*nāqilān-i akhbār*) relate that in the days of yore the *ʿajam* [non-Arab] kings, especially the Sasanians and among them most notably the just King Anushirvan, avidly craved the collecting of information about those who had passed away, and the correcting (*taṣḥīḥ*) of their conditions and their stories.
>
> Constantly he used to send out messengers in all directions to the remote parts of the earth, so that in every kingdom they scrupulously researched and verified the stories of the kings of that place, along with other stories worthy of remembrance. They placed a copy of these [materials] (*noskha-yi ān*) in his library.
>
> When it reached the time of Yazdegerd-i Shahriyār, the collection of those historical accounts had been arbitrarily (*motafarriqan*) assembled in his treasury. He ordered Dāneshvar the Dehqān, who was among the elders of Madaʾin and who combined courage with learning and wisdom, to organize a list of chapters and arrange them in order from the beginning of the reign of Kayomars to the end of the reign of Sultan Khosrow Parviz. And every word not mentioned there he asked about from among the *mobad*s and the learned (*dānāyān*), and he added to it. And so a chronicle that reached the outer limits of perfection was assembled.
>
> When it came to the time that Saʿd b. Waqqāṣ seized as loot the treasure of Yazdegerd, they brought that chronicle, which fell as part of the loot, to Amir al-Muʾminin Omar, may God be pleased with him. He ordered a translator to inform him of the book's contents. He [the translator] recounted a portion of this book, about the principles of

23. *Shāhnāma* VIII: 655, ll. 3460–4.

> justice and equity of the Pishdadians and other precepts (*ʿazāʾim*) of the kings of the ʿAjam, their prudence and wise opinions. He [Omar] was elated and ecstatic and ordered them to translate it into Arabic. However, other parts contained passages that were contrary to reason and unworthy, and when Omar heard about the beliefs of the sun-worshippers and the fire-worshippers, the codes of the Sabians, the story of Zāl and the Simorgh and the like, he decreed that this book did not merit inspection or careful study, because it bore an exact semblance to this world, and this world was not worthy of consideration and care.
>
> They asked: "In what sense is it like this world?"
>
> He said: "I heard from the Prophet that the world was of so little importance to its Lord that he mixed its *ḥarām* with its *ḥalāl*. That is to say, this world is so worthless before God that he mixed in it what is lawful and unlawful, and in this book too the lawful and unlawful are mixed together: I mean the true and the false."[24]

In this passage, the *Shāhnāma* is depicted as a prototypical book of prose that provides the ideological foundation for Ferdowsī's poetry, and the Caliph's reaction to the book is symbolic of the reaction of Islam to the pre-Islamic poetry of the Persians. The BP represents this world-view in a negative light. From such a point of view, it implies, the pre-Islamic poetic traditions of the Persians might as well be relegated to such unlikely places as Abyssinia. In striking contrast, in the world-view of Persian poetry, the very remoteness of Abyssinia provides the opportunity for a return, by way of the back door, to the cultural prestige of the Persia that once had been. As I have suggested above, the narrative of the BP slips from Abyssinia to India, envisaged as the ultimate source of cultural prestige. From India, the poetry of the Persians is poised to stage its grand re-entry into legitimacy, following the legitimating roadmap of *Kalīla and Dimna*.

Furthermore, in the mythologizing narrative of the BP, the accretive and inclusive character of the *Shāhnāma* contrasts with the reductionist and exclusionary "correctness" represented by the Caliph. The process of accretion involved in the genesis of the *Shāhnāma* emerges as a distinguishing virtue. In the narrative logic of the BP, the *Shāhnāma*, as an accretive and inclusive book, is identified with an accretive and inclusive world — a world that goes beyond the world represented by the Caliph. For Persian civilization, the Book of Kings *is* the world, in all its beautiful unruliness.

24. BP, in Riyahi 1993, 368–70. The translation is the author's.

Bibliography

Bertels, Y. E. et al., eds. (1960–71), *Ferdowsī: Shāhnāma*, 9 vols., Moscow.

Bosworth, C. E. (1989), "Balʿamī, Abuʾl-Fażl Moḥammad," *EIr* III: 573–4.

Davidson, O. M. (1994/2006), *Poet and Hero in the Persian Book of Kings*, Ithaca, New York: Cornell University Press. 2nd ed. Bibliotheca Iranica: Intellectual Traditions Series No. 12, Los Angeles, CA: Mazda Press.

—— (1998), " The Text of Ferdowsī's *Shāhnāma* and the Burden of the Past," *Journal of the American Oriental Society* 118: 63–8.

—— (2000), *Comparative Literature and Classical Persian Poetry*, Bibliotheca Iranica: Intellectual Traditions Series No. 4, Los Angeles, CA: Mazda Press.

——(2001), "Some Iranian Poetic Tropes as Reflected in the 'Life of Ferdowsi' Traditions," *Philologica et Linguistica: Festschrift für Helmut Humbach*, ed. M. G. Schmidt and W. Bisang, Trier: Wissenschaftlicher Verlag, Supplement, 1–12.

Minorsky, V. (1964), " The Older Preface to the Shāh-nāma," *Iranica: Twenty Articles, Tehran: University of Tehran*, 260–73. First published in *Studi Orientalistici in onore di Giorgio Levi Della Vida*, Rome: Instituto per l'Oriente, 1956, 159–79.

Nagy, G. (2004). "L'aède épique en auteur: la tradition des *Vies d'Homère*." *Identités d'auteur dans l'Antiquité et la tradition européenne*, ed. C. Calame, and R. Chartier, 41–67. Grenoble.

Qazvini, M. (1944), "Muqaddama-ye qadīm-e *Shāhnāma*," *Hazāra-ye Ferdowsī*, Tehran, 123–48. First published in *Bīst maqāla-yi Qazvīnī*, Tehran 1934, 1–64.

Riyahi, M. A., ed. (1993), *Sar-chashma-hā-ye Ferdowsī-shenāsī*, Tehran: Muʾassasa-yi Mutalaʿat va-Tahqiqat-i Farhangi.

Shahbazi, A. S. (1991), *Ferdowsi: A Critical Biography*, Costa Mesa: Mazda Press.

Biography and the Image of a Medieval Historian: The *Tārīkh-i jahān-goshā* of ʿAṭā-Malek Jovaynī

Mohammad Jafar Mahallati

The *Tārīkh-i jahān-goshā* (*The History of the World Conqueror*, 658/1260) of ʿAṭā-Malek Jovaynī (623–81/1226–83) has been called, with some justice, "unquestionably the best and most authoritative account" of Mongol history.[1] In form, the work is relatively compact, especially in comparison with the more comprehensive *Universal History* (*Jāmeʿ al-tavārīkh,* (ca. 711/1311) of Rashīd al-Dīn (ca. 645–718/1247–1318).[2] One of the qualities that distinguishes Jovaynī's work from that of some other medieval observers is that the author writes not only as a historian, but also as a player in the unfolding drama of the royal court, and thus as a maker of the very history he relates.[3] Jovaynī's work consists of more than a general account of the era in which he lived; it offers an intimate reflection of the author's life and thoughts, and accordingly provides readers with a richer context for the developments it recounts. The present article represents an endeavor to look into the mirror of this text in search of the author, a man who has given us one of the shrewdest and most thoughtful accounts of the turbulent era in which he lived. The article also attempts to shed light, through the lens offered by Jovaynī, on this crucial stage in Iranian history, and to trace its effects and implications for later periods.

Incentives and Ironies

According to Jovaynī and other historians of the period, the Mongol incursions into Iran destroyed, along with other social strata, much of the scholarly and literary establishment.[4] Yet, paradoxically, though he was him-

I am grateful to Professor Donald Little and most especially Mohsen Ashtiany of *Encyclopaedia Iranica* for comments on earlier versions of this article, able editorial assistance and many lively conversations on Persian history.

1. Browne 1912, I: XIII.
2. For a partial comparison of the two works, see Boyle 1962.
3. This authorial posture is not, of course, unique to Jovaynī; see Daniel 2004; Melville 2004; and comparisons with Bayhaqī in the present article.
4. Early in his preface, Jovaynī writes:

self a highly cultured and urbane scholar, Jovaynī was invited by the Mongol invaders to serve at their court in the early days of their domination over Iran. He is well aware of this irony and takes upon himself the task of reviving the literary and scholarly community and restoring its tarnished dignity and prestige. In the preface to his *History*, he embarks on a daring tirade against contenders for the higher echelons of the Mongol administration:

> Every market lounger in the garb of iniquity has become an emir; every hireling has become a minister... every stableboy the lord of dignity and honour... every cruel man a competent man; every nobody somebody, every churl a chief, every traitor a mighty lord and every valet a learned scholar....
>
> The back of learning was utterly broken that day when these ignorant ones leant their backs upon the cushion.[5]

Jovaynī's invective continues, and his criticism of Mongol policies is as forthright as he can make it. Following these jeremiads, however, the historian attempts to place the unfortunate developments in some perspective. He pauses to consider the sequence of events that occasioned the trends that he finds so lamentable. Jovaynī was certainly aware of the immediate reasons for the Mongol invasion: the conflict that erupted between Sultan Moḥammad Khvārazmshāh (r. 596–617/1200–20) and Chingiz Khan (r. 603–24/1206–27), who initially sought peace (at least on paper), but felt betrayed when the Khvārazmshāh and his governor responded by putting his emissaries and a group of Mongol merchants to death.[6] Jovaynī may also have heard the rumor that the caliph al-Nāṣir (r. 575–622/1180–1225) had invited Chingiz Khan's invasion in order to check the increasingly threatening power of the Khvārazmshāh.[7] But he surely felt that there were no proportional and logical links between cause and effect, between the murder of a few hundred Mongol merchants and the subsequent massacre of

---

> ... [B]ecause of the fickleness of Fate, and the influence of the reeling heavens, and the revolution of the vile wheel, and the variance of the chameleon world, colleges of study have been obliterated and seminaries of learning have vanished away; and the order of students has been trampled upon by events and crushed underfoot by treacherous Fate and deceitful Destiny; they have been seized by all the vicissitudes of toils and tribulations; and being subjected to dispersion and destruction they have been exposed to flashing swords; and they have hidden themselves behind the veil of earth.
>
> All learning must now be sought beneath the earth, because all the learned are in the belly of the earth (Boyle 1958, I: 5–6).

5. Boyle 1958, I: 7–8.
6. Spuler 1985 = Miraftab 1986, 27.
7. Spuler 1985 = Miraftab 1986, 24.

hundreds of thousands, and the sack of numerous human habitations on a hitherto unprecedented scale. Therefore Jovaynī seeks broader teleological explanations, and ultimately places the blame on the Islamic nation (*umma*) as a whole. He stresses that six centuries after the advent of Islam, Muslim societies had gone astray. By succumbing to thorough corruption, they had made themselves into deserving candidates for such a calamity. The end result of this upheaval involved, however, more than the punishment of the Islamic nation. In fact, Jovaynī argues, one of the greatest of all divine marvels was the conversion of the Mongols themselves to Islam. "Any light that becomes bright by means of darkness is most remarkable and extraordinary," he exclaims.[8]

Jovaynī then embarks on an explanation of the motives that prompted his work. He refers to both worldly and spiritual factors. Quoting the early sixth/twelfth-century poet Sanāʾī, he declaims:

> Take either hope or fear, the Sage hath created nothing vain
> In the world whatever is gone and whatever is to come and
> whatever is must be so.[9]

The worldly purpose of his narrative of Mongol history, Jovaynī contends, is that "the intelligent man may learn without the pain of experience and be edified by the study of these discourses."[10] As for the spiritual purpose, Jovaynī avers that history serves to broaden a person's view of life, enabling him to see how the affairs of the world are governed by wisdom and towards a moral end, no matter how harsh they may appear at the time and how cruel and fickle a role fate might play.

It is appropriate at this point to consider Jovaynī's observations within the context of Persian history and the notions of the past embedded in it. The Mongol invasion was hardly the only watershed in Persian history, nor was Jovaynī by any means the only, or the first, Persian historian to comment on the violent temper of his times. In a vivid antecedent to Jovaynī's poignant remarks, Ferdowsī (d. 411/1020) concludes his *Shāhnāma* (completed in 400/1010) with the famous prophecy of Rostam-i Farrokhzād, who, in the era of the last Sasanian ruler, Yazdegird III (d. 31/651), evokes a grim vision of a world turned upside down, where thrones and cities are destroyed and good breeding, as well as true merit, disappear in an atmosphere of enmity and ethical chaos. In another example, the surviving volumes of the *Tārīkh-i Masʿūdī*, the massive history of the Ghaznavids composed by Abū

8. Jovaynī, *Tārīkh-i jahān-goshā*, I: 9.
9. Boyle 1958, I: 12.
10. Boyle 1958, I: 43–44.

l-Fażl Bayhaqī (385–470/995–1077), deal with the reign of Sultan Masʿūd (r. 421–32/1030–41) and his ultimate defeat at the hands of the Turkman Seljuks at Dandanqan in 431/1040. This surviving section of Bayhaqī's work likewise comprises a study of decline, defeat, and shrinkage, even if it is observed in slow motion over the course of several years. Indeed, it might even be argued that lamentations for the glories of the distant past and acerbic assessments of the calamities that have befallen in the immediate past are part and parcel of many a medieval historian's art. Such devices enable the writer to praise the present ruler as a restorer of former glories and as a harbinger of prosperity and peace. Medieval historical texts, after all, often incorporate unmistakably panegyric elements.

A closer consideration of the three texts referred to above, the *Shāhnāma*, the *Tārīkh-i Masʿūdī* and the *Tārīkh-i jahān-goshā*, reveals important distinctions, however. Seen through Rostam's pro-Sasanian, Zoroastrian eyes, the *Shāhnāma*'s Arabs execute the same function that the Mongols would perform some centuries later: namely, they tear the fabric of a society apart. The Arabs are accordingly demonized, depicted as grotesque, snake-eating hordes, bereft of shame and wisdom. At the same time, Rostam is a portrayed as a military commander facing certain defeat; he harbors no hope of survival, let alone of integration in the new world order that will emerge. He regards himself as a victim of the ruthless cyclical nature of history, and Ferdowsī portrays him as a spent force.

For Bayhaqī, on the other hand, the categories of "them" and "us" are less self-evident. Bayhaqī's patrons, the Ghaznavids, had, after all, been nomadic Turks themselves, and although Sultan Masʿūd's own learning and style are praised, the 'men of the sword', the Turkish commanders of the troops, are often portrayed as thoroughly illiterate and not much more urbane than the nomads who finally defeat them. Even their defeat is depicted in a somewhat lowly style. In contrast to the downfall of members of the bureaucracy, evoked with the often memorable rhetoric of vicious repartee and clinching parting words, the demise of the Turkish commanders is presented in a simple fashion: one, for example, is induced to drink vast quantities of wine, an uncomplicated strategy given his love for the bottle, until he becomes effectively "legless" and can be pounced upon and put in fetters without much of a struggle by him or his followers. The distinctions between "them" and "us" are thus less clear and fall as much within the Ghaznavid society as between them and their enemies outside.

Jovaynī's case is different again. Like Rostam-i Farrokhzād, he belongs to a distinguished family with a long record of service. Unlike Rostam, he is a survivor and a Muslim, and although he sees the Mongols as the scourge referred to in the Qurʾan and sent by the Almighty to chasten mankind, he means to do his utmost to ameliorate the situation. At the same time, in his descriptions of the Mongol army, Mongol manners and mores, he appears as a bedazzled outsider, at times admiring and at times thoroughly disgusted. His elaborate accounts of organized hunts and military raids, and his detailed descriptions of the structure and conduct of the army, which he depicts as a highly efficient killing machine of men and beasts in bulk, are imbued with a strong element of wonder. In the *Tārīkh-i Masʿūdī*, one of Bayhaqī's major objectives was to assist his readers in attaining a better understanding of the self; with reference to the hadith "Whoever knows himself knows his God," Bayhaqī seeks to promote self-knowledge in his readers as a path to greater spiritual insight.[11] By contrast, Jovaynī seeks to focus his readers' attention on others, on a community that is different from his own. In this regard the two historians adopt different approaches, but perhaps both aim at the identical goal of moving a society forward to a more harmonious state. Jovaynī also has a more immediate and mundane purpose in mind when he maintains that prompt submission to the Mongols allows people to save their own lives, whereas the alternative route of resistance, given the weight of past evidence, leads only to more massacres and further bloodshed. Accordingly, Jovaynī calls on people to accept peace and to blame themselves for the carnage that they have witnessed:

> To complain of fate is useless; whatever befalleth us is our own doing.[12]

The spirit of self-criticism that Jovaynī seeks to promote among his readers has a psychological importance. It instills, in its own way, a sense of confidence crucial to the devastated and traumatized subjects. Had Jovaynī explained the cataclysmic events solely in terms of alien factors beyond human control and the blind turn of the wheel of fortune, it would have led to an even stronger sense of despair and helplessness among the people and would have made it even harder for them to defend themselves against injustice.

In the introduction to his translation of the *Tārīkh-i jahān-goshā*, John Andrew Boyle advances the argument that "as an official in their [the Mongols'] service, Juvaini had to justify the invasion itself. This he has done by representing the Mongols as the instrument of the divine will."[13] With reference to the historical evidence as well as earlier Persian historiography, the present article suggests that the fatalistic attitude suggested by this assessment is more complex than it may at first appear.

As an initial qualification, it should be noted that while the Mongol

11. Bayhaqī, *Tārīkh-i Bayhaqī*, I: 154.
12. Boyle 1958, I: 18.
13. Boyle 1958, I: xxxiii. See further Boyle 1962, 133.

incursions caused devastation and loss of life on an unprecedented scale, the immediate pre-Mongol history of Iran and the region was hardly peaceful. Iran and Transoxiana experienced perpetual conflict among and within various dynasties, including the Ghaznavids and Seljuks. The death and hardships occasioned by constant warfare were compounded by widespread drought and crop failure, which badly compromised urban life in many areas,[14] and brought socio-economic instability to the entire region. If the scale of the destruction wrought by the Mongol invasions was unparalleled, the savagery of the Mongol onslaught was not without precedent. According to Bayhaqī, the approach to warfare of Sultan Maḥmūd (r. 388–421/998–1030) was characterized by a similar ruthlessness: "Since Sultan Maḥmūd found himself victorious in all these [preliminary] wars, he established for himself a schedule of two campaigns a year: one conquest in India, and another in Khurasan, Sistan and western Iran [*bilād-i ʿAjam*]."[15] Bayhaqī reports further, "... [Sultan Maḥmūd] set out for the [Indian] kingdom of Nanda, and for six months, he burnt everywhere he went; when he came to the border of that land, he sent envoys, together with Indian translators, [to the king]; he wrote a letter in which he conveyed the message that ... he would not leave Hindustan until he had made all the people Muslims, or else he would enslave all the women and children and kill all the men."[16] Maḥmūd was also responsible for the murder of a Fatimid emissary, and after his conquest of Rayy, he ordered the execution of the city's Shiite population and had the books in the library burnt beneath their hanging corpses.[17] Such examples suggest that the Ghaznavid's conduct in war differed little in its severity and cruelty from that of Sultan Moḥammad Khvārazmshāh or even the Mongols. Furthermore, it is significant that in connection with the massacre and burning of books in Rayy, Bayhaqī reminds his readers of similar events perpetrated by the Ghuzz army in Khurasan, where many Shiite ulema were killed in the same manner. Apparently, the historian regarded such acts as commonplace sequels to conquest.[18]

Given this history and its representation, it is not altogether surprising to find Jovaynī taking an active part in the book burning of the Ismaʿili library at Alamut. In this context, it was possible for Jovaynī to perceive the Mongols within the conceptual and moral framework associated with the warlords who had preceded them, possibly more destructive, but in the role of carriers and instruments of God's vengeance for the misdeeds perpetrated in the pre-Mongol eras.

14. See Bulliet 1994.
15. Nafisi 1963, I: 43; see also I: 356.
16. Nafisi 1963, I: 45.
17. See Nafisi 1963, I: 589, 562, 568.
18. Nafisi 1963, I: 568.

Elites beyond Regimes

According to biographical sources, Jovaynī came from a learned and distinguished family that had served under various and sometimes mutually hostile political regimes from mid-eighth century onwards.[19] He, his father Bahāʾ al-Dīn (d. 651/1253) and his brother Shams al-Dīn (d. 683/1284) served at the highest ranks in various Mongol courts till the sudden demise of the entire family towards the end of the thirteenth century.[20] Bahāʾ al-Dīn and Shams al-Dīn both held the office of *ṣāḥib-dīvān*, and ʿAṭā-Malek was appointed as governor, or functioned as acting governor, for a total of about two decades during the reigns of the Ilkhans Hülegü (r. 654–63/1256–65), Abaqa (r. 663–80/1265–82), and Sultan Aḥmad Takūdār (Tegüder) (r. 680–3/1282–4). A few of Jovaynī's descendants likewise held positions at the court for a brief period until the family vanished during the reign of Arghun (r. 683–90/1284–91). In other words, this learned family survived more than five centuries of continuous political turmoil and was capable of serving under various caliphs, dynasties, and sultans, only to disappear abruptly and entirely from public life in a very short period of time.

The Jovaynī family's long historical experience points to two implications. First, it indicates that all the new political and military entities, regardless of their background, almost immediately became cognizant of the fact that they would not be able to sustain their rule without tapping the resources of, and incorporating, learned indigenous figures. Second, the scarcity of educational institutions that were open to all meant that the heritage of the scholarly traditions within specific families was conducive to the continuity of a successive lineage of learned figures, thereby ensuring the preservation of a family's social and political status in spite of frequent dynastic upheavals. The migration of poets and scientists from one court to another was not a phenomenon confined to the Mongol period. However, the religio-political volte-face of some contemporary members of the elite was quite remarkable. The prominent scientist and scholar Naṣīr al-Dīn Ṭūsī (597–672/1201–74), for example, served the mutually opposing Ismaʿili and Mongol regimes. Such cases also point to the religious open-mindedness of the Mongols as described by Jovaynī in his historical account.

The Abrupt Demise

The Jovaynī family's early good fortune under the Mongols was noteworthy, but their later demise followed a well-established pattern illustrated perhaps most dramatically by the tragic destruction of the Barmakī fam-

19. Boyle 1958, I: xv–xxv.
20. Barthold-Boyle 1996; Spuler 1996; Browne 1912, XLVII–XLIX.

ily under the Abbasid Caliph Hārūn al-Rashīd (r. 170–93/786–809).[21] The fall of the Barmakīs involved a series of events that gained an emblematic quality among "men of the pen" in subsequent generations and to which repeated references were made in later historical works, including that of Bayhaqī, as will be seen below. Even at the threshold of modernity, in the nineteenth century, there are lithograph illustrations of Nāṣir al-Dīn Shāh (r. 1264–1313/1848–96) and his hapless Grand Vizier, Amīr Kabīr, depicted as Hārūn al-Rashīd and Jaʿfar the Barmakid (d. 187/803) respectively. The principal elements in this familiar sequence include the vizier's amassing of wealth and titles, the engendering of local jealousies, intrigues, a pervading sense of threat within the court, and finally the demise of an entire family within a short period. This pattern characterized many of the authoritarian dynasties of medieval Iran, in a phenomenon that has undermined and damaged the educated elites of the country till the present day.[22] In the case of the Jovaynī family, it should be observed that although the instrument of the purge is the foreign (Mongol) ruler, its real instigator and catalyst is domestic, in the form of Majd al-Molk, a court rival of the Jovaynī brothers. Although Majd al-Molk had been a patron of the Jovaynīs and had secured the governorship of a large province for himself, he stopped at nothing, even risking his own life and fortune, in order to destroy those he envied.[23] The repetition of such events can only have fostered a deep sense of insecurity among many social groups. The savage reaction of Majd al-Molk's enemies, when his luck ran out, is a gruesome part of the same sequence. "Once he was mutilated, his murderers roasted parts of his body and devoured them; then they sent the remnants to different corners of the world; his head to Baghdad, his hands to Iraq, his feet to Fars, and a person bought his tongue for a hundred dinars.... Majd al-Molk's associates were also stoned, mutilated and burned in the same manner."[24] This particular vicious cycle came to a halt within six months, during which time ʿAṭā-Malek died, and his brother and their descendants were rapidly executed. Looking at the ends of both enemies, Jovaynī's frequent refrain seems apposite:

> To complain of fate is useless; whatever befalleth us is our own doing.[25]

21. On the Barmakid family, see Sourdel 1960, Abbas 1989.

22. See Reza-Qoli 1998, a widely discussed book that topped the best-seller list in the nonfiction category in Iran during the 1990s. Reza-Qoli invokes many instances in which despotic rulers in the past two centuries of Iran's history systematically eliminated the most promising talents.

23. Browne 1912, XLV.

24. Qazvini 1912, نح.

25. Boyle 1958, I: 18 and *passim*.

The sudden demise of the Jovaynīs, including all the younger members of the family, took place on the order of Ilkhan Arghun (r. 683–90/1284–91), who had been won over by the intrigues of the anti-Jovaynī factions. But it should again be noted that it was not the Mongols who initiated this pattern of behavior; on the contrary, the Ilkhans merely perpetuated a well-established practice, to which the medieval historians themselves often appear to give only a fatalistic explanation.

Theological Concepts of History Common to Jovaynī and Bayhaqī

The fatalistic-seeming worldviews of historians of the Mongol period are in continuity with the historical outlooks of their predecessors. Bayhaqī, for instance, witnessed perhaps as many military expeditions in India and Central Asia as Jovaynī witnessed within a much larger geographical compass. Their common observation is that cities, societies and lives, no matter how far apart from one another they may be, are sacked, devastated, and destroyed in consequence of the same underlying causes and assumptions. Some of those killed share the same faith, others do not, but in their efforts to formulate an all-encompassing explanation, both historians arrive at the same conclusion: namely, that these afflictions are above all a trial and a test by the Almighty. If the defeated society or enemy is Muslim, then they have suffered defeat as a punishment for past sins. If, on the other hand, the defeated society is composed of infidels, it is either punished for its lack of faith, or is blessed (at some price) by being introduced to Islam, thereby reaping the subsequent rewards of following God's chosen path. After each successful military venture on the part of their masters, the two historians frequently register two somewhat contradictory conclusions: first, they express gratitude for the victory; second, they reconfirm for the reader the notion that the present life is ephemeral, and should not be spent in transgression and disobedience to God. Life, they aver, is unpredictable. This shared worldview is evident in many passages from the two works of history.

Jovaynī, for instance, describes the way in which fate brought him to the writing of his *History*: "In the year 650/1252–3 Fate was kind to me, and Fortune smiled, and there befell me the honour of kissing the threshold of the Court of the World-Emperor."[26] In his account of the Mongols' rise to power, he writes in a similar vein:

> When the phoenix (*humā*) of prosperity wishes to make the nest of one

26. Boyle 1958, I: 4.

> man its abode, and the owl of misfortune to haunt the threshold of another, though their stations be widely different, the one in the zenith of good fortune and the other in the nadir of abasement, yet neither scarcity of equipment nor feebleness of condition prevents the fortunate man from attaining his goal –
> Whoever hath been prepared for Fortune, though he seek her not, Fortune seeketh him – [27]

In portraying Chingiz Khan as the instrument of God's punishment, he writes: "There has been transmitted to us a tradition of the traditions of God which says: 'Those are my horsemen; through them shall I avenge me on those that rebelled against me,' nor is there a shadow of doubt but that these words are a reference to the horsemen of Chingiz-Khan and to his people."[28] On the occasion of the fall of Bukhara, Chingiz Khan delivers the following speech to the public:

> "O, people, know that you have committed great sins, and that the great ones among you have committed these sins. If you ask me what proof I have for these words, I say it is because I am the punishment of God. If you had not committed great sins, God would not have sent a punishment like me upon you."[29]

Faced with the carnage wrought by the Mongol sack of the city, two eminent spiritual figures engage in an exchange that seems in complete accord with the Khan's statement: Imam Jalāl al-Dīn Zaydī, leader of the *sayyids* of Transoxiana, asks, "That which I see do I see it in wakefulness or in sleep, O Lord?"[30] Imam Rokn al-Dīn Imāmzāda, the accomplished scholar, responds, "Be silent: it is the wind of God's omnipotence that bloweth, and we have no power to speak."[31]

Jovaynī implies that in the mundane world, actions follow one another, and each action leaves a trace and a set of consequences. In connection with Chingiz Khan's conquests in Central Asia, Jovaynī repeatedly cites Ferdowsī:

> If thou doest evil, thou dost punish thyself; the eye of Fate is not asleep.
> Bizhan's picture is still painted on the walls of palaces; he is in the prison of Afrasiyab.[32]

27. Boyle 1958, I: 19.
28. Boyle 1958, I: 24.
29. Boyle 1958, I: 105.
30. Boyle 1958, I: 104.
31. Boyle 1958, I: 104.
32. Boyle 1958, I: 81.

> We are all destined to die, young and old; no one remaineth in this world for ever.[33]
>
> Such is the way of high heaven; in the one hand it holds a crown, in the other a noose.[34]

The historian employs similar language of his own in pointing out that individuals cannot escape and should not clash with destiny:

> Nor was it concealed from the Sultan's discernment that to struggle with the contentious Heavens and to persevere against fickle Fate is [vain] toil and trouble; that the course of all events is predestined ... and that it is not in your hands or mine to restore our luck when it is gone, nay the world itself is a snare of calamity, a deceitful coquette.
>
> Shun care, for worldly-wise men have found no shore to the sea of the world.
>
> Why shouldst thou blindly put thy trust in oppression and chicane? For the affairs of this world are all oppression and chicane.[35]

Again, the seemingly fatalistic tone of these passages must be considered in its historical and its literary contexts. As noted above, Bayhaqī had anticipated Jovaynī's attitude toward history in several respects. Of several passages in the *Tārīkh-i Masʿūdī* that illustrate the worldview of this remarkable historian, Bayhaqī's much-studied account of the fall of Ḥasanak, whom Maḥmūd had appointed to the vizierate in 416/1025, is especially striking for the understated manner in which it draws connections between fate and human agency.[36] The narrative opens with a preliminary sketch of the villain of the piece, the restless and over-ambitious courtier and official Bū Sahl Zawzanī (d. ca. 440–50/1050–59). Bayhaqī draws an explicit contrast between Bū Sahl and the former head of the chancery, Bū Naṣr-i Mishkān (d. 431/1039), whom Bayhaqī had served as an assistant:

> This Bū Sahl descended from a line of religious scholars and was distinguished, learned, and cultivated. But a streak of wickedness and malevolence was engrained in his nature – "There is no changing what God has created" (Q. 30: 30) – and along with that wickedness went a certain lack of compassion and he was forever on the lookout for a mighty and willful monarch to become angry with a retainer, and have him arrested and chastised. This man would then pounce from a corner,

33. Boyle 1958, I: 85.
34. Boyle 1958, I: 86.
35. Boyle 1958, II: 400.
36. Of the many scholarly treatments of this celebrated extract, see especially Meisami 1995, Waldman 1980, 166–76 and *passim*.

> exploit the opportunity, and stir up things and inflict much suffering on the retainer. He would then boast that, "It was I who brought the downfall of so-and-so, and he got what he deserved," but the wise knew that this was not so; they would shake their heads and scoff in private, and dismiss him as a braggart. But the case of my master, Bū Naṣr-i Moshkān, proved an exception, for in spite of all his intrigues against him, he could not procure his fall. He was unable to achieve his desire regarding him because the divine decree did not favor and support him in his plans to make mischief. Moreover, Bū Naṣr was a farsighted man. In the time of Amir Maḥmūd, and without betraying his own master, he kept himself in Sultan Masʿūd's good graces in all matters, for he knew that after the father, the royal throne would be his.
>
> Ḥasanak's case was different. For the sake of Amir Moḥammad, and keen on maintaining the affections of Maḥmūd and obeying his orders, he offended this prince and said and did things which his peers would find intolerable, let alone a king; and this is all too similar to the manner in which Jaʿfar the Barmakid and his relations conducted themselves as viziers in the time of Hārūn al-Rashīd, when they suffered the same fate that was meted out to this vizier.[37]

The passage demonstrates not only Bayhaqī's skill in evoking a dramatic scene and its actors within very few lines, but also his ironical juxtaposition of certain underlying themes: fate, divine decree, human foresight and human foibles. The role of fate notwithstanding, Bayhaqī makes it abundantly clear that human beings possess the capacity either to chart a course to safety or, if they succumb to their weaknesses (and sometimes even if they remain true to their deeper loyalties), to effect their own ruin. Bayhaqī's seemingly whimsical ordering of the factors involved in Bū Naṣr's survival, in which he mentions the crucial quality of farsightedness last, almost as if it were an afterthought, is in fact a deliberate strategy, designed not to minimize but to accentuate the importance of individual human control.[38]

In short, on closer examination of their works of history, it becomes clear that, despite their frequent references to the unalterable course of destiny, for both Jovaynī and Bayhaqī, the matter of causality is not rooted entirely in fatalism. Like the texture of their syntax, with its continued use of quotations and evocations of the past, their conceptions of history are in fact less deterministic and more open-ended than they may at first appear.

37. Bayhaqī, *Tārīkh-i Bayhaqī*, I: 226–7. The translation is the author's; compare Waldman 1980, 167.

38. In the same way, as Meisami has pointed out, Bayhaqī leaves the reader in no doubt that Ḥasanak brought his downfall upon himself (Meisami 1995, 357).

The Uses of Intertextuality: Talking Between the Lines

The heavy dose of literature, Qur'anic references, hadith, poetry, prose and proverbs, in Arabic and Persian, that Jovaynī employs in his analysis reflects the wide extent of his knowledge in all these fields. His deployment of these literary excerpts and quotations also functions to convey, explicitly or tacitly, several ideas and conclusions to the reader. Jovaynī's presentation of his philosophical and theological explanations for the Mongol invasion and its effects has already been discussed. In addition, however, Jovaynī's citations from poetry and proverbs enable him to express his thoughts "between the lines."

A good example of this literary strategy is Jovaynī's use of the epic poetry of Ferdowsī, through which the historian points to at least two important features of the monumental events that he recounts. First, he portrays the chivalry and bravery of Sultan Jalāl al-Dīn Khvārazmshāh (r. 617–28/1220–31) in his battles with the Mongols and others. By depicting Chingiz Khan's admiration for Jalāl al-Dīn, Jovaynī implies to the reader that good virtues are universal, such that even the Mongol conqueror is compelled to praise his staunchest enemy in front of his troops:

> The Sultan, for his part, seeing that the day of action was arrived and the time of battle, set his face to combat with the few men that were still left to him. He hastened from right to left and from the left charged upon the Mongol centre. He attacked again and again, but the Mongol armies advanced little by little leaving him less space to manoeuvre and less room to do battle; but still he continued to fight like an angry lion.
>
> Whithersoever he spurred on his charger, he mingled dust with blood [Ferdowsī].
>
> Since Chingiz-Khan had ordered them to take him prisoner, the army were sparing with their lances and arrows wishing to execute Chingiz-Khan's command. But Jalal-ad-Din was too quick for them and withdrew. He was brought a fresh horse, and mounting it he attacked them again and returned from the charge at the gallop.
>
> Like the lightning he struck upon the water and like the wind he departed.
>
> When the Mongols saw him cast himself in the river they were about to plunge in after him. But Chingiz-Khan prevented them. From excess of astonishment he put his hand to his mouth and kept saying to his sons, 'Such a son must a father have.'
>
> When Isfandiyar gazed behind him, he descried him on the dry land on the far side of the stream.

> He said: 'Call not this being a man – he is raging elephant endued with pomp and splendour.'
> So he spoke and gazed thitherwards where Rustam went seeking his way [Ferdowsī].[39]

Secondly, Jovaynī's quotations from the *Shāhnāma* imply parallels between Sultan Jalāl al-Dīn and the epic heroes Rostam, his son Sohrāb, and Esfandiyār, and between the Sultan's Mongol enemies, including Chingiz Khan, and Afrasiyāb and Ashkabus, both of whom symbolize Iran's enemies:

> [T]he Sultan led his army in an attack on Tekechük and Molghor. He slew a thousand men of the Tartar vanguard; and his army being larger in numbers, the Mongols withdrew across the river [probably the Panjshir], destroying the bridge, and encamped upon the other side. The river thus formed a barrier between the two armies, and they [simply] discharged arrows at one another till nightfall. Then at midnight the Mongol army retreated, and the Sultan also retired ...Then he returned to Parvan.
> When news of this reached the ear of Chingiz-Khan and he learnt how the Sultan had mended his affairs and restored them to order -
> Tidings came to Afrasiyab that Suhrab had cast a boat upon the water.
> From the army there were chosen many horsemen, veterans in war -
> He [Chingiz-Khan] dispatched Shigi-Qutuqu with 30,000 men.[40]

Occasionally, such as in his narration of Jalāl al-Dīn's courageous passage of the River Indus following his defeat by Chingiz Khan, Jovaynī invokes the full story more than once.[41] Such repetition suggests that he attaches particular importance to the episode and wishes to convey a significant message to his readers. Jovaynī's casting of Chingiz Khan in the role of the archetypal antagonist, even while he was in service at the court of his son, is a bold act in itself. The historian calls on the consciousness of his compatriots and reminds them of the heroic legacies of the past. His praise of virtue does not stop, however, at the borders of his Iranian homeland.

Seeing Jewels in the Rubble

Jovaynī's invocation and citation of the *Shāhnāma* against the Mongol invaders clearly attest to his ethnic allegiances. Moreover, his incorporation

39. Boyle 1958, I: 134–5. Teresa Fitzherbert has demonstrated how early miniature paintings of the encounter between Jalāl al-Dīn and the Mongols emphasize the former's heroism (Fitzherbert 1994).

40. Boyle 1958, II: 405–6. See also Jovaynī, *Tārīkh-i jahān-goshā*, I: 73, 107, 110; II: 136, 139, 173.

41. Jovaynī, *Tārīkh-i jahān-goshā*, I: 107; II: 143.

of extensive religious materials into his historical account is an indication of his firm faith in Islam. Here and there in the text, the reader perceives Jovaynī's lamentations for the calamities that had befallen the Dār al-Islām. Jovaynī nevertheless served at the Mongol court, and his brother Shams al-Dīn held the most powerful position in the administration after the head of the state. To a degree, Jovaynī was in a position to implement the Mongol policies. For example, he was dispatched to the Alamut library and, while he rescued many precious manuscripts, he set fire to and burnt the books that remained.[42] He seems to have had few scruples in the matter. How could he accommodate these diverse, conflicting and seemingly contradictory views and sentiments?

Jovaynī's evaluation and praise for certain Mongol virtues may provide an explanation beyond that of mere conformism. It seems that Jovaynī sought to ground his value judgments in a broadly construed Islamic worldview, rather than in a narrower or sectarian outlook. It is from this perspective that he surveys Mongol culture. Although he feels and expresses his revulsion at certain rituals, he also praises some Mongol values, apparently with the intention of fostering a similarly objective and critically thoughtful outlook among his readers.

First and foremost among the virtues that he perceives in Mongol culture, Jovaynī emphasizes the high level of solidarity, family allegiance and loyalty among the court members, and their total submission to their master. He then compares this system to what he has observed in his homeland, and expresses deep regret about the unfortunate contrast: "[O]ur purpose in relating this much was to show the harmony which prevails among them as compared with what is related concerning other kings, how brother falls upon brother and son meditates the ruin of father till of necessity they are vanquished and conquered and their authority is downfallen and overthrown.... Whereas by mutual aid and assistance those khans of the children of Chingiz-Khan that succeeded him on the throne have conquered the whole world and utterly annihilated their enemies.'"[43] The unmistakable implication of these lines is that conditions in the Dār al-Islām have lapsed. Furthermore, Jovaynī has no difficulty in finding contrasts to the family solidarity of the Mongols. At a time when the destructive power of the Mongol invaders was beyond any doubt, he observes that the sons of Sultan Moḥammad, namely Jalāl al-Dīn, Qoṭb al-Dīn, Rokn al-Dīn, and Ghiyāth al-Dīn, were busy fighting and killing one another.[44]

42. Qazvini 1912, کح.
43. Boyle 1958, I: 43.
44. Spuler 1985 = Miraftab 1986, 35– 6.

Jovaynī praises, as well, the Mongols' tolerance of other religions, in the sense that they allowed all people to follow their own beliefs and practices as long as they did not interfere in the affairs of the state. In his words: "Being the adherent of no religion and the follower of no creed, he [Chingiz Khan] eschewed bigotry, and the preference of one faith to another, and the placing of some above others; rather he honoured and respected the learned and pious of every sect, recognizing such conduct as the way to the Court of God. As for his children and grandchildren...they still for the most part avoid all show of fanaticism and do not swerve from the *yasa* of Chingiz-Khan, namely, to consider all sects as one and not to distinguish them from one another.'"[45] It was therefore no surprise, according to Jovaynī, that Chingiz Khan's heirs and successors felt totally free to choose whatever religion they liked: "As for his children and grandchildren, several of them have chosen a religion according to their inclination, some adopting Islam, others embracing Christianity, others selecting idolatry and others again cleaving to the ancient canon of their fathers and forefathers and inclining in no direction; but these are now a minority."[46] Jovaynī is similarly impressed by Mongol generosity, and he notes the Mongol custom whereby a new head of state, almost immediately after the demise of his predecessor, shares his fortunes among his army and the members of his court.[47] In a similar vein, he reports:

> They have a custom that if an official or a peasant die, they do not interfere with the estate he leaves, be it much or little, nor may anyone else tamper with it. And if he has no heir, it is given to his apprentice or his slave. On no account is the property of a dead man admitted to the treasury, for they regard such a procedure as inauspicious.[48]

Jovaynī notes with approval the Mongol avoidance of excessive and unnecessary ceremonies at court. He relates: "It is one of their laudable customs that they have closed the doors of ceremony, and preoccupation with titles, and excessive aloofness and inaccessibility ... When one of them ascends the throne of the Khanate, he receives one additional name, that of Khan or Qa'an ..."[49]. He also praises the Mongols' bravery and discipline in military ventures: "... [F]rom the time of Adam down to the present day ... it can be read in no history and is recorded in no book that any of the kings that were

45. Boyle 1958, I: 26.
46. Boyle 1958, I: 26.
47. Jovaynī, *Tārīkh-i jahān-goshā*, I: 25. See also the many anecdotes about the generosity of Ögedei Khan, I: 174–90.
48. Boyle 1958, I: 34.
49. Boyle 1958, I: 26.

lords of the nations ever attained an army like the army of the Tartars, so patient of hardship, so grateful for comforts, so obedient to its commanders both in prosperity and adversity; and this not in hope of wages and fiefs nor in expectation of income or promotion ... In time of action, when attacking and assaulting, they are like trained wild beasts out after game, and in the days of peace and security they are like sheep, yielding milk, and wool, and many other useful things."[50]

As these examples show, Jovaynī faces squarely the destruction wrought by the Mongol conquests, but sifting through the rubble, he finds and appreciates many an unexpected jewel.

Jovaynī the Successful Governor

As mentioned above, an important and distinguishing feature of Jovaynī's historical account is the fact that the author was himself an important participant in some of the events he describes. A number of earlier historians had some involvement in government and administration – Bayhaqī, for example, was a high-ranking member of the Ghaznavid bureaucracy – but Jovaynī's association with the Mongol administration was particularly extensive, especially when the position of his brother Shams al-Dīn, the *ṣāḥib-dīvān*, is taken into account.[51] Jovaynī writes not only as a learned observer and author, nor as a somewhat submissive secretary resigned to executing the whims of his masters. His position acquainted him with the daily intricacies of administration and enabled him to strike a balance, in his writings, between theory and practice, ideals and reality. His governorship of Iraq and part of Syria entailed great challenges, particularly given the fact that the economy of the entire region had been devastated by the Mongol conquests. Marshall Hodgson posited that the economic destruction caused by the Mongol incursions, combined with a phase of global economic contraction, contributed to the beginnings of a new era (the Later Middle Period), set apart from the preceding (Earlier Middle) period.[52] Even under these difficult conditions, Jovaynī was reportedly able to implement successful economic policies during his governorship. With reference to Qazvīnī, E. G. Browne writes, "His [Jovaynī's] efforts were constantly directed to furthering the prosperity of the lands over which he held sway and the well-being of their inhabitants. He lightened the taxes by which the peasants and villagers were oppressed, and exerted himself to bring barren land

50. Boyle 1958, I: 29–30.

51. On Bayhaqī's first-hand observation of and participation in many of the events he describes, see Meisami 1999, 289.

52. Hodgson 1974, II: 373, 386.

under cultivation and to create new villages and watercourses. From the Euphrates he cut a canal from Anbár ... to Kúfa and Najaf, and on this work alone expended more than 100,000 *dínárs* of red gold, founding one hundred and fifty villages on the banks of this canal, and converting the hitherto desert land lying between these two places into verdant and smiling groves and pastures.... Agriculture was eagerly pursued and the revenues of ʿIráq-i-ʿArab were doubled."[53].

Qazvīnī's account indicates that Jovaynī's economic policies were successful. It was this very success, however, that proved Jovaynī's undoing: it brought him wealth, reputation and influence, and provoked jealousy and intrigue against him. As an author Jovaynī was in the position of judging major historical actors, but eventually, he was himself judged and finally overwhelmed by malevolent rivals. These developments have left little trace in his *Tārīkh-i jahān-goshā*, but they do imbue his last work, the *Tasliyat al-ikhwān,* which contains melancholic reflections on the historian-governor's final struggles during the reign of Arghun Khan, when his family had already suffered reversals of fortune.

Conclusion

Both of the historians considered in this article, Jovaynī and his precursor Bayhaqī, maintain a palpable authorial presence throughout their writings. Both wrote works of history and both, especially Jovaynī, actively took part in shaping it. Jovaynī was only twenty-seven years old when he began to write. As many scholars have observed, it is a pity that as soon as he started his administrative career in Baghdad, he stopped writing, except for a brief spell at the end of his life. Nevertheless his historical account, which grew over a period of seven to eight years, is rich in detail and analysis. His witnessing of the rise and fall of individuals, of the full cycles of political lives, and of the ways in which subjects, including the learned, judged their rulers, endowed him with a particular kind of mental flexibility. He was able to see the Islamic world from the outside as well as from within, and he thereby developed an ability to think critically and pragmatically about his own society. In this way, he identified certain defects in both the court and society at large. Through his employment of a highly sophisticated literary language, he repeatedly reminded the current holders of power and authority that sooner or later their terms would come to an end, and that they, like their predecessors, should be mindful of their legacies.

Like the Barmakids before them, the Jovaynī family was annihilated quite suddenly and terminally. But they were instrumental in effecting the

53. Browne 1912, XXIX–XXX.

transformation of a succession of nomadic warlords into courtly rulers, who appreciated and promoted knowledge, literature, and moral codes of conduct. As Hodgson put it, "The Mongols from the first acted in a spirit of monumental achievement: they destroyed in the grand manner, they built in the grand manner too."[54]

Bibliography of Works Cited

Abbas, I. (1989), "Barmakids," *EIr* III: 806–9.

Barthold, W. [J. A. Boyle] (1996), "Djuwaynī, ʿAlāʾ al-Dīn ʿAṭā-Malik," *EI²* II: 606–7.

Bayhaqī, Abū l-Fażl Moḥammad, *Tārīkh-i Bayhaqī*, ed. Khalil Rahbar, 3 vols., Tehran: Enteshārāt-i Saʿdī, 1368/1989.

Boyle, John A. (1958), *The History of the World-Conqueror*, 2 vols., Manchester: Manchester University Press, Cambridge, Mass.: Harvard University Press.

Boyle, J. A. (1962), "Juvaynī and Rashīd al-Dīn as Sources on the History of the Mongols," in: *Historians of the Middle East*, ed. Bernard Lewis and P. M. Holt, London: Oxford University Press, 133–7.

Browne, Edward G. (1912), "Introduction," *The Taʾríkh-i-Jahán-Gushá of ʿAláʾu ʾd-Dín ʿAṭá Malik-i-Juwayní*, ed. Mirza Muhammad Qazvini, 3 vols. Leiden: E. J. Brill, London: Luzac, XIII–XCIII.

Bulliet, Richard W. (1994), *Islam: The View from the Edge*, New York: Columbia University Press.

Daniel, Elton (2004), "Historiography: iii. Early Islamic Period, " *EIr* XII: 330–48.

Fitzherbert, Teresa (1994), "Portrait of a Lost Leader: Jalal al-Din Khwarazmshah and Juvaini," in: *The Court of the Il-Khans 1290–1340*, ed. Julian Raby and Teresa Fitzherbert, Oxford University Press, 63–77.

Hodgson, Marshall G. S. (1974), *The Venture of Islam, Conscience and History in a World Civilization*, 3 vols., Chicago and London: The University of Chicago Press.

Jovaynī, ʿAlā al-Dīn ʿAṭā-Malek, *The Taʾríkh-i-Jahán-Gushá of ʿAláʾu ʾd-Dín ʿAṭá Malik-i-Juwayní*, ed. Mirza Muhammad Qazvini, 3 vols. Leiden: E. J. Brill, London: Luzac, 1912–37.

Meisami, Julie Scott (1995), "Exemplary Lives, Exemplary Deaths: The Execution of Ḥasanak," *Actas XVI Congreso UEAI*, ed. Concepción Vázquez de Benito and Miguel Ángel Manzano Rodríguez, Salamanca, 357–64.

—— (1999), *Persian Historiography to the End of the Twelfth Century*, Edinburgh: Edinburgh University Press.

54. Hodgson 1974, II: 405.

Melville, Ch. (2004), "Historiography: iv. Mongol Period," *EIr* XII: 348–56.
Nafisi, Said (1342/1963), *Dar pīrāmūn-i Tārīkh-i Bayhaqī shāmil-i āthār-i gom-shodeh-yi Abu l-Fażl Bayhaqī va-Tārīkh-i Ghaznaviyyān*, 2 vols.,Tehran: Forūghī.
Qazvini, Mirza Muhammad (1912), "Editor's Introduction," *The Taʾríkh-i-Jahán-Gushá of ʿAláʾu ʾd-Dín ʿAṭá Malik-i-Juwayní*, 3 vols. Leiden: E. J. Brill, London: Luzac.
Reza-Qoli, Ali (1998), *Jāmeʿa-shenāsī-yi nokhba- koshī*, Tehran: Enteshārāt-i Nashr-i Nay.
Sourdel, D. (1960), "al-Barāmika," *EI*[2] I: 1033–6.
Spuler, Bertold (1985), *Die Mongolen in Iran: Politik, Verwaltung und Kultur der Ilchanzeit 1220–1350*, Leiden: E. J. Brill. Translated into Persian by Mahmud Miraftab, Tehran: Sherkat-i Enteshārāt-i ʿIlmī va-Farhangī, 1365/1986–7.
—— (1996), "Djuwaynī, Shams al-Dīn Muḥammad," *EI*[2] II: 607.
Waldman, Marilyn Robinson (1980), *Toward a Theory of Historical Narrative: A Case Study in Perso-Islamicate Historiography*, Columbus: Ohio State University Press.

A Glorious Past and an Outstanding Present: Writing a Collection of Biographies in Late Persianate Central Asia

Maria Szuppe

Har ke az mā konad be nīkī yād
nām-ash andar jahān be nīkī bād
(Malīḥā, *Modhakker al-aṣḥāb*)

THE POST-TIMURID PERIOD OR LATE MEDIAEVAL PERIOD in the Muslim East is generally characterised by the division of the Timurid political "space" into three large domains: Safavid Iran, the Uzbek states in Central Asia, and Mughal India. This diversity in the political sphere is not mirrored in other areas, and especially not in the cultural sphere. On the contrary, a clear perception of belonging to a single cultural space was maintained over this geographically vast area for centuries after the "Empire" of Timur's descendants had disappeared in the years following 1506.[1] This perception derives partly from the use in these regions of the Persian language as the dominant idiom of literary expression,[2] as well as from a common adherence to the Perso-Islamicate cultural-social system of education, behaviour, and good manners, or *adab*, which provided a common basis for the educational and cultural references shared in particular by the literate middle and upper classes of society. This shared cultural framework seems to have been sustained by regular contacts among individuals, family groups, and social groups functioning within the political units of the post-Timurid space. Individuals and groups of people travelled frequently between Central Asia, Iran, and India, thus promoting cultural, literary, and spiritual exchanges through direct personal contacts, and generating an overall climate of profound interest in literary trends, accomplishments, and production in all these parts of the Persianate world.[3]

The Timurid period saw several rich literary developments, including

1. Foltz 1998b; Fragner 1999; Szuppe 2004.
2. Other prevalent literary languages were Chaghatay Turkish and, more rarely, Arabic.
3. See for example Haneda 1997 (and his bibliography); Foltz 1998a, 12–14; but also McChesney 1990; Szuppe 2004.

the formal refinement of specific genres (such as the *moʿammā*, or poetical riddle) on the one hand, and expansion of the contents of literary and historical works in response to new social and intellectual interests on the other.[4] One significant aspect of this change in mentality, which finds expression in the writings of the late fifteenth and following centuries, was the strong interest of the literati in the events of "real life." Through the introduction of elements of realism and reminiscences drawn from current developments and conditions, this new mentality facilitated a number of modifications of earlier literary conventions.[5] In this era, literary writings not only provide realistic descriptions of places and monuments, as opposed to canonical poetic descriptions, but also exhibit a marked attention to the individual and, especially, to contemporary society. An important expression of this new social worldview can be seen in the appearance of works containing a significant element of autobiographical material. The *Bābor-nāma* or Memoirs of Bābor (r. 932–37/1526–30), a Timurid of a junior branch and the founder of the Mughal dynasty in India, is the best known work of this kind, but other examples include the *Homāyūn-nāma*, a narrative of the reign of the Emperor Homāyūn b. Bābor (r. 937–63/1530–56) written by his sister, Golbadan Begom (*ca.* 929–1011/1523–1603), as well as, in Safavid Iran, the *Tadhkera* by Shāh Ṭahmāsp I b. Esmāʿīl Ṣafavī (r. 930–84/1524–76).[6] These and similar writings represent, in Maria Subtelny's term, a sort of "political 'memoir' ";[7] they contain important biographical and autobiographical elements. While all the above-mentioned works originated in courtly settings, the Memoirs of Zayn al-Dīn Vāṣefī of Herat (d. before 964/1551), entitled the *Badāyeʿ al-vaqāyeʿ* and written *ca.* 939/1532–33 in Tashkent, represent an early and rare example of "autobiographical" writings by an author belonging to an urban middle-class milieu.[8] In extensive passages, this text contains a

4. In an interesting article on the dispute between the "old" and the "new" in Timurid Herat, Aftandil Erkinov shows the crucial importance of reconciling the demands of formal literary codes with the need to modify or modernise the contents of literary works at the end of the fifteenth century (Erkinov 1999).

5. Several traditional literary genres underwent such transformations; as Michele Bernardini (2003) has recently argued, the *shahrāshūb* writings constitute a good example.

6. The *Bābor-nāma* was originally written in Chaghatay Turkish, and then translated into Persian (see Golchīn Maʿānī 1363sh./1984, II: 459–66; Storey/Bregel' 1972, II: 828–38, for the list of Chaghatay and Persian manuscripts). For a modern edition of the original text, see *Bābor-nāma*, ed. E. Mano, Kyoto, 1995. There are numerous translations into major eastern and western languages. For further discussion, see the article of Stephen Dale in the current volume. The *Tadhkera-ye Shāh Ṭahmāsp-e Ṣafavī* has been edited by ʿAbd al-Shakūr (Berlin-Charlottenburg: "Kaviani," 1343/1965), and by Amrallāh Ṣafarī (Tehran: Enteshārāt-e Sharq, 1363sh./1984 [2nd edition]).

7. Subtelny 1984, 139.

8. Golchīn Maʿānī 1363sh./1984, II: 467–82. The text was also published by A. N. Boldyrev (Moscow: Nauka, 1961; new edition, Tehran: Bonyād-e Farhang-e Īrān, 1970). For the author's

direct account of the author's life, especially during his youth, and gives expression to his feelings and opinions. However, none of these works can be considered an autobiography *stricto sensu*, a genre that does not fully appear in Persian literature until modern times.[9]

Simultaneously, collections of biographies of famous people, and especially biographical poetical anthologies (*tadhkera*) count among the literary genres that evolved mainly from the end of the fifteenth century onwards. They enjoyed growing popularity and continued to be extremely widespread in Central Asia, Iran, and Mughal India in the later period.

I. Collected Biographies of Poets in Persian by Late Central Asian Authors

Biographical dictionaries have a long tradition in Muslim historiography, having been in existence since the early years of Muslim literature.[10] Usually arranged by social categories (*ṭabaqāt*), or devoted to one particular socio-professional group, they describe the lives of "famous people." These biographies are generally short and far from exhaustive; in some cases, the biographical data are supplemented by samples of poetry composed by individuals listed in the dictionary. As a rule, this type of biographical writing is strongly codified in form and in contents, and mostly devoted either to saintly, religious and administrative personalities, or to literati and learned men and, sometimes, women.[11]

In Persian tradition, the collection of biographies of outstanding poets

---

biography, see Boldyrev 1957. There has been a recent renewal of interest in this text; see for example Subtelny 1984; Rota 1996.

9. Lambton 1962, 149. It should be noted, however, that many Central Asian *tadhkera* writers include an entry devoted to themselves, and sometimes to the members of their family; such "autobiographical" entries are found, for example, in Khvāja Ḥasan Nethārī (see Nethārī [d. 1004/1595–96], *Modhakker al-aḥbāb*, 300–10), and in Malīḥā (see Malīḥā [d. after 1103/1692], *Modhakker al-aṣḥāb*, 506–11, and *passim*); the latter includes a regular entry on "Malīḥā-ye Samarqandī," the author himself (see below). More generally, autobiographical information is scattered throughout the text.

10. On biographical writings in earlier Muslim literature, and particularly in Arabic, the basic references have been gathered in the revised edition of Rosenthal 1968², in Gibb 1962, as well as in the relevant articles of the *Encyclopaedia of Islam*, 1st and 2nd editions (Leiden: E. J. Brill). See especially the entries "Ṭabaḳāt" (Heffening repr.1987; and Gilliot 2000), "Taʾrīkh. II. Historical Writing" (Humphreys 1998 for Arabic, and Lambton 1998 for Persian). More recently, numerous publications have appeared pertaining to general or particular aspects of the mediaeval Muslim biographical collections; among other examples, see Abiad 1979; al-Qadi 1995; Cooperson 2000; Robinson 2003, and their respective bibliographies.

11. See Roded 1994, and the article of Devin Stewart in the present volume. For a sixteenth-century *tadhkera* by Fakhrī Heravī devoted to learned women and poetesses, see Szuppe 1996, and below, nn. 18 and 22.

and literati was usually called *tadhkera*.[12] Especially following the *Tadhkerat al-shoʿarā* (892/1487) written in Herat by Dawlatshāh Samarqandī (d. *ca.* 900/1494), which established a new model for *tadhkera*s for centuries, the "Timurid" perception of society opened the *tadhkera* genre to the massive inclusion of contemporary material. This turn in perspective brought about certain changes in the composition of *tadhkera*s, most visibly in matters of content and structure. Although in Central Asia the post-Timurid *tadhkera*s of poets are still, strictly speaking, biographical anthologies of poetical writings that attest to a glorified classical past and an outstanding present, in practice the historical part was strongly reduced and the modern part expanded, often disproportionally.

The change of focus on the part of later Central Asian authors led to the incorporation into their works of more and more biographies of contemporary poets, many of whom were still active at the time of the composition of the *tadhkera*. It must be strongly underlined that expressions of literary life were present at all levels of society; this widespread activity was typically encouraged by the larger tradition of oral literary transmission, as well as by the importance in Muslim society in general of at least elementary schooling that was accessible to all social classes. Numerous examples from the Central Asian *tadhkera* sources show that poets, literati, and calligraphers originated not only from the upper administrative, military and religious classes, but also from the middle and even lower milieus of post-Timurid society. Moṭrebī of Samarqand (b. 966/1559; d. after 1037/1627) indicates that "the common people" (*ʿavāmm*) participated in literary gatherings (*soḥbat*) held at the house of Khvāja Ḥasan Nethārī Bokhārī (d. 1004/1595–96), a central figure in Bukharan literary circles in the second half of the sixteenth century and, incidentally, himself the author of a major *tadhkera*.[13] Various sources quote a poet court official or bazaar scribe side by side with a poet craftsman or peasant.[14]

The great majority of the people quoted in Central Asian *tadhkera*s were not professional but amateur or occasional poets; few of them made a living by writing poetry. According to the practice of the time, any person, and es-

12. For a general overview of the Persian *tadhkera*, see de Bruijn 1998; also Lambton 1962. On some particularities of post-Timurid Central Asian *tadhkeras*, see Szuppe 1999, esp. p. 100.

13. On both these authors, see below.

14. Moṭrebī (d. after 1037/1627), *Noskha*, 133. Some examples: Moḥammad-Bāqī Kaffāsh Samarqandī, the shoemaker (Moṭrebī [d. after 1037/1627], *Tadhkera*, 255–56, under "Bāqī Kaffāsh"), Ghaẓanfarī the peasant, *mard-e keshāvarzī* (Kāmī Qazvīnī [d. after 1004/1595–96], *Nafāyes al-moʾāther*, MS. Tashkent, fol. 85b; on this source, see Golchīn Maʿānī 1363sh./1984, II: 362–91; Naqavī 1347sh./1968, 100–08); Ahlī of Herat who was of "low origin," see Bābor (d. 937/1530), *Bābor-nāma*, 290 and n. 6. For other examples, see Szuppe 1999, 101 and nn. 9–12.

pecially any literate person, could and should be able to compose verses. The *tadhkeras* quote names, short biographies and samples of verses of hundreds and, sometimes, thousands of people who at some point in their lives wrote poetry, and have thus been recorded by each particular *tadhkera* author. Some of these poets were widely renowned, others were known only locally and at a particular period. These historical-literary sources often bring up rare and even unique data on persons unknown from other historical writings. Many samples of literary compositions quoted in these *tadhkeras* are likewise unattested in other collections of verse. Thus, the *tadhkeras* appear as very valuable sources on all aspects of contemporary life.

This new attitude towards composing collections of biographies — "for remembering" (*tadhkera*) — brought with it another important transformation. During the sixteenth to the nineteenth centuries, the *tadhkera* effectively evolved from being a collection of model lives and literary creations for the benefit of posterity towards becoming a picture, indeed a "remembrance," of literary life in each author's time. The classical *tadhkera* assembled biographies of outstanding poets, with samples of their verses considered as perfect examples of a particular genre or style, in a sort of model biographical anthology. But, as mentioned above, the post-Timurid *tadhkera* collected also, if not principally, biographies of contemporary and living authors, often the author's friends and relations, or people he had met here and there in the course of his visits and travels. How many of these "poets" would have otherwise survived the test of time? How many of them have been saved from oblivion by the fact of having their names recorded in a *tadhkera* just because the author had met them or had heard their verses on a certain occasion? In post-Timurid Central Asia, the criteria for entering a poet's name into a *tadhkera* differ from those of earlier periods.

Generally, a Central Asian *tadhkera* followed some basic rules of the early-established formal traditions, which themselves remain somewhat poorly understood. The entries were arranged according to certain generally accepted principles, such as the alphabetical order of poets' names (or, more often, their poetical pennames, *takhalloṣ)*, and also social categories (rulers, state dignitaries, religious men, and so on).[15] However, Central Asian *tadhkeras* include a characteristic division that reflects their authors' new scope of interest: poets of the past are grouped in a chapter apart, while

15. Some monumental *tadhkeras* include special chapters devoted to women poets, such as the *Mer'āt al-khayāl* written in 1102/1690–91 by the Mughal author Shīr-Khān Lūdī, who adds a chapter with seventeen names of female poets, and, in Iran, the *Āteshkada* of Loṭf-ʿAlī Beg Shāmlū Ādhar, completed *ca.* 1174/1760–61, which contains a sub-chapter with eight names (see Szuppe 1996, 124 and nn. 26–28).

contemporary poets are arranged in chapters according to the personal criteria of the author, the basic distinction being whether or not the author was personally acquainted with the poet.[16] Each category could be more precisely situated by sub-division into poets who "have died since" and those who "are still alive," or poets who "wrote under the rule of such and such a sovereign." These typologies were not exclusive of each other, and could combine at different levels; usually the alphabetical order of the names was maintained inside each division and sub-division.

As the *tadhkeras* are concerned with poets and learned men predominantly writing in Persian, in some cases the biographers will especially acknowledge poets who composed verses in other languages, mainly Chaghatay Turkish, and, exceptionally, Arabic. In his *Toḥfa-ye Sāmī* (957/1550), the Herat-educated Sām Mīrzā Ṣafavī (923–74/1517–67) groups in a special chapter the poets "who wrote in *torkī*," that is Chaghatay Turkish or Turki, with samples of their poems.[17] In *ca.* 963/1555–56, Solṭān-Moḥammad-e Amīrī, known as Fakhrī Heravī (d. after 963/1555–56, possibly *ca.* 970/1562–63), wrote the *Javāher al-ʿajāyeb*, a short *tadhkera* in Persian exclusively dedicated to learned women and female poets; in his work, Fakhrī takes for granted that these poetesses composed in Persian, and always notes explicitly if one or another of them was also known for composing verses in Turki.[18] In one of the entries in his biographical anthology of poets, Moṭrebī mentions the literary bilingualism (*dū-zabānī; goftan-e sheʿr be dū zabān fārsī va-torkī*) of Amīr Dūst Vafā Bīy Dūrmān, who composed verses not only in Persian but also in Turki under the penname of Vafāʾī.[19]

Finally, the authors' interest in contemporary poets and literati generated particular requirements for gathering source material, and involved special methods that were developed for writing a *tadhkera* according to this model. As will be demonstrated below, the Central Asian *tadhkera* writers paid particular attention to the accuracy, originality, and richness of the contemporary material to be included in their collections of biographies.

16. This arrangement can typically be seen in the works of Khvāja Ḥasan Nethārī (*Modhakker al-aḥbāb*, written in 974/1566), and Moṭrebī Samarqandī (*Tadhkerat al-shoʿarā*, written in 1013/1604–05, and *Noskha-ye zībā-ye Jahāngīr*, the greater part of which was written in 1036/1627).

17. See Sām Mīrzā (d. 974/1567), *Toḥfa-ye Sāmī*. The author, a younger brother of the Safavid ruler of Iran Shāh Ṭahmāsp, spent his childhood in Herat as governor of Khurasan, in 927–35/1521–29 and 940–41/1534–35.

18. For example, at Samarqand, Moghūl Khātūn, daughter of Solṭān-Moḥammad Khān of Tashkent, and wife first of the Uzbek khan Moḥammad Shaybānī (d. 916/1510), then, after his death, of ʿObaydallāh Khān (d. 946/1540); see Fakhrī Heravī (d. after 963/1555–56), *Javāher al-ʿajāyeb*, 127–28.

19. Moṭrebī, *Noskha*, 235–37; and Moṭrebī, *Tadhkera*, 332.

II. The Author's Workshop

The author's reasons for engaging in the long and complicated process of writing a collection of poetical biographies are not always explicitly stated in the text, and even where such reasons are noted, they often appear to be formulated in a standard and impersonal way. Some authors provide more details than others and there are cases where the introductory part of the work includes a special chapter or paragraph on "the reasons for writing [the book]," *sabab-e taʿlīf[-e ketāb]*.

Putting together a collection of biographies with a selection of poetry could rarely be a short-term enterprise, and thus composing a *tadhkera* was, in most cases, a project of many years. Time was needed not only to assemble historical and poetic material, but also to organise and edit it according to general rules and, ideally, according to a preconceived plan. The importance for the writer of conformity to the established formal canon is illustrated by the misadventure of one Central Asian author, Moḥammad-Ṣādeq known as "Ṣādeqī," who wrote a *tadhkera* entitled *Riyāḍ al-shoʿarā* (composed in the late sixteenth-early seventeenth century). As soon as the book had been "released," it met with strong criticism from the author's fellow literati because it did not contain a chapter devoted to "difficult or astonishing poems," a category that was traditionally expected to be present in such a work. Moḥammad-Ṣādeq was so devastated by the criticism that he destroyed his work, and then wrote a second version of it that conformed formally in all points to the established rules.[20] Unfortunately, neither the first nor the second versions of his *tadhkera* are extant today, but the work was evidently well known during the author's lifetime and for some time afterwards, as it is quoted as a source by another Central Asian writer a century later.[21]

In addition, many shorter *tadhkera*s existed, such as those composed by Fakhrī Heravī in the middle of the sixteenth century.[22] These types of

20. This anecdote is narrated by Moṭrebī, who was well acquainted with Moḥammad-Ṣādeq (see Moṭrebī, *Tadhkera*, 605). In addition, see Davidson 2001, on the problem of the publication and release of texts in the mediaeval Muslim context.

21. For example, it is quoted among the written sources used by Malīḥā-ye Samarqandī. The recent edition prints the name as "Ṣāmī" (Malīḥā, *Modhakker al-aṣḥāb*, 52), which obviously is a misreading for "Ṣādeqī." The name is clearly legible in the Tashkent manuscript, MS. 4270: Malīḥā, *Modhakker al-aṣḥāb*, fol. 40a. See also below and n. 28.

22. Fakhrī Heravī wrote the already mentioned *Javāher al-ʿajāyeb*, a *tadhkera* of learned women where he quotes between nineteen and twenty-three names (the actual number varies according to different manuscripts), and in 960/1553, he completed another *tadhkera*, entitled the *Rawḍat al-salāṭīn*, where several dozen poets are listed (Golchīn Maʿānī 1363sh./1984, I: 644–49). The latter work has been published in Hyderabad together with the *Javāher al-ʿajāyeb* quoted here (see Bibliography), as well as in Tabriz as [Solṭān-Moḥammad b. Amīrī], *Tadhkera-ye Rawḍat al-salāṭīn*, ed. A. Khayyāmpūr, Tabriz 1345sh./1966.

writings contain on average three to four hundred short biographies, while major *tadhkeras* can list as many as a thousand, sometimes more, poets, as in the case of the *ʿArafāt al-ʿāsheqīn*, composed *ca.* 1024/1615 by Taqī Awḥadī (d. after 1039/1629) in India, the *Āteshkada* (*ca.* 1174/1760–61) by Loṭf-ʿAlī Beg Shāmlū Ādhar in Iran, and others.[23]

In the seventeenth century, the above-mentioned Moṭrebī Samarqandī wrote two major *tadhkeras* in more than twenty years: the *Tadhkerat al-shoʿarā*, finished in 1013/1604–05, and the *Noskha-ye zībā-ye Jahāngīr*, the main part of which was completed in 1036/1627. Although they are two different texts, these *tadhkeras* cross-reference each other, and some entries present in the later text constitute an updated version of the earlier one. The task of writing the *Noskha-ye zībā-ye Jahāngīr*, the second of the two texts, took two years for the main body of the book, from Rajab 1034/April 1625 to Jomādā II 1036/February-March 1627, and another year or more, until 1037/1627–28 or some time afterwards, for the Epilogue (*khātema*) which is an important part of this book as it recounts the author's stay at Jahāngīr's court.[24]

A lesser known author named ʿAbdallāh Kābolī (d. after 1035/1625–26), a contemporary of Moṭrebī, spent about twenty years (990–1010/1582–1601) in writing his somewhat different *tadhkera*, which consisted of historical biographies illustrated by chronograms (*tārīkh*).[25] The text was partly revised and augmented at least once during this period: the modifications and updating process can be traced from one of the three known manuscripts, which represents the author's working copy (*noskha-ye taḥrīr*).[26] Elāhī or Mīr ʿEmād al-Dīn Maḥmūd Ḥosaynī (d. *ca.* 1063/1653), another interesting but little known author from Central Iran who emigrated to Kabul, Delhi, and Kashmir, composed his collection of biographies of Iranian, Indian, and Central Asian poets, the *Khazīna-ye ganj*, over several years, most probably between 1042–52/1632–43.[27] At the end of the seventeenth century, Moḥammad-Badīʿ Samarqandī, known as Malīḥā (b. *ca.* 1051/1641; d. after 1103/1692), took seven years from 1093/1682–83 to 1100/1697–98 to write his *tadhkera*

23. On Taqī Awḥādī's *ʿArafāt al-ʿāsheqīn*, see Golchīn Maʿānī 1363sh./1984, II: 3–24, and Naqavī 1347sh./1968, 151–63. On the *Āteshkada*, of which there are editions, see Golchīn Maʿānī 1363sh./1984, I: 2–17. Interestingly, the Bibliothèque nationale de France (Paris) possesses an important manuscript of the work (*Supplément persan 1327*), which had been collated with an autograph copy.

24. See Moṭrebī, *Noskha*, 267–344. R. C. Foltz's translation into English of the *khātema* has recently been published (see Foltz 1998a, where references to earlier editions are also provided).

25. ʿAbdallāh Kābolī (d. after 1035/1625–26), *Tadhkerat al-tavārīkh*, MS. Tashkent 2093. This author used the poetical pennames of Gonāhī and ʿAbdī, see Szuppe 2006, 348, 350. On ʿAbdallāh Kābolī, see also Nūr al-Dīnūf [Nuriddinov] 1365sh./1986.

26. For details, see Szuppe 2006, 349–50.

27. Naqavī 1347sh./1968, 191–92.

of Persian-language poets, entitled the *Modhakker al-aṣḥāb*; later, he added a Supplement (*mulḥaqāt*), composed between 1100/1689 and 1103/1693, containing updates with the names of poets who had been overlooked in the main part of the text.[28] ʿĀsheq ʿAẓīmābādī (b. 1194/1780; d. in or after 1252/1836–37) started to write his huge *tadhkera* of Persian-language poets of India, Iran, and Central Asia, called the *Neshtar-e ʿeshq*, in 1224/1809–10; he finished it only eight years later, in 1233/1817–18.[29]

In order to produce such a collection of biographies, the author had to plan his work carefully and proceed in stages. Firstly, he had to conceive the project, and define the particular field of interest and the scope of his *tadhkera*. Secondly, he had to gather the necessary factual and literary material, according to his criteria of selection, then organise and edit it. Finally, he had to check and update the working copy, so that the final authorised version could be prepared and released.[30] How were all these stages actually accomplished, in practical as well as intellectual terms?

II. 1. Conceiving the project: motivation

Many, if not the majority of *tadhkera*s contain an introductory part that provides a sequence of interesting albeit standard pieces of information, such as the title and the date of the work, the name of the author, and the name of the author's patron or dedicatee. Quite often, the structure and contents of the work are announced in a table of contents (*fehrest*), and the reasons and purposes that motivated the writer to produce the work are explained. In practice, however, the data contained in these introductory sections are rarely comprehensive. Rather, different introductions contain different pieces of information drawn from the ideal list given above, and frequently,

28. The only edition, quoted here, is that of Kamāl al-Dīn ʿAynī [Kamoliddin Aïni]: Dushanbe 1385sh./2006. In addition, among numerous manuscripts of Malīḥā Samarqandī's text known to be held at Saint Petersburg, Tashkent, and Dushanbe, we refer to the "Biruni" Oriental Institute copy (Tashkent), MS. 4270 (autograph "working copy," undated; described in SVR, IX, no. 6076. For a general description of the text, see Akhmedov 1985, 173–78, especially p. 175.

29. ʿĀsheq, *Neshtar-e ʿeshq*, MS. Tashkent 2096, fol. 20b. On the author, and the manuscripts and edition of the text, see below and nn. 45 and 47.

30. The question of "publication," while interesting, remains outside the scope of this paper. On the importance of public reading in Muslim society, see Davidson 2001. In the present case, it is important to underline the interest of the process of "release" of a new text, and the circulation of writings in the literary milieu of the time. Most probably, the text was released directly in writing. Even for a public recitation — the most widespread means of literary publication — the existence of at least one copy, the original, seems to have been indispensable, considering the nature and size of a standard *tadhkera*. Did this one original copy, circulating at first among a necessarily restricted group of readers, constitute "publication" of a text? The misadventure of Moḥammad-Ṣādeq, narrated above, seems to confirm this supposition.

to gain a more complete picture, many elements must be sought indirectly in relevant remarks and facts indicated in the core of the work.

Turning to the introductory parts of the *tadhkera*s produced in the post-Timurid cultural domain is nevertheless a profitable means of discovering the factors that motivated the authors to engage in the long and difficult literary process of compiling their texts. Even if such introductions conform in part to the conventions of literary expression inherent in the historiographical genre, their articulations of authorial motivations are advanced by the writers themselves and addressed to their contemporary readers; in some cases, as will be seen, they include an obviously personal note. How, then, did post-Timurid authors comprehend and justify their *tadhkera*-writing activity?

In late sixteenth-century Bukhara, the house of Khvāja Ḥasan Nethārī, one of the most prominent literary and spiritual figures of the times, was a visiting "must" for local poets and literati, as well as for foreign travellers, who came especially to attend the literary gatherings (*soḥbat* or *majles*) that were regularly held there. Nethārī is also the author of an important *tadhkera* of poets, the *Modhakker al-aḥbāb* (974/1566), which established a direct point of reference for later *tadhkera* writers of Central Asia. In the introductory part of his work, the author inserts a special section on his "reasons for writing the book," *dar sabab-e ta'līf-e ketāb.*[31] According to his explanation, Nethārī had been urged to write a *tadhkera* by some "brothers" (*akhvān*)[32] and "learned men" (*foḍalā*) of his entourage. They argued that, since the release of the *Majāles al-nafāyes* (in 896/1490–91) by Mīr ʿAlī-Shīr Navāʾī (d. 906/1501) — a well-known *tadhkera* of the late Timurid period originally written in Turki and immediately translated into Persian[33]— there had been no other *tadhkera* registering the names of the famous khans, sultans, and other persons, so that they might live on in the memory of their disciples (*ṭālebān*). This, Nethārī asserted, was why he picked up a pen and gathered together (*jamʿ nemūda*) the names of nobles and grandees, thus composing his *tadhkera* and dedicating it to the ruler ʿAbdallāh Khān II (r. 991–1006/1583–98) of the Shaybanid Uzbeks.[34] Several lines further down the text, Nethārī quotes,

31. Nethārī, *Modhakker al-aḥbāb*, 6–7.

32. Nethārī was affiliated to the powerful Naqshbandi Sufi order, and this is probably why the word *akhvān* is used here, as well as *ṭālebān*, further down the page.

33. The text was first translated into Persian and extended by the above-mentioned Fakhrī Heravī. His Persian version, also known as the *Laṭāyef-nāma*, includes an additional section on the early sixteenth-century poets, i.e. the translator's own contemporaries.

34. On different aspects of the relationship between authors and representatives of political power, see the collective volume Gruendler and Marlow (eds.) 2004; on the question of dedicating works to a patron in particular, see Touati 2000b.

first, a few words from a hadith and, second, from the Qurʾan to illustrate the importance of the process of "remembrance."[35]

In the early seventeenth century, Moṭrebī Samarqandī, who was a follower and admirer of Nethārī, wrote (as already mentioned) two important *tadhkera*s of poets of Central Asia, Iran and India: the *Tadhkerat al-shoʿarā*, and the *Noskha-ye zībā-ye Jahāngīr*.[36] In the first of these two texts, after quoting the Qurʾan and the hadith, Moṭrebī explains that in every period of time there has existed a learned man who produced a written copy (*noskha*) of the collected poems and sayings of famous and pious people, as a means of remembering them (*be yādgārī*).[37] He gives three examples of such "celebrated books": the *Tadhkera* by Amīr Dawlatshāh [Samarqandī], the *Majāles al-nafāyes* by Amīr Kabīr ʿAlī-Shīr [Navāʾī], and finally the *Modhakker al-aḥbāb* by "my deceased master (*ostādh*), His Excellency Ḥasan Khvāja Nethārī Bokhārī." In order to follow this outstanding example, Moṭrebī took it upon himself to note the names of people of renown, including his own contemporaries, and put in writing "the verses, the hadiths, and the stories (*ḥekāyat*)" associated with them.[38]

The introductory part is also quite developed in Moṭrebī's second *tadhkera*, the *Noskha-ye zībā-ye Jahāngīr*. In this work the author defines more precisely certain points concerning the writing of this particular book, but some of his remarks apply more generally to the practice of *tadhkera*-composition. Moṭrebī, now seventy years old and his memory full of many names and poems, expresses his wish to gather together in one volume (*dar yek jeld jamʿ sāzad*) all that he has seen and heard, so that these compositions might remain and possibly bring some pleasure to a future reader.[39]

At the end of the seventeenth century, in the opening paragraphs of his *Modhakker al-aṣḥāb*, Malīḥā Samarqandī explains the motives for his own embarking on the long process of *tadhkera*-writing; although the explanation is more detailed, the ultimate reason given by the author conforms with the general trend.[40] Having been reluctant to pursue the path of learning, Malīḥā Samarqandī had spent his younger years doing nothing in particular until he realised at some point that in this way nothing would remain of him by which he might be remembered after his death. Accordingly he set

35. Nethārī, *Modhakker al-aḥbāb*, 7; the Qurʾanic quotation is taken from *Sūrat al-Insān* (Q. 76: 29).

36. On the author and his writings, see Akhmedov 1985, 165–73, and his bibliography p. 231, for articles in Russian and Uzbek. See also Foltz 1996, and Foltz 1998a.

37. Moṭrebī, *Tadhkera*, 126.

38. Moṭrebī, *Tadhkera*, 126–27.

39. Moṭrebī, *Noskha*, 14.

40. Malīḥā, *Modhakker al-aṣḥāb*, 49–51.

about participating in literary meetings (*soḥbat*), gathering pieces of poetry, and also composing some himself, before finally deciding to assemble the verses of others into one book so that they would be recorded (*ḍabṭ*) forever. Malīḥā insists on the fact that a trace would thus be left forever of each of these persons (*va az har yek neshānī mānad*); this should be, according to him, reason enough to "justify [the creation of] the 'remembrance' (*tadhkera*) and [the reciting of] the *fāteḥa*."[41]

In this way, Malīḥā adds, the good names of all the people of the past (*goẕashtegān*) who wrote poetry would be remembered. But additionally, his own name would not be forgotten; on the contrary, it would be quoted among the "people of renown" (*nāmdār*). It is also of importance, continues Malīḥā a few paragraphs later, to record the words of one's contemporaries.[42] He refers to his famous predecessors, especially Dawlatshāh Samarqandī, who quotes in his *tadhkera* not only Arabic and Persian poets of the early age but also scholars (*foḍalā*) of his own time, such as Jāmī and other prominent people. He also refers to the works of Mīr ʿAlī-Shīr Navāʾī, who "wrote in Turki," and of Khvāja Ḥasan Nethārī, for the "past" authors, and to a certain Moḥammad Bāltū, known as Mollā Ṣāmī/Ṣādeqī Samarqandī, for the "present" authors.[43]

Among the texts of the early nineteenth century, the work of Āghā Ḥosayn-Qolī Khān ʿAẓīmābādī (d. 1252/1836 or later),[44] an Indo-Persian author from a family of remote Khurasanian extraction,[45] is very explicit. Known under the penname of ʿĀsheq,[46] he wrote a huge *tadhkera* containing nearly 1,500 biographies arranged in alphabetical order and entitled *Neshtar-e ʿeshq*.[47] Although written in the territory of Mughal India, it is

41. Malīḥā, *Modhakker al-aṣḥāb*, 48.

42. Malīḥā, *Modhakker al-aṣḥāb*, 54.

43. Malīḥā, *Modhakker al-aṣḥāb*, 52. In the main manuscript used for the printed edition (i.e. MS. Ayni), the name of Ḥasan Nethārī is spelled Thanāʾī, evidently a mistake, as indicated in n. 1, where other manuscripts are quoted. For Mollā "Ṣāmī"/Ṣādeqī Samarqandī's printing error, see n. 21 above.

44. According to Naqavī (1347sh./1968, 518), a contemporary source mentions him as "presently living" in Lucknow (cf. n. 100).

45. The author's great-grandfather, ʿĪsā Khān (d. 1165/1751–52), emigrated to Dehli from Jām in Khurasan, before the middle of the eighteenth century. Since then the family had remained in the service of the Mughal emperors (Naqavī 1347sh./1968, 516–18). The author succeeded his father, Āghā ʿAlī Khān Shāhjahānābādī, in the office of *taḥṣīldār* (tax collector) in the financial administration of several districts (Naqavī 1347sh./1968, 517).

46. His *kunya* was Abū Moḥammad (Naqavī 1347/1968, 516). The known sources on the author and his biography are listed in Naqavī 1347sh./1968, 521.

47. The *tadhkera* is described in Naqavī 1347sh./1968, 515–21, and in Golchīn Maʿānī 1363sh./1984, II: 357–60. Five manuscripts of the *Neshtar-e ʿeshq* are listed (Naqavī 1347sh./1968, 520–21; Golchīn Maʿānī 1363sh./1984, II: 358), all in Indian and Pakistani libraries. To this list

clearly a work of the post-Timurid tradition of Central Asia and eastern Iran: it deals without distinction among the Persian poets of India, Central Asia, and Iran. It is therefore of immediate interest to us here, and we will refer to it alongside the earlier texts, especially as the introduction to the work contains an important *sabab-e taʿlīf* section (see Fig. 1).[48]

ʿĀsheq ʿAẓīmābādī explains how on his official travels he used to meet and converse with many people, often engaging in poetical meetings (*soḥbat*) during which he collected verses that were recited and exchanged among the participants. As a result, he came to possess a collection of about two thousand *bayts* of poetry by different individuals. The immediate impulse for compiling his own anthology of poets' biographies arose from a meeting with a local financial officer, called Mīr Moḥammad Jaʿfar. This person had at home a copy of a well-known Safavid biographical collection, the *Riyāḍ al-shoʿarā* by ʿAlī-Qolī Khān Dāghestānī, known as Vāleh (d. 1169/1755–56).[49] ʿĀsheq read this book from cover to cover, and took many notes. So, he says, he gradually formulated the idea of his own *tadhkera*, which would assemble the biographies and samples of verses of all the poets who wrote specifically on the theme of love (*ʿeshq*), from the period of Rūdakī to the contemporary period.[50]

There is no doubt that each author includes in the introduction of his compilation a quite conventional presentation of his work. In some cases, the writer modestly attributes his literary initiative to his companions' request, with which he simply complies; sometimes, he ascribes his undertaking to sudden inspiration. On a broader level, the author's literary activity is situated in relation to a realisation of the importance of preserving the literary heritage of the past and present for future generations of readers. This stand might be justified by the author's direct links with literary and intellectual milieus, as in the case of Ḥasan Nethārī, or could result from his contact with a particular book, as for ʿĀsheq. In other instances, the personal desire of the author for his name to be remembered after his death appears as the main and legitimate purpose for compiling the *tadhkera*. Recording the names of famous people to avert their loss from memory could only be considered good and beneficial both for the society and for the individual, as the authors suggest by quoting — if perhaps rather as an afterthought — basic religious authoritative writings, the Qurʾan and hadith.

---

should be added Tashkent and Dushanbe copies. The copy used here is held at the "Biruni" Oriental Institute, Tashkent, MS. 2096 (copied by Shaykh ʿAbdallāh Jaʿfar in the first half of the nineteenth century), and described in the printed catalogue of this collection (see SVR, I, no. 328). A non-critical edition was published in Dushanbe in 1981–88 (see Bibliography).

48. ʿĀsheq, *Neshtar-e ʿeshq*, MS. Tashkent 2096, fol. 18b.

49. See Naqavī 1347sh./1968, 273–310, on the author and his work.

50. ʿĀsheq, *Neshtar-e ʿeshq*, MS. Tashkent 2096, ff. 36a–b, 37b.

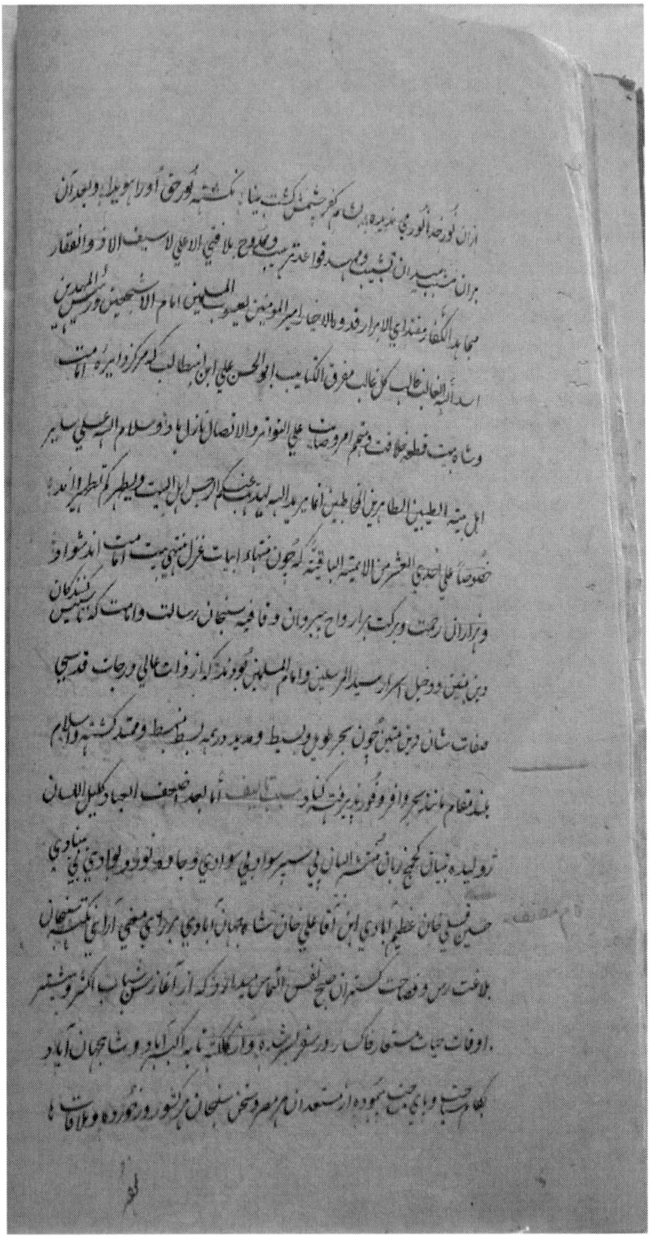

Fig. 1: Beginning of the *sabab-e taʿlīf* section in ʿĀsheq's *Neshtar-e ʿeshq* (1233/1817–18), MS. Tashkent, 2096, fol. 18b. © Courtesy of the "Biruni" Oriental Institute, Uzbek Academy of Sciences, Tashkent.

II.2. Structuring the book

As previously mentioned, before starting to write and edit his work, the author was obliged to spend long years in gathering the material, organising it, double checking it, and, frequently, updating it, right up to the point of release. The information included in the texts, together with analysis of the extant manuscript copies, illuminate the processes by which these writers actually worked. Thus, for example, the autograph copy of the historico-biographical *Tadhkerat al-tavārīkh* (1010/1601) by ʿAbdallāh Kābolī witnesses to the process of checking, correcting, and re-writing the original version of the text;[51] another example is the introduction added by ʿĀsheq ʿAẓīmābādī to his *Neshtar-e ʿeshq* (1233/1817–18), which explains the circumstances of his gathering of materials.

The author organises his compilation according to a formal plan. It is possible to observe this structure from the final form of the text contained in the manuscript copies, and in addition, in many cases, the author provides his original table of contents, and sometimes adds even more information about the process of his work.

In the Introduction to his model work *Modhakker al-aḥbāb*, Nethārī Bokhārī includes a sub-chapter on "the arrangement (*tartīb*) of the book into parts (*faṣl*) and chapters (*bāb*)." Here he provides the table of contents, consisting of a *maqāla* (an introductory section on sovereigns, subdivided in two *rokns*), followed by four chapters (*bāb*), each subdivided in parts (*faṣl*), and ending by an epilogue (*khātema*) on the author's ancestors.[52] Following Nethārī's example, Moṭrebī explains in detail the structural framework of his *Noskha-ye zībā-ye Jahāngīr*. The text, he announces, is composed of two parts, each called a "chain" or "lineage" (*selsela*), and an epilogue (*khātema*). The first *selsela* is devoted to "the Chaghatay sultans and the poems of their times, the collections (*dīvān*) of which are found in Māvarāʾ an-nahr (Transoxiana)." This part opens with a chapter on "Akbar Pādshāh," that is the Mughal Emperor Akbar (r. 963–1014/1556–1605), father of Jahāngīr (r. 1014–37/1605–27). The second *selsela*, concerned with "the Uzbek sultans and scholars (*afāḍel*) who lived in their kingdoms," is further divided into two sections, devoted to "those who belong to the line of Tīmūr" and "those descended from Chingiz Khan." The Epilogue recounts the events (*vaqāyeʿ*) of the reign of the author's royal patron.[53] This structure is indeed reflected in the final version of the work as it has come down to us.

Moṭrebī chose the same procedure for his earlier work, the *Tadhkerat*

51. Szuppe 2006, 341, 349–50; the contents of one chapter (*bāb*) in particular have been totally modified.

52. Nethārī, *Modhakker al-aḥbāb*, 9–10.

53. Moṭrebī, *Noskha*, 15.

al-shoʿarā, where he also carefully explained the rules adopted in his arrangement of the chapters: here the items, or descriptions (*tasmīya*), listed in alphabetical order by penname (*takhalloṣ*), are divided into three parts, designated "name" (*esm*). The most interesting third *esm*, concerning the contemporary period, is further divided into three sections, each called a "point" (*noqṭa*): the first "point" is devoted to rulers whom the author had met and with whom he had conversed; the second treats rulers whom the author had seen (from afar) but not met in person; the third deals with rulers whom the author had neither met in person nor seen, as well as with the scholars and poets whose *takhalloṣ* starts with the corresponding letter. This second part of the third *noqṭa* is still further sub-divided according to a more precise system of classification: scholars with whom the author was acquainted and whose verses were known to him; scholars whom the author had seen, but not met directly, and whose verses were made known to him through the intermediacy of other people; and poets whom the author had neither met nor seen, and whose verses were made known to him through other people.[54] In this regard, Moṭrebī again follows closely the model of Nethārī's *Modhakker al-aḥbāb*, which carefully classifies individuals into separate chapters according to the closeness of their relationship to the author. As these *tadhkera*s were destined for immediate release and were obviously read and directly commented on by the author's contemporaries, this kind of detailed structural classification of the contents was considered necessary in order to establish the seriousness of the work.

Supplementary information can be found in Malīḥā Samarqandī's *Modhakker al-aṣḥāb*. This *tadhkera* includes a passage that gives an idea of how a biographical entry was supposed to be structured in order to prevent future criticism (*eʿterāḍ*).[55] The principal objections of the reader and critic, says Malīḥā, always proceed from the evaluation of the criteria used for including individual biographies in the compilation. Thus the author should specify clearly the identity of the poet or writer, his literary works, his nature and personality, and, above all, the particular qualities that make him worthy of inclusion in the *tadhkera*. Interestingly, Malīḥā declares immediately his total disagreement with this prevailing opinion, which, it seems to him, is erroneous. The inclusion of some people's names and exclusion of others amounts to, effectively, the "killing" of the poets whose names are omitted. Malīḥā thinks that all contemporary poetry deserves to be noted for the benefit of posterity, and consequently that all writers should be included in biographical anthologies.[56]

54. Moṭrebī, *Tadhkera*, 129, for the list of chapters.
55. Malīḥā, *Modhakker al-aṣḥāb*, 58.
56. Malīḥā, *Modhakker al-aṣḥāb*, 58.

II.3. Gathering the biographical material: fieldwork and library research

Two main methods were employed in gathering the biographical and literary material: learned research, which included reading through written sources, and direct investigation, which involved the registering of oral information. As stated above, the most valuable aspect of the Central Asian *tadhkera*s is the presence in them of detailed contemporary material. In most cases, this material circulated orally and was transmitted directly in the course of literary gatherings (*majles*) at courts, private homes, mosques, bazaars and elsewhere. By contrast, the chapters containing the biographies of classical poets and literati for the most part recapitulated information that could be found in earlier biographical, historical, or literary works. Authors used copies of these works as reference books, thus positioning themselves in a universally acknowledged tradition of bio-historical writing.

(a) Use of oral sources and fieldwork

While the authors of the Central Asian *tadhkera*s underlined their personal experience, they rarely acknowledged directly the oral sources exploited in the composition of their works. Such sources were, however, highly significant for all the biographical data concerning these authors' contemporaries. Although, with the exception of Moṭrebī, they rarely quote their informants, the Central Asian authors make a general distinction concerning the reliability of the oral information processed, according to whether it originated in the direct experience of the author, a first-hand account, or diverse second-hand accounts. As discussed above, this distinction is often reflected in the structural arrangement of the text, which separates the biographies of people whom the author had "met personally" from those whom he had not met in person but of whom he had heard an eye-witness or a second-hand account.

The oral material was collected through direct methodical investigation. This gathering of material can be compared to the modern practice of fieldwork research. The locales chosen for investigation were usually places where literary people gathered together, such as princely and private assemblies of erudite persons, but also bazaars and especially booksellers', calligraphers' and paper-makers' shops, as well as the courtyards of mosques and *madrasa*s, traditional sites for literary discussions and exchange, and — especially in Iran — coffee-shops (*qahva-khāna*).[57] All of these locations constituted important gathering places for all groups of society.

57. See McChesney 1990, 61, on poets' meetings at *qahva-khāna*s and *madrasa*s in Safavid Iran, as recounted by Malīḥā.

Such fieldwork was conducted over several seasons; as we have seen above, the compiling of a *tadhkera* stretched over many years. Writers were acutely aware of the need to update periodically the literary and biographical information intended for the *tadhkera*, and they did so during repeated series of travels across the region, the country, and abroad. The material was gathered in the course of "interviews" with individuals who represented precisely defined categories of the population: scholars and literati, but also copyists and, especially, booksellers, whose shops were systematically visited by all the other categories and who were most familiar with the full range of literary novelties and news.[58]

As already noted, the scope of the Central Asian *tadhkera* typically includes poets in Persian from Iran and India, a feature that is particularly evident in the case of contemporary and near-contemporary biographies. This inclusive approach is readily explained by the general interest in literary creation in Persian, as well as by the active participation of all the authors in the learned life of their own times, and strong curiosity regarding literary novelty and exchange in all parts of the Persianate Muslim East.[59] Authors such as Moṭrebī, Elāhī, Malīḥā, or ʿĀsheq, who spent many years of their lives travelling, are good examples of this approach. Moṭrebī, having left Bukhara, his "place of origin" (*vaṭan*),[60] spent time at the princely court of Balkh, where he witnessed ghazal contests, but also at Lahore, and finally at the court of the Emperor Jahāngīr in Delhi. As has been seen above, his two *tadhkera*s were separated by a period of twenty years, but the later text partly repeats information from the earlier one, in an updated form. A systematic comparison of the entries devoted to poets who appear in both sources promises to reveal other aspects of the Central Asian author's methodology.[61]

How the writer of a *tadhkera* proceeded while working on and updating his text can be inferred by analysis of the autograph copy of the *Tadhkerat al-tavārīkh*, started in 990/1582 by ʿAbdallāh Kābolī. It is known that ʿAbdallāh Kābolī, who later in his life was established in Sind, travelled a lot between

58. For the role played by booksellers in circulating the literary novelties in Central Asia in the sixteenth to eighteenth centuries, see examples in Szuppe 1999, 108–10. Bookshops (*ketāb-forūshī*) are especially mentioned as places for discussion and casual meetings among literati.

59. See Foltz 1998b, especially pp. 68–92; and Szuppe 2004.

60. For the evolution of the meaning and contents of the classical term *vaṭan* in the Timurid official historiography, see Bernardini 2006.

61. One good example of how Moṭrebī worked on updating his material, quoted in Szuppe 2006, 350–52, concerns the biographical information on ʿAbdallāh Kābolī: Moṭrebī updates the information on the basis of an account provided by an informant while the author was travelling to India.

Kabul (and possibly Herat), Bukhara, and places in India.[62] The manuscript represents a working copy of his text; it bears traces of the author's many alterations and additions during the final revision of his work in 1010/1601.[63] Notably, Kābolī modified the contents of his text to take into account the new political circumstances in Sind: the name of the royal dedicatee of the work, the Emperor Akbar, has been added in a long note in the margin, and the place for the insertion of this addition is indicated by the sign "v," commonly used by copyists to mark an omission or an insertion (see MS. Tashkent, No. 2093, f. 2b, line 10). Moreover, the original list of contents, where the author had specified the chapters of his work, has also been modified, in order to conform with the final text. Chapter Five was initially to have dealt with different "nobles and commoners" (*khavāṣṣ va-ʿavāmm*), but was later revised to constitute the "Chapter on the Emperor Akbar": the correction is visible in the margin of the list of contents (Ibid., f. 2b, line 14). The actual Chapter Five (Ibid., ff. 239a–248a) is indeed devoted to the events of the life of Akbar. Also, the margins of the autograph manuscript contain important additions, some of which expand the original biographical material of particular items, while others add new biographies to the collection. In most cases, these additions concern either the lives of the author's contemporaries, or the lives of major Sufi sheikhs, past or present, belonging to the Naqshbandi order of which ʿAbdallāh Kābolī was a follower. Incidentally, he sometimes mentions that he has heard a certain piece of information "from one [or some] of the disciples" (*az baʿḍī morīdān shenīda ast*).[64]

Intellectual curiosity provided a powerful incentive for these post-Timurid writers, and the practice of travel was essential for the gathering, cross-referencing and updating of their biographical and literary materials. Travelling for the satisfaction of curiosity became more acceptable in the later period than it had been during the first centuries of Islam. Authors not only travelled frequently themselves, but also received travellers from other regions and countries. Moṭrebī mentions the stay in his house of a scholar from eastern Iran with whom he led nightly discussions on numerous subjects; he introduced his guest to other literati in Samarqand, who were eager for news from Safavid Iran.[65] But Moṭrebī especially underlines the interest in political and cultural news from Central Asia that he met with at the

62. Szuppe 2006, 350–55.

63. Szuppe 2006, 338–42, 349–50.

64. ʿAbdallāh Kābolī, *Tadhkerat al-tavārīkh*, MS. Tashkent 2093, fol. 77b (right margin).

65. The visitor was Mollā Nāẓerī Mashhadī. Samarqand was just a stop for him on his long trip across Central Asia leading ultimately to India (via Tashkent and the Ferghana valley); see Moṭrebī, *Noskha*, 189.

Mughal court.[66] The Iranian Elāhī is reported to have arrived in India during the reign of the Emperor Jahāngīr, probably in Delhi. After some time he continued his travels to Kabul, where he spent several years, and remained at least until 1040/1630–31. He then returned to the court of Shāh-Jahān (r. 1037–68/1628–57), and eventually departed for Kashmir,[67] where he died without being able to finalise his collection of about 400 biographies, mostly of contemporary poets, the *Khazīna-ye ganj*.[68] Malīḥā, being particularly

Table: Some Authors' Itineraries (sixteenth to nineteenth centuries)

Date	*Authors*	*General itineraries*
1st half 16th c.	Vāṣefī	1) Herat - Mashhad - Nishapur - Herat 2) Herat - Bukhara - Tashkent - Samarqand - Tashkent
late 16th/early 17th c.	ʿAbdallāh Kābolī	[Kabul?] - Bukhara - Kabul - Herat - Sind
early 17th c.	Moṭrebī	Samarqand - Bukhara - Balkh / Bukhara - Kashghar / Bukhara - Lahore - Delhi [and return]
1st half 17th c.	Maḥmūd b. Valī	Balkh - Herat - Delhi - Ceylon [and return]
mid-17th c.	Elāhī	Hamadan -Shiraz - Isfahan - Kabul - Delhi - Kashmir - Delhi - Kashmir
late 17th c.	Malīḥā	Samarqand - Nishapur - Semnan - Kashan - Isfahan [and return]

interested in what was going on "elsewhere," embarked on a three-year tour of Safavid Iran, where he stopped in Nishapur, Mashhad, Kashan, Isfahan, and several other places. In all these locations, Malīḥā participated in literary meetings and held conversations with numerous poets, including the renowned Mīrzā Moḥammad Ṭāher Naṣrābādī, with whom Malīḥā became acquainted in Isfahan and who was himself the author of a large *tadhkera* (*ca.* 1090/1679).[69] This attitude of curiosity, which was prevalent among learned

66. Szuppe 2004, 1013–16.

67. Cf. Naqavī 1347sh./1968, 191–92. Elāhī was given the governorship of Kashmir from 1042/1632–33 to 1048/1638–39, and then from 1051/1641–42 until his death in *ca.* 1063/1652–53.

68. The text has remained practically unknown: not only does it lack an introduction and an epilogue, but the core of the work is unfinished (Naqavī 1347sh./1968, 194). Of the two manuscripts recorded, one is an autograph copy kept in Berlin (see *Verzeichniss der persischen Handschriften ... Berlin*, 1888, MS. 626), and the other a copy at the Oudh Library (described in Sprenger 1854, no. 11/1, who also gives the list of poets' names on pp. 67–87).

69. On this important Safavid *tadhkera*, see Afshar 1993; a short bibliography of Persian studies on this text is given in his n. 1.

persons of the time, is probably best expressed by Maḥmūd b. Amīr Valī (d. after 1050/1640–41) whose family, originally from Kasān in the Ferghana valley, established itself and prospered in Balkh: after many years of travel in the Indian subcontinent, he noted in his historico-geographical work, *Baḥr al-asrār* (*ca.* 1050/1640–41), that he had set out on his journey in order to "see through his own eyes the astonishing marvels" of all these countries.[70]

(b) Written sources and library research

In addition to the oral sources collected during their "fieldwork" travels, when they were mostly concerned with securing the fullest possible coverage of contemporary literary production, the biographers used an important mass of written sources. In some cases, authors acknowledged these sources in a heading or an introductory phrase, such as "the discourse on the life [lit. 'states' or circumstances] of each of them (has been taken) from the books mentioned below..." (*ṣoḥbat-e aḥvāl-e har yek az rū-ye kotob-e masṭūra...*).[71] These books are cited in lists of titles that constitute in effect a form of authoritative "bibliography" to the *tadhkera*, as well as in occasional references scattered among the biographical entries.

The use of written sources is one of the crucial issues involved in the process of composing biographical collections. The names of authors and titles that many *tadhkera* writers cite directly or mention indirectly shed light on their methods of investigation and of assembling materials in preparation for the writing of their biographical anthologies. These references also furnish valuable indications of the cultural and educational backgrounds of individual authors, as well as of *tadhkera* writers in general. Furthermore, they serve as a measure of the popularity of particular texts over the centuries and on a wider geographical scale, namely the Persianate Muslim East, in the context of cultural and literary trends. Such considerations remain outside the scope of the present paper, but they are certainly of relevance for the *longue durée* approach to cultural history, textual studies, and the history of mentalities.

Examination of their bibliographical lists not only brings to light the types of writings used by *tadhkera* authors, but also shows their means of gaining access to these sources. In the long introduction to his *Neshtar-e ʿeshq*, ʿĀsheq ʿAẓīmābādī states the reasons for writing his bio-bibliographical

70. Maḥmūd b. Amīr Valī (d. after 1050/1640–41), *Baḥr al-asrār*, MS. India Office 575, fol. 389a. Among other places in India, he visited Peshawar, Delhi, Hyderabad, Calcutta, Bihar (ff. 389a–408b). See Szuppe 2004, 1013, for more details on this author, and pp. 1010–17 for some other Central Asian examples of travels; and McChesney 1990, 73–78, for other interesting, and sometimes very entertaining, examples of poets' and intellectuals' travels across Central Asia, Iran, and India.

71. Quoted after ʿĀsheq, *Neshtar-e ʿeshq*, MS. Tashkent 2096, fol. 20a.

work, and supplies a list of the written sources of which he availed himself in order to compile it.[72] At this point, ʿĀsheq goes into quite a detailed explanation of how he used these sources, which include several other *tadhkeras* but also chronicles and *dīvāns* (poetical collections, usually of poems by a single author).[73] In order to consult these writings, he searched for them in many places, drawing on a network of personal relationships. Once he had located a copy of a work in a library or in an individual's private possession, he either took volumes on loan or bought them for his own library "regardless of the great expense." These books came from "everywhere," not only from his own place of residence, Azimabad (that is Patna), or from the neighbouring regions of Akbarabad (Agra) or Shahjahanabad (Dehli), but also from such distant places as Belgram, Farrokhabad, and Aligarh.

ʿĀsheq's account demonstrates the importance of book circulation on the local and regional levels. Books were circulated through lending as well as through selling and buying, sometimes as a result of private contacts, as when, for example, the author read the *Riyāḍ al-shoʿarā* of Vāleh Dāghestānī which was lent to him by an acquaintance, and sometimes thanks to the existence of public or semi-public libraries at mosques and *madrasas*.[74] Many authors had recourse to personal contacts in order to gain access to a particular book, or to a whole library collection; such activation of intellectual relations was evidently common practice. Moṭrebī is especially detailed on this subject as we follow him on his travels across Central Asia: in Samarqand he had access to the home library of "good books" owned by his first patron, the governor of the city Ḥājjī Atālıq Qushchī (d. 1019/1610); in Kashghar, he handled books of the reigning khan, ʿAbd al-Karīm Solṭān (r. *ca.* 967–99/1560–91); in other places, he used to consult volumes deposited at the booksellers' (*ketāb-forūsh*).[75] Additionally, in one of many autobiographical passages in his text, Maḥmūd b. Amīr Valī gives an explicit account of how he gained access to the rich library of his teacher in Balkh, and was thus able to discover and study many different books.[76]

If the *tadhkera* contains a list of sources, they are usually mentioned without any particular arrangement, in most cases by the name of the author and/or the short title of the book. The lists vary in length; some examples

72. ʿĀsheq, *Neshtar-e ʿeshq*, MS. Tashkent 2096, fol. 37a.

73. The author provides no further details regarding this category of sources.

74. Circulation of books through private and library loan is well attested in the mediaeval and late mediaeval periods, especially through handwritten annotations added by readers, and the use of the *ʿarḍ* (library register and control annotations) inscribed on manuscript volumes; library loans were not free of charge. On this aspect of book history in the eastern Iranian manuscript tradition, see Afshar 1997.

75. For more details, see Szuppe 1999, 107–10; and, Szuppe 2004, 1004, 1006–07.

76. Maḥmūd b. Valī, *Baḥr al-asrār*, MS. Tashkent 1375, fol. 4a.

refer to a small number of basic but relevant titles, as in the case of the work of Elāhī, while others are highly detailed, such as the lists of ʿAbdallāh Kābolī, who records twenty-five works, and ʿĀsheq ʿAẓīmābādī, who mentions as many as thirty-two titles.[77] Writers more particularly linked with the Timurid tradition in Central Asia, eastern Iran, and northern India, the already mentioned Khvāja Nethārī, Moṭrebī and Malīḥā, as well as ʿAbdallāh Kābolī and certainly Elāhī, can be viewed as forming quite a homogenous group. The list of written sources given in ʿĀsheq's work is one of the most detailed of its kind, and it is also distinguished by its inclusion of a particularly large number of late references, especially from Mughal India. It cannot, however, be considered atypical in the context of Persianate learning. On the contrary, the writer, who lived very late in the period under consideration and was connected with the Mughals more closely than others, followed exactly the same lines of procedure as his predecessors in using and including contemporary and local writings.

Among the sources quoted by the *tadhkeras*, two basic types of writings can be distinguished. The first group consists of historical chronicles (*tārīkh*); the second consists of other biographical compilations (*tadhkera*). In some cases, quotations are drawn (often implicitly) from the collections of works by particular poets (*dīvān*), and, occasionally, from dictionaries (*farhang*). The historical writings belong to the classical Persian repertoire of the mediaeval period. With the exception of ʿĀsheq, who cites several later Mughal historians, the latest universal chronicle quoted is Khvāndamīr's *Ḥabīb al-siyar*, which was written at the beginning of the sixteenth century. By contrast, the literary-biographical *tadhkera* sources used by our authors date predominantly from the later period — from Timurid times onwards — except for such classics as the early thirteenth-century *Tadhkerat al-awliyāʾ* of Farīd al-Dīn ʿAṭṭār Nīshāpūrī, quoted by ʿAbdallāh Kābolī.[78]

There can be little doubt that, in general, the *tadhkera* writers considered all written texts equally valuable as source material. The authors refrain from critical judgement of their written sources, and rarely follow any particular typology, chronological or thematic, when listing them for the reader. A remarkable exception is ʿAbdallāh Kābolī, who presents his list of sources for his collection of "historical" biographies, illustrated by verses and chronograms, according to a detectable order (see Fig. 2). The list opens with *Siyar al-nabī*, a classical biography of the Prophet Moḥammad, follows with a series of historical or quasi-historical works (chronicles, genealogies

77. The sources of the main *tadhkera* writers quoted in this paper are listed in the Appendix. See especially the list for ʿAbdallāh Kābolī, who does not appear in Naqavī 1347sh./1968. For ʿĀsheq's sources, see also Naqavī 1347sh./1968, 519.

78. See Appendix.

Fig. 2: List of sources given by ʿAbdallāh Kābolī in his *Tadhkerat al-tavārīkh* (1010/1601), MS. Tashkent 2093 [autograph copy], fol. 2a. © Courtesy of the "Biruni" Oriental Institute, Uzbek Academy of Sciences, Tashkent.

and religious biographies), and ends with several literary *tadhkeras*. All these works are arranged in a roughly chronological order, from the earliest Islamic period to Timurid times. The list thus demonstrates the author's effort to produce a systematic presentation of his sources.[79] A similar effort can be detected in ʿĀsheq's compilation, where all *tadhkeras* but one are grouped at the beginning of the list, and all historical chronicles and dictionaries follow.[80]

Even a cursory examination of the main literary biographies referred to in Central Asian *tadhkeras* during the later mediaeval period reveals some interesting features. Firstly, and not surprisingly, a standard group of particular texts appears, regardless of the date and place of the composition of the *tadhkera*; these texts form a core of "neo-classical" sources, and serve as universally authoritative references for *tadhkera* writing. These classics are common to texts from Central Asia as well as from other parts of the Muslim East, especially eastern Iran and northern India. It is tempting to explain their presence across the centuries by the persistence of the strong Khurasanian (if not Timurid) tradition of historiography, of which biographical anthologies of the later period can be seen as a particular branch. It should not be forgotten that these texts were created to function within the largest possible circle of readership, in social as well as spatial and temporal terms.

Not surprisingly, among such universally quoted authorities in the sixteenth to nineteenth-century *tadhkeras* are two paradigmatic Timurid authors, Dawlatshāh Samarqandī and Mīr ʿAlī-Shīr Navāʾī, the latter frequently being specified as the author of a model *tadhkera* for Turki poets. Contemporary and near-contemporary sources are continually added by each subsequent author; this process is especially visible in later Indian *tadhkeras*, as demonstrated by the list of sources in ʿĀsheq's work. As a result, some sixteenth-century *tadhkeras* are quoted among the written sources of later authors and pass into the category of "neo-classical" representatives of the Persianate *adab* in the region. The best example of this trend is certainly Khvāja Ḥasan Nethārī's *Modhakker al-aḥbāb*, but there is also the *Toḥfa-ye Sāmī* of Sām Mīrzā Ṣafavī, one of the main sources used for example by Elāhī in the seventeenth century and by ʿĀsheq in the early nineteenth century. Other authors and texts, such as Moḥammad-Ṣādeq Samarqandī, a contemporary of Moṭrebī, and his *Riyāḍ al-shoʿarā* (mentioned above), seem

79. ʿAbdallāh Kābolī, *Tadhkerat al-tavārīkh*, MS. Tashkent 2093, fol. 2a. See below, Appendix I.1–25, for details of the twenty-five titles listed. In its initial part, this list is remarkably close, in terms of the titles quoted and their order of appearance, to the one contained in Ḥamdallāh Qazvīnī's *Tārīkh-e gozīda* (which is itself one of ʿAbdallāh Kābolī's authoritative references). Qazvīnī's list of sources is indicated in Browne 1928, 88.

80. See Appendix, V.1–17 and V.29; and V.18–28, and V.30–32.

to enjoy popularity with some writers for a certain period of time. Interestingly, Fakhrī Heravī's unique collection of biographies of female poets of Timurid and post-Timurid Herat, the *Javāher al-ʿajāyeb*, written in Sind in the mid-sixteenth century, is quoted (under the generic title of *Tadhkerat al-nesāʾ*) a century later by Taqī Awḥadī in his major work *ʿArafāt al-ʿāsheqīn*, by Elāhī in his *Khazīna-ye ganj*, and by one or two other Mughal writers in the seventeenth century.[81]

By explicit reference to classics and to literary models of the *tadhkera* genre, the Central Asian writers place themselves directly in the line of the dominant literary tradition of Khurasanian historiography, and more precisely that of Timurid Herat. This is evident in the case of the late sixteenth-century Bukharan author and Naqshbandi sheikh, Khvāja Ḥasan Nethārī, whose *Modhakker al-aḥbāb*, in turn, was added by later authors to the list of "classic" authorities, and was consequently invoked as a leading literary model alongside the works of Dawlatshāh and Navāʾī. Not only in Bukhara where Ḥasan Nethārī lived and wrote, but also elsewhere in Central Asia and in Mughal India, he came to be considered as the link between later Central Asian *tadhkera* literature and the writings of the "Golden Age" of Timurid Herat.

III. Some Remarks on Persianate Learning and the Profane Reading Curriculum

The above observations concerning the use of written sources by the authors of literary biographies entail yet another series of considerations pertaining to the existence of a standard literary erudition shared by inhabitants of the post-Timurid "space." This "Persianate learning" involved a body of common cultural and historical references, especially as embodied in the literary canon, taste in classical and modern literature, and more general intellectual trends.[82]

As has previously been noted, given the high consideration traditionally granted to oral creation and the transmission of knowledge through the process of audition, that is, by listening and memorizing, it is possible to dissociate literacy in the strict sense of knowing how to read and write from the pursuit of learning and erudition in the literary field. An orally based way of learning had been highly valued during the first centuries of Islam, when it was regarded as the only right way of acquiring knowledge. Taking notes while listening and reading books in the absence of the teacher assumed

81. See Naqavī 1347sh./1968, 157 and 193, respectively.
82. Szuppe 2004, 1010, 1018.

significance only very gradually and quite late.[83] In the post-Timurid period, the importance of oral transmission was still remarkable. The Mughal Emperor Akbar, for instance, acquired most of his erudition in the process of learning by audition.[84] This method seems to have been particularly adapted to suit the transmission of literary learning, in which memorizing texts and poems facilitated their recitation, either in their entirety or in part as appropriate to the situation — a highly prized ability in a well-educated person, and crystalised in the paramount institution of the Timurid literary *majles* or *soḥbat*.[85] For hundreds of poets quoted in Central Asian *tadhkeras* of the later period, no information has survived except for their biographical entries and the few verses quoted as examples of their works. In his *Javāher al-ʿajāyeb*, Fakhrī Heravī includes nineteen contemporary poetesses; in only two cases, he emphasises, was there a written *dīvān* of their poems, which he saw.[86] Many, if not the majority, of the poems in circulation in late Central Asia were exclusively spoken and recited orally; they appear to have been rarely, if ever, committed to writing. The preservation of these verses, which might otherwise disappear, was, as has been mentioned above, among the objectives of the authors of *tadhkeras* as they set about composing their literary-biographical collections.

In Central Asia, as elsewhere, the transmission of knowledge took place within the *maktab* and the *madrasa* systems, but also outside these institutions, especially in the case of subjects that did not enter the traditional religious-legal curriculum, such as universal history and geography. Recent research by Maria Subtelny and Anas Khalidov has shed new light on the *madrasa* curriculum during the Timurid period, and has shown its strong focus on readings in Arabic grammar, prosody and rhetoric on the one hand, and on Qurʾanic, legal and theological studies on the other. Interestingly, the documentation analysed by Subtelny and Khalidov demonstrates that most *madrasa* subjects were taught according to two systems: the "reading method" (*al-maqrūʾāt*) allowed for the use of particular manuals and books, while the "audition method" (*al-masmūʾāt*; *samaʿa min...*) applied to specific scholarly works that teachers were individually authorised to transmit.[87]

83. On these questions, see Schoeler 2002 (cf. his bibliography); also Touati 2000a, 119–21, on the practice of *vijāda*, that is, acquisition of knowledge through book reading in the physical absence of the authorised teacher.

84. See Szuppe 1999, 108; Szuppe 2004, 1006–08.

85. The best presentation and analysis of a Timurid *majles*, based on the first-hand account by Vāṣefī of Herat in his *Badāyeʿ al-vaqāyeʿ*, is Subtelny 1984.

86. See Fakhrī, *Javāher al-ʿajāyeb*, 132, for the *dīvān* of Bībī ʿEṣmatī, sister of the governor of Khvāf; and Fakhrī, *Javāher al-ʿajāyeb*, 134, mentioning the *dīvān* of ghazals by Seyyed Begom Shāh-Molk, daughter of Seyyed Ḥasan Kār Kiyā of Gorgān.

87. Subtelny and Khalidov 1995, and especially pp. 226–36, where the authors provide lists

Current explorations of provincial manuscript collections from the former Bukhara, Khiva, and Kokand khanates, most of which consist of books that had previously belonged to *madrasa*s and local men of learning, suggest that even if the variety of books studied diminished considerably over time, the contents of the *madrasa* readings seem not to have changed much during the later period in Central Asia. As in earlier times, the Central Asian *madrasa* education was heavily based on religious, theological, and legal matters. It also paid great attention to the teaching of Arabic grammar and vocabulary, which provided access to higher education in the above-mentioned fields, since the relevant textbooks were mostly written in Arabic, though sometimes in Persian, and very rarely in Turki. Manifestly, late Central Asian scholars and students used Persian as the main language of learning: the Arabic textbooks frequently display marginal and interlinear explanations, translations and commentaries that have been inscribed in Persian by readers and students.[88]

With the exception of the works of major poets and poetical collections, such as the classical *dīvān*s of Ḥāfeẓ and Bīdel, *madrasa* libraries in later Central Asia usually contained very few books related to literature, and no textbooks on such profane subjects as universal or dynastic history, or geography. These and other non-religious fields had to be learned outside the formal *madrasa* system through private teaching, frequently with a parent, and if possible with a renowned master. Travelling long distances in order to study with a prominent teacher, or to gain access to a celebrated library, was quite common, and the biographies of poets often describe such journeys. Numerous sources record the educational trajectories of individuals, since such information was considered an important element in biographical writings; together with narratives that reflect a non-religious education, these data facilitate the construction of a reasonably coherent picture of literary and cultural formation.

With reference to the seventeenth century, for which considerable interesting information has come to light, the case of Elāhī, author of the

---

of titles for all these manuals and books. In general, on *madrasa* education and the transmission of knowledge, see Makdisi 1981; Berkey 1992; Vajda 1983.

88. This research is part of the current international project "Patrimoine manuscrit: fonds d'Asie centrale" begun in 2000 and coordinated by M. Szuppe (CNRS research team "Mondes iranien et indien"); see http://www.iran-inde.cnrs.fr/spip.php?rubrique49. Also, see the respective introductions to the two catalogues of manuscripts already published: M. Szuppe and A. Muminov, *Catalogue des manuscrits orientaux du Musée régional de Qarshi (Ouzbékistan)*, Series Catalogorum I, Istituto per l'Oriente "C. A. Nallino"–"Monde iranien," CNRS (IPO: Roma 2004); A. Muminov, M. Szuppe and A. Idrisov, *Manuscrits orientaux du Musée régional de Nukus (République autonome du Karakalpakstan, Ouzbékistan): Fonds arabe, persan,* turkī *et karakalpak*, Series Catalogorum II, Istituto per l'Oriente "C. A. Nallino"– "Mondes iranien et indien," CNRS (IPO: Roma, 2007).

Khazīna-ye ganj, has already been mentioned: Elāhī narrates that he left his native village of Asadābād near Hamadan for Isfahan and then Shiraz, all in "search of learning" (*be qaṣd-e taḥṣīl*).[89] The historian and geographer Maḥmūd b. Amīr Valī explains in his *Baḥr al-asrār* that, at the age of nineteen — that is, certainly after having received the initial, or even secondary, *madrasa* formation — he became a disciple (*morīd*) of a Sufi sheikh, Seyyed Mīrak-Shāh Ḥosaynī, a renowned traditionist (*moḥaddeth*), jurist (*faqīh*) and specialist in medicine (*ṭebb*), who incidentally was the husband of his elder sister.[90] Maḥmūd remained by Seyyed Mīrak-Shāh's side for ten years, making extensive use of the sheikh's private library; he studied various books, among which were the classics of Muslim geography, such as the works of Moqaddasī and Eṣṭakhrī (Iṣṭakhrī), and the works of the most prominent Persian historians, such as Bayḍāvī, Vaṣṣāf, Rashīd al-Dīn, Jovaynī, Mīrkhvānd, and some others.[91] Maḥmūd's scholarly interests also included botany, mineralogy, medicine, and other subjects: he wrote several treatises on legal and theological matters, and he composed poetry. Later in his life, he held the post of chief court librarian at Balkh.[92]

In his *Modhakker al-aṣḥāb*, Malīḥā includes a long entry devoted to his own life and entitled "Malīḥā-ye Samarqandī."[93] Written in the first person and quite detailed, it appears as an autobiographical account, and supplements the elements of the author's biography that were inserted into the introduction to the *tadhkera*. Malīḥā explains that, after leading a somewhat carefree life in his "youth," at the age of eleven, his education was taken in hand by his father, Moḥammad-Sharīf, who was the mufti of Samarqand.[94] He learned to read and write (*bayāḍ-e dīda be savād-e khaṭṭ āshena karda-am*), to understand and to compose poetry, and studied the foundations of logic, theology, philosophy, and Arabic. He studied for many years under the guid-

89. Naqavī 1347sh./1968, 191. He spent three-and-a-half years in Isfahan before leaving for Shiraz, in 1015/1606.

90. Maḥmūd b. Amīr Valī, *Baḥr al-asrār*, MS. India Office 575, ff. 336a–b, 338a, 362a. According to Akhmedov 1977, 4–5, Maḥmūd b. Amīr Valī stayed with the sheikh from 1023/1614 to 1033/1624. In 1034/1625, only after the death of the sheikh, did he set off from Balkh on his long travels across India.

91. Maḥmūd b. Amīr Valī, *Baḥr al-asrār*, MS. Tashkent 2372, ff. 3b–4a. Of this list, Bayḍāvī, Jovaynī, and Mīrkhvānd are also specifically mentioned among the sources indicated by ʿAbdallāh Kābolī, and by Motrebī; see Appendix. For a general presentation of Persian historiography, see now the series of articles by different authors, grouped under the heading "Historiography" in *Encyclopaedia Iranica* (E. Yarshater [gen. ed.], Center for Iranian Studies, Columbia University, New York: The Encyclopaedia Iranica Foundation), vol. XII (2003–2004): 323–402.

92. Akhmedov 1977, 5. No manuscript of any of his other works is known to exist today.

93. Malīḥā, *Modhakker al-aṣḥāb*, 506–11, and MS. Tashkent 4270, ff. 221a–226b.

94. Malīḥā, *Modhakker al-aṣḥāb*, 506–08. Malīḥā speaks very warmly about his deceased father, who appears to have been a major figure in his life.

ance of his father, until the latter's death when the author was thirty years old; at this time Malīḥā inherited his father's estate and possessions, including all of his numerous books.[95] Just like Maḥmūd b. Amīr Valī, who set out on his Indian travels after his master's death, Malīḥā departed for Iran for a period of three years. It was only after his return that he embarked on his studies with other teachers, friends of his deceased father, in Samarqand and in Bukhara, where he spent seven years learning such sciences (*ʿelm*) as Arabic, law (*feqh*), exegesis (*tafsīr*), and hadith.[96] Some complementary information is supplied in the entry devoted to the life of Malīḥā's second principal teacher, Qāḍī Loṭfallāh Shāker, with whom he studied the religious sciences and poetry, and also astronomy.[97] In 1100/1689, Malīḥā was given the position of teacher at the Shaybānī Khān Madrasa in Samarqand, where he completed the writing of his *tadhkera*.[98]

In the *Neshtar-e ʿeshq*, ʿĀsheq, who belonged to a family of financial administrators of the Mughal state, also supplies some information on his education. Until the age of fourteen, most of his time was spent in learning the Persian language (*zabān-e fārsī*), history (*tārīkh*), and the basics of [Arabic] grammar (*ṣarf-o-naḥv*).[99] Interestingly, another source, written when ʿĀsheq was still living, reports that he had not learned the Arabic language (or perhaps, he had not learned it well enough), for which reason his *tadhkera* contained many errors.[100] In his youth, ʿĀsheq accompanied his father during his professional travels to different places in the country. These trips gave him his first opportunity to attend literary sessions, where he heard poets reciting verses. ʿĀsheq's lively interest in poetry led him, in his adulthood, to follow his father's example in attending literary sessions wherever he went and whenever possible, and, as noted above, finally motivated him to compile his own *tadhkera* of poets.

95. Malīḥā, *Modhakker al-aṣḥāb*, 507: "four hundred and forty-four" books, to be taken as "very many."

96. Malīḥā, *Modhakker al-aṣḥāb*, 508.

97. Malīḥā, *Modhakker al-aṣḥāb*, 310. The relevant passage mentions two books on astronomy, which Malīḥā read with his teacher. The works are the *Sharḥ-e Chaghmīnī*, a commentary by Seyyed Sharīf ʿAlī Gorgānī/Jurjānī (d. 816/1416) on Chaghmīnī's *al-Mulakhkhas fi-l-hayʾat*, and "the treatise in Persian by Mollā ʿAlī Qūshchī," i.e. the commentary on the Astronomical Tables (*Zīj*) of Ulugh Bek. See Akhmedov 1985, 173 and nn. 34 and 35. Qāḍī Loṭfallāh himself wrote an astronomical treatise in Persian; he was also an excellent poet, and composed lyric and epic works, such as ghazals, qasidas, and mathnavis (Malīḥā, *Modhakker al-aṣḥāb*, 310).

98. Malīḥā, *Modhakker al-aṣḥāb*, 508.

99. References in Naqavī 1347sh./1968, 517.

100. *az taḥṣīl-e ʿarabī bī-bahra mānda*: the remark is quoted in Naqavī 1347sh./1968, 517, after the *Golshan-e bī-khār* by Moḥammad-Moṣṭafā Khān, a *tadhkera* of Urdu poets who also wrote Persian verses, written in *ca.*1250–52/1834–35 – 1836–37, which includes a biographical entry on ʿĀsheq. On *Golshan-e bī-khār* itself, see Naqavī 1347sh./1968, 540–41, no. 24.

A group of sources from seventeenth-century Mughal India provides a valuable comparative viewpoint. In a recent article, Muzaffar Alam and Sanjay Subrahmanyam analyse the secular dimension of the Persianate educational standards expected from holders of secretarial positions (*monshī*), especially among the Hindu families from which *monshī*s of the Mughal administration were frequently recruited.[101] Fluency in the Persian language being of primary importance in the educational curriculum of an "ideal" *monshī*, it was advisable for the student to learn Persian by studying the works of Saʿdī and Jāmī, and continuously to improve his linguistic skills by reading the works of other Persian poets.[102] The remaining recommended readings, apart from textbooks on norms and ethics, consisted of a series of historical writings, all of them classical histories. Notably, many of these works, such as the chronicles of Ṭabarī, Ḥamdallāh Qazvīnī, Mīrkhvānd, Khvāndamīr, and Abū-l-Faḍl ʿAllāmī, appear among the sources quoted by the *tadhkera* writers, too.[103]

An unusual autobiographical account, *Tadhkerat al-safar va-toḥfat al-ẓafar*, written by the end of the seventeenth century by Nīk Rāy, member of a Hindu *monshī* family, gives many details on books and readings at different stages of pre-secretarial training.[104] According to this text, Nīk Rāy first learned the rudiments of reading and writing in Persian, in two years, from the age of five to seven, before taking up the study of Persian literature by reading the works of Saʿdī. At the next stage, when he was about ten years old, he studied other Persian poetical texts, but also the writings of Jāmī and Abū-l-Faḍl, before turning to more complex works by Amīr Khosraw Dehlavī, Khāqānī, and others, including contemporary Mughal and Safavid poets. Then, he integrated into his readings *tadhkera*s of poets, such as the Timurid *Majāles al-ʿoshshāq*, as well as the literary sections of classical chronicles, for example that of Khvāndamīr.[105] Nīk Rāy seems to have completed his literary education in Persian, with several different teachers, when he was about fourteen years old.[106]

Some elements of an "educational scheme" emerge from these few examples of autobiographical passages. Secular education started at an early

101. Alam and Subrahmanyam 2004.

102. Alam and Subrahmanyam 2004, 62–63, quoting the text of the Letter of Chandhraban to his son, a sort of a model reading list for a "perfect" education. The number of poets recommended for reading amounts to more than forty names.

103. Alam and Subrahmanyan 2004, 63. For the sources quoted by the *tadhkera* writers, see Appendix.

104. Alam and Subrahmanyam 2004, 64–70, giving a detailed and annotated paraphrase of the text.

105. See Appendix, I.23 and I.13, for the mention of these two texts among the sources used by authors of *tadhkeras*.

106. Alam and Subrahmanyam 2004, 69.

age, and was accomplished in Persian, even if the fundamentals of Arabic were present. Proficiency in the Persian language, both in reading and writing, and mastery of Persian literature, classical and contemporary, were essential. On another level, the importance of individual initiative and interest on the part of the student is evident in most of the narratives quoted, as well as the influence played by an esteemed teacher, frequently a member of the family or close entourage of the student. The teacher's private library, in particular, appears as a key instrument for more advanced readings: it provided the means for students to obtain and study books that were not part of the standard *madrasa* set of manuals. The lists of recommended readings and of authoritative historical and literary references are similar in Central Asia, Iran, and Mughal India, and formed the core of Persianate education in the later period.

APPENDIX

Texts quoted as authoritative sources in *tadhkeras* of the later period (in the order given in the text):

I. *Tadhkerat al-tavārīkh*

Author: ʿAbdallāh Kābolī (d. after 1035/1625–26)
Date of text: 990–1010/1582–1601
References: Storey/Bregel, I: 416, no. 276 [134a]; MS. "Biruni" Oriental Institute Tashkent, no. 2093 (list of sources on fol. 2a).
Sources quoted:

(I.1) *Siyar al-nabī,*
A biography of the Prophet Moḥammad; certainly not the work by Moʿīn b. Maḥmūd, which is explicitly mentioned below (I.15), but probably the Persian translation of Ibn Hishām's ninth-century work, completed *ca.* 612–20/1215–23 in Iran; see Storey/Bregel, I: 537–38.

(I.2) *Tavārīkh*, by Moḥammad-e Jarīr Ṭabarī,
= *Ta'rīkh al-rosūl wa-l-molūk* of Abū Jaʿfar Moḥammad b. Jarīr Ṭabarī; a major chronicle in Arabic composed in the first quarter of the tenth century; see *GAL*, I: 142.

(I.3) *Zubdat al-tavārīkh*, by Jamāl al-Dīn Kāshī,
A general chronicle by Jamāl al-Dīn ʿAbdallāh b. ʿAlī Kāshānī, compiled at the beginning of the fourteenth century; see Storey/Bregel, I: 320–22.

(I.4) *Neẓām al-tavārīkh*, by Qāḍī Nāṣer al-Dīn Bayḍāvī,
A chronicle by ʿAbdallāh b. ʿOmar Bayḍāvī, composed in 674/1275; see Storey/Bregel, I: 298–301.[107]

107. On this text, see now Melville 2001, and Melville 2007.

(I.5) *ʿOyūn al-tavārīkh*, by Abū Ṭāleb Baghdādī,

= *Jāmeʿ* al-*mukhtaṣar fī unwān al-tavārīkh va-ʿoyūn al-siyar*, a world history by Tāj al-Dīn Abū Ṭāleb ʿAlī b. Anjab b. al-Sāʿī al-Khāzin al-Baghdādī, known as Ibn al-Sāʿī (d. 674/1275); see GAL SB, I: 590.

(I.6) [*Tārīkh-e*] *Jahān-goshā-ye Jovaynī*,

= *Tārīkh-e Jahān-goshā* by ʿAlāʾ al-Dīn ʿAṭā-Malek Jovaynī; a chronicle composed in 658/1260; see Storey/Bregel, II: 757–65.

(I.7) *Siyar al-molūk*, by Neẓām al-Molk,

= *Siyāsatnāma* by Ḥasan b. ʿAlī b. Isḥāq Ṭūsī Neẓām al-Molk, composed in 484/1091.[108]

(I.8) *Seljūq-nāma*, by Ẓahīrī Nīshāpūrī,

A chronicle composed in 571/1176 by Ẓahīr al-Dīn Nīshāpūrī; see Storey/Bregel, II: 743–45.[109]

(I.9) *Dīvān al-nasab*,

A genealogical work, no precise identification.

(I.10) *Qeṣaṣ al-anbiyā*,

Works of various authors are known under this title; for works in Persian, some of which remain anonymous, see Storey/Bregel, I: 510, 511, 512, 516, 519, 531–33, 535, 11413; on one particular anonymous *Qeṣaṣ al-anbiyā* of the pre-Mongol period, see Daniel 2004, 330b.

(I.11) *Tadhkerat al-awliyāʾ*,

Biographies of saintly figures, by Farīd al-Dīn ʿAṭṭār Nīshāpūrī, composed in the early thirteenth century; see Storey, I/2: 930–33, no. 1250.

(I.12) *Moṭūn al-khabar*,

This work remains unidentified.

(I.13) *Ḥabīb al-siyar*,

= *Tārīkh-e Ḥabīb al-siyar fī akhbār afrād al-bashar*, a major Timurid chronicle by Ghiyāth al-Dīn b. Homām al-Dīn Moḥammad Ḥosaynī Heravī, known as Khvāndamīr, the first redaction of which was finished in Herat in 930/1524; see Golchīn Maʿānī 1363sh./1984, II: 602; Storey/Bregel, I: 379–93 on the author and his works, and especially pp. 383–93, on this history.

(*I.14) *Dorj al-dorar*, by Amīr Aṣīl al-Dīn,[110]

= *Dorj al-dorar va-barj al-ghorar fī bayān mīlād seyyed al-bashar*, a short history of the Prophet Moḥammad, composed by Amīr Seyyed Aṣīl al-Dīn

108. On this important work, see Meisami 1999, 145–62. For some aspects of its historiographical importance, see Simidchieva 2004.

109. On this text, see Meisami 1999, 229–34. A critical edition has recently been published by A. H. Morton (*The Saljūqnāma of Ẓahīr al-Dīn Nīshāpūrī...*, E. J. W. Gibb Memorial Trust, 2004).

110. All book titles marked with an asterisk (*), that is, items I.14, I.15, I.16, and I.25, appear in the margin of fol. 2a in the MS.

ʿAbdallāh al-Ḥosaynī Dashtakī Shīrāzī in or after 858/1454 in Herat; see Storey/Bregel, I: 557.

(*I.15) *Siyar-e Mollā Moʿīn al-Dīn* called *Maʿārej al-nobovvat*,

= *Maʿārej al-nobovva fī madārej al-fotovva*, a biography of the Prophet Moḥammad also referred to as *Siyar-e sharīf* and *Siyar-e Moʿīnī*, composed *ca.* 891/1486 by Moʿīn al-Dīn Farāhī Heravī, known as Moʿīn al-Meskīn; see Storey/Bregel, I: 565–68.

(*I.16) *Rawḍat al-aḥbāb*, by Mīr Jamāl al-Dīn,

= *Rawḍat al-aḥbāb fī siyar al-nabī va-l-āl va-l-aṣḥāb*, a biography of the Prophet and the members of his family and entourage, written by Amīr Jamāl al-Dīn ʿAṭāʾallāh al-Ḥosaynī Dashtakī Shīrāzī in 900/1494–95 in Herat; see Storey/Bregel, I: 569–73.

(I.17) *Nafaḥāt al-ons*,

= *Nafaḥāt al-ons min ḥaḍarāt al-qods*, a collection of saintly biographies by Nūr al-Dīn ʿAbd al-Raḥman Jāmī, compiled in 883/1478–79; see Golchīn Maʿānī 1363sh./1984, II: 800; Storey, I/2: 954, no. 1274.

(I.18) *Rashaḥāt al-qods*,

= *Rashaḥāt-e ʿayn al-ḥayāt* by Fakhr al-Dīn ʿAlī b. Ḥosayn Vāʿeẓ Kāshefī Heravī, composed in 909/1503–04; see Storey, I/2: 964, no. 1277.

(I.19) *Jāmeʿ al-ḥekāyāt*,

= *Javāmeʿ al-ḥekāyāt va-lavāmeʿ al-revāyāt*, a collection of anecdotes by Moḥammad ʿAwfī Bokhārī, composed *ca.* 628/1230–31; see Storey, I/2: 781–82, no. 1088.

(I.20) *Majmaʿ al-maqāmāt*,

Probably one of the Naqshbandi *maqāmāt*; quite possibly, the *Maqāmāt-e Khvāja Naqshband(ī)* (i.e. Bahāʾ al-Dīn Naqshband), a version of the *Anīs al-ṭālibīn va-ʿoddat al-sālekīn* composed by Ṣalāḥ b. Mobārak Bokhārī. Bokhārī was a disciple of the successor of Bahāʾ al-Dīn, the sheikh ʿAlāʾ al-Dīn ʿAṭṭār (d. 802/1400), who figures prominently among the Naqshbandis included in the book, which was composed at an unspecified date (probably after 791/1389); see Storey I/2: 947–48, no. 1263.[111]

(I.21) *Tārīkh-e gozīda*,

By Ḥamdallāh b. Abī Bakr Mostawfī Qazvīnī; a chronicle completed in 730/1330; see Golchīn Maʿānī 1363sh./1984, II: 549–50; Storey/Bregel, I: 327–34.

(I.22) *Tadhkerat al-shoʿarā-ye Dawlatshāhī*,

By Dawlatshāh b. ʿAlāʾ al-Dawla Bakhtīshāh Samarqandī, completed in

111. In any case, not the *Jāmeʿ al-maqāmāt* devoted to the life of Aḥmad Kāsānī Dahbedī (d. 549/1452) known as "Makhdūm-e Aʿẓam," composed by Khvāja Abu'l-Baqā in 1026/1617 (on this source, see Akhmedov 1985, 179–82). On the Naqshbandi *maqāmāt*, see Paul 1998, 5–15, and especially pp. 10–12 on the problem of dating the *Maqāmāt-e Khvāja Naqshband(ī)*, and the existence of several different versions of this text; see also his n. 28, concerning the misunderstanding about the author.

892/1487 in Herat; see Golchīn Maʿānī 1363sh./1984, I: 264–66; Browne 1928, 436–37; Storey, I/2: 784–89, no. 1093.

(I.23) *Majāles al-ʿoshshāq*, [which is] the *Tadhkera* of Mīrzā Solṭān-Ḥosayn,

= The work written by Amīr Kamāl al-Dīn Ḥosayn Tabasī Gāzorgāhī in 908/1502, for Solṭān-Ḥosayn Bāyqarā, the last significant Timurid ruler of Herat; see Golchīn Maʿānī 1363sh./1984, II: 707–09; Storey, I/2: 961–62, no. 1276, with an incorrect attribution to Solṭān-Ḥosayn Bāyqarā.[112]

(I.24) *Majāles al-nafāyes* [which is] the *Tadhkerat al-shoʿarā* of Mīr ʿAlī-Shīr,

= The *tadhkera* by Mīr ʿAlī-Shīr Navāʾī, which was composed in Turki, in 896/1490–91, and in the 1520s translated into Persian by Fakhrī Heravī as *Laṭāyef-nāma*, and by Ḥakīm Shāh Moḥammad b. Mobārak Qazvīnī as *Hasht behesht*; see Golchīn Maʿānī 1363sh./1984, II: 118–20, 120–23 (for the two versions), and 123–25 (for the later translation by Shaykh-zāda Fāyeḍ); Storey, I/2: 789–95, no. 1094; also, Browne 1928: 437–39.

(*I.25) *Tadhkera-ye Mawlānā Banāʾī*,

Apparently, a work by Kamāl al-Dīn Shīr-ʿAlī Banāʾī of Herat (d. 918/1512 in Qarshī); he wrote a history of the Shaybanid Moḥammad Khān, the two versions of which are known as *Shaybānī-nāma* and *Fotūḥāt-e khānī*; see Storey/Bregel, II: 1116–19. He is also the author of a treatise on music, *Resāla-ye mūsīqī*, the manuscript of which (dated 888/1484) has recently been discovered in a private collection; see Wright 1994, esp. n. 71 on the identification of the author;

And others (*va-ghayra*).

II. *Tadhkerat al-shoʿarā*

Author: Moṭrebī al-Aṣamm Samarqandī

Date of text: 1013/1604–05

References: Akhmedov 1985, 165–73.

Contains no special list of sources, but some scattered references:

(II.1) *Majāles al-nafāyes yā Tadhkera-ye Mīr ʿAlī-Shīr*,

See I.24.

(II.2) *Tadhkera-ye Khvāja Ḥasan Nethārī*,

= *Modhakker al-aḥbāb*, by Seyyed Bahāʾ al-Dīn Khvāja Ḥasan *naqīb al-ashrāf* Bokhārī "Nethārī," composed in 974/1566; see Golchīn Maʿānī 1363sh./1984, II: 219–35; see Storey, I/2: 802, no. 1102; Storey/Bregel, II: 842.

(II.3) *Riyāḍ al-shoʿarāʾ*,

Probably the early seventeenth-century work by Moḥammad-Ṣādeq Samarqandī "Ṣādeqī," for which no extant manuscript is known.

(II.4) *Tadhkerat al-shoʿarāʾ*

See I.22.

112. The author himself ascribes the authorship of the *tadhkera* to his Timurid royal patron (see Browne 1928, 457–58, quoting the *Bābor-nāma*); on his identification, see Richard 1997, 197.

III. *Khazīna-ye ganj*

Author: Mīr ʿEmād al-Dīn Maḥmūd Ḥosaynī Hamadānī "Elāhī"
Date of text: *ca.* 1042–52/1632–1642–43
References: Naqavī 1347sh./1968, 191–94 (list of sources, p. 193); Golchīn Maʿānī 1363sh./1984, I: 518–24; Storey, I/2: 815–16, no. 1121.
Sources quoted:

(III.1) *Tadhkera-ye Dawlatshāh-e Samarqandī,*
See I.22.

(III.2) *Toḥfa-ye Sāmī,*
By Sām Mīrzā b. Shāh Esmāʿīl I Ṣafavī, brother of the Safavid ruler of Iran Shāh Ṭahmāsp I; a *tadhkera* composed in 957/1550; see Golchīn Maʿānī 1363sh./1984, I: 155–57; see Storey, I/2: 797–800, no. 1100.

(III.3) *Majāles al-nafāyes,*
See I.24.

(III.4) *ʿArafāt al-ʿāsheqīn,*
= *ʿArafāt al-ʿāsheqīn [/al-ʿārefīn] va-ʿaraṣāt al-ʿārefīn [/al-ʿāsheqīn],* completed in 1024/1615 at Jahāngīr's court by Taqī Awḥadī, or Taqī b. Moʿīn Moḥammad al-Ḥosaynī Awḥadī Daqāqī Eṣfahānī; see Golchīn Maʿānī 1363sh./1984, II: 3–24; Naqavī 1347sh./1968, 151–66; Storey, I/2: 808–11.

(III.5) *Javāher al-ʿajāyeb,* by Fakhrī,
= Solṭān-Moḥammad-e Amīrī "Fakhrī" Heravī; a *tadhkera* of contemporary women poets written in Sind *ca.* 963/1555–56; see Golchīn Maʿānī 1363sh./1984, I: 417–32; Naqavī 1347sh./1968, 96–100; Storey, I/2: 795–97, no. 1099.[113]

(III.6) *Tadhkera-ye Khvāja Amīn al-Dīn Ḥasan Nethārī,*
See II.2.

(III.7) *Maqālat al-abrār* or *Tadhkera-ye ṣūfīya,*
By Rashkī b. Dīvān Manū Lāl Falsafī; see Storey, I: 1065, no. 1411(115); listed in Naqavī 1347sh./1968, 756, no. 144.

(III.8) *Majāles,* by ʿAbd al-Qāder Marāghī,
Apparently, ʿAbd al-Qāder b. Ghaybī al-Ḥāfeẓ al-Marāghī (d. 838/1435 at Herat), author of two celebrated treatises on the theory of music, but also several other works (although it is unclear if one of his recorded works or an unknown text might be referred to here). He was also known as a poet and painter; on him and his works in Persian, see Storey II/3: 412–13, no. 702.[114]

IV. *Modhakker al-aṣḥāb*

Author: Moḥammad-Badīʿ "Malīḥā" Samarqandī
Date of text: 1093–1100/1682–1690

113. On this *tadhkera* and its context, see Szuppe 1996.
114. See further Wright 1994–95.

References: Golchīn Maʿānī 1363sh./1984, II: 236–41; Akhmedov 1985, 173–78.
Contains no special list of sources, but some scattered references:

(IV.1) Mawlānā Dawlatshāh b. Bakhtshāh Samarqandī,
See I.22.

(IV.2) ʿAbd al-Raḥmān Jāmī,
Among the numerous works of Jāmī (d. 898/1492) are the *Nafaḥāt al-ons* (see I.17) and the *Bahārestān*, written in 892/1487 (see Golchīn Maʿānī 1363sh./1984, II: 485–86); either or both of these works may be intended here.

(IV.3) Mīr ʿAlī-Shīr who "wrote in Turki,"
See I.24.

(IV.4) Mawlānā Khvāja Ḥasan Nethārī,
See II.2.

(IV.5) Mollā "Ṣāmī" (?) Samarqandī whose personal name was Moḥammad Bāltū,
Probably to be corrected as "Mollā Ṣādeqī Samarqandī," the form of the name that appears in the "Biruni" Oriental Institute (Tashkent) manuscript (MS 4270, fol. 40a), i.e. maybe the author of *Riyāḍ al-shoʿarā*, Moḥammad-Ṣādeq "Ṣādeqī" Samarqandī; see II.3.

(IV.6) Mīrzā Ṭāher Naṣrābādī,
= Mīrzā Moḥammad Ṭāher Naṣrābādī Eṣfahānī, who completed his *Tadhkerat-e Naṣrābādī* in 1090/1679; see Golchīn Maʿānī 1363sh./1984, I: 397–404; Storey, I/2: 818–21, no. 1130.

(IV.7) *Rawḍat al-ṣafā*,
= *Rawḍat al-ṣafā fī sīrat al-anbiyāʾ va-l-molūk va-l-kholafāʾ*, a universal chronicle by Moḥammad b. Khvānd-shāh, known as Mīrkhvānd, written in Herat *ca.* 900/1494–95; see Golchīn Maʿānī 1363sh./1984, II: 636–38; Storey/Bregel, I: 361–78, no. 260.

(IV.8) *Qandīya*,
= *Qandīya-ye khord*, which seems to be the sixteenth-century Persian version (?) of ʿOmar b. Moḥammad al-Nasafī's (d. 537/1142) *Kitāb al-Qand fī taʾrīkh Samarqand/fī ʿulamāʾ Samarqand*; see Storey/Bregel, II: 1112–13.[115]

V. *Neshtar-e ʿeshq*

Author: (Āghā) Ḥosayn-Qolī Khān "ʿĀsheq" ʿAẓīmābādī
Date of text: 1233/1817–18
References: Golchīn Maʿānī 1363sh./1984, II: 357–60; Naqavī 1347sh./1968, 515–21 (list of sources, p. 519); and "Biruni" Oriental Institute, Tashkent, MS. 2096 (list of sources on fol. 20a).

115. On the problems related to the Persian *Qandīya*, and its editions, see Paul 1993. A recent edition of the Arabic *Kitāb al-Qand* by Y. al-Hādī (Tehran: Mīrāth-e Maktūb, 1378sh./1999) has since appeared.

Sources quoted:

(V.1) *Toḥfa-ye Sāmī*, written by the late (*marḥūm*) Sām Mīrzā,
See III.2.

(V.2) *Hamīsha bahār*, by Ekhlāṣ Dehlavī,
Or Keshan Chand "Ekhlāṣ" Jahānābādī; a *tadhkera* composed in 1136/1723–24; see Golchīn Maʿānī 1363sh./1984, II: 414–16; Naqavī 1347sh./1968, 229–31; Storey, I/2: 826, no. 1137.

(V.3) *Ḥayāt al-shoʿarā*, by Moḥammad-ʿAlī Khān Kashmīrī,
Composed in the second half of the twelfth/eighteenth century, according to Golchīn Maʿānī 1363sh./1984, I: 462–64; listed by Naqavī 1347sh./1968, 710, no. 5b/2, among the *tadhkeras* of which no manuscript is known to exist today.

(V.4) *Mardom dīda*, by Ḥākem Lāhūrī,
= ʿAbd al-Ḥakīm "Ḥākem" Lāhūrī; a *tadhkera* composed in 1175/1761–62; see Golchīn Maʿānī 1363sh./1984, II: 786–87; Naqavī 1347sh./1968, 415–24; Storey, I/2: 829–30, no. 1146.

(V.5) *Khulāṣat al-afkār*, by Mīrzā Abū Ṭāleb,
= Abū Ṭāleb Khān b. Ḥājjī Moḥammad-Beg Khān Tabrīzī Eṣfahānī;[116] a *tadhkera* composed in 1206–07/1791–93; see Golchīn Maʿānī 1363sh./1984, I: 564–90; Naqavī 1347sh./1968, 477–89; Storey, I: 878, no. 1178(1); Storey/Bregel, I: 463–65.

(V.6) *Khezāna-ye ʿāmera*, by Mīrzā Gholām-ʿAlī "Āzād" Belgrāmī,
A *tadhkera* composed 1176/1762–63; on the text, see Golchīn Maʿānī 1363sh./1984, I: 513–18; Naqavī 1347sh./1968, 435–37; Storey, I/2: 864, no. 1162 (17). On this renowned author (1148–1200/1736 – 85/86) and his numerous works in Arabic and Persian, including V.7 and V.8, see Naqavī 1347sh./1968, 255–70, and Storey, I/2: 855–67, no. 1162.

(V.7) *Sarv-e Āzād*, by Mīr-e Mamdūḥ,
= Mīrzā Gholām-ʿAlī "Āzād" Belgrāmī (see V.6), who composed this *tadhkera* in 1166/1752–53; see Golchīn Maʿānī 1363sh./1984, I: 706–07; Naqavī 1347sh./1968, 383–90; Storey, I/2: 864, no. 1162(16).

(V.8) *Yad-e bayḍā*, by Seyyed-e Mabrūr,
= Mīr(zā) Gholām-ʿAlī "Āzād" Belgrāmī (see V.6), who compiled this *tadhkera* in 1145/1732–33, revised it in 1148/1735–36, and again at a later date; see Golchīn Maʿānī 1363sh./1984, II: 418–20; Naqavī 1347sh./1968, 271–73; Storey, I/2: 863–64, no. 1162(15).

(V.9) *Gol-e raʿnā*, by Lachhmī Narāyan Shafīq,
A *tadhkera* composed in 1181–82/1767–69 by Rāy Lachhmī Narāyan Shafīq

116. Mughal author of Iranian origin, also called "Landanī" owing to his travel to London in 1798–1803, and his account of his journey, entitled *Masīr-e Ṭālebī* (1219/1804) (see Storey, I: 704, no. 934).

Awrangābādī "Shafīq"; see Golchīn Maʿānī 1363sh./1984, II: 46–50; Naqavī 1347sh./1968, 438–45, also on the author and his other historical and literary works; Storey, I/2: 867, no. 1165(2).

(V.10) *Bī-naẓīr,* by Mīr ʿAbd al-Vahhāb Dawlatābādī,

A *tadhkera* composed in 1172/1758–59; the author's *takhalloṣ* was "Eftekhār"; see Golchīn Maʿānī 1363sh./1984, I: 194–203; Naqavī 1347sh./1968, 393–96; Storey, I/2: 854, no. 1157.

(V.11) *Riyāḍ al-shoʿarā*, by ʿAlī-Qolī Khān "Vāleh" Dāghestānī,

An important *tadhkera* composed in 1161/1748–49; see Golchīn Maʿānī 1363sh./1984, I: 650–66; Naqavī 1347sh./1968, 293–310; Storey, I/2: 830–33, no. 1147.

(V.12) *Tadhkerat al-moʿāṣerīn*, by Shaykh Moḥammad-ʿAlī "Ḥazīn" Lāhejānī,

An important *tadhkera* composed in 1165/1752; see Golchīn Maʿānī 1363sh./1984, I: 349–59; Naqavī 1347sh./1968, 341–76; Storey, I: 848, no. 1150(2).

(V.13) *Majmaʿ al-nafāyes*, by Serāj al-Dīn ʿAlī-Khān "Ārezū,"

A *tadhkera*, composed in 1164/1750–51; see Golchīn Maʿānī 1363sh./1984, II: 158–66; Naqavī 1347sh./1968, 322–41, especially pp. 337–41; Storey I/2: 839, no. 1149. See also V.30.

(V.14) *Montakhab al-laṭāyef*, by Raḥm-ʿAlī Khān Īmān Farrokhābādī,

A rare *tadhkera* written in 1190/1776 as an abridgment of the author's earlier work entitled *Jāmeʿ al-laṭāyef* (*ca.* 1184/1770–71);[117] the author's name is given as Mawlavī Raḥm-ʿAlī Khān Farrokhābādī "Īmān" b. Bahramand Khān, and his date of death indicated on 16th of Ṣafar 1224 (= 2 April 1809) by Sprenger 1854: 645, in his comments on the sources of the *Neshtar-e ʿeshq*.[118]

(V.15) *Kalimāt al-shoʿarāʾ*, by Mīr Moḥammad Afḍal "Sarkhūsh" Dehlavī,

= Mīrzā Mīyān Moḥammad Afḍal "Sarkhūsh" b. Moḥammad Zāhed, born in Kashmīr into a family of Badakhshani origin; a very popular *tadhkera*, completed in 1093/1682; see Golchīn Maʿānī 1363sh./1984, II: 32–41; Naqavī 1347sh./1968, 210–20; Storey, I/2: 821–23, no. 1132.

117. See the Introduction to the recent edition: Raḥm-ʿAlī Khān Īmān, *Montakhab al-laṭāyef*, ed. Ḥosayn ʿAlī-zāda and Mehdī ʿAlī-zāda, Tehran: Ṭahūrī, 1386sh./2007. The editors used the manuscript kept at the University Library at Dehli.

118. Apparently identical with "Muḥammad Raḥm ʿAlī Khān b. Bahramand Khān Sekandarpūrī," author of a work on *materia medica* entitled *Badīʿ al-navāder* (see Rieu, III: 1026a, MS. Or. 1762 [xxvii]), and "Raḥm ʿAli Khān b. Bahramand Khān Pordelkhānī Sekandara-Rāoʾī," who wrote a treatise on Persian grammar, *Meṣbāḥ al-ṣebyān* (see Rieu, III: 1043b, MS. Or 2017 [iv]). Cf. Sprenger 1854: 645, who adds that the author of the *Montakhab al-laṭāyef* was "a good Arabic and Persian scholar." The work is also mentioned as one of the sources for the *Takmelat al-shoʿarā-ye jām-e Jamshīd* (1199/1784–85) by Moḥammad Qodratallāh Shawq (see Naqavī 1347sh./1968: 470).

(V.16) *Mer'āt al-khayāl*, by Shīr Khān Lūdī,

A *tadhkera* composed in 1102/1690–91; see Golchīn Ma'ānī 1363sh./1984, II: 242–46; Naqavī 1347sh./1968, 220–28; Storey, I/2: 823–25, no. 1135.

(V.17) *Kharīṭa-ye jawhar*, by Mīrzā Jān-e Jānān Maẓhar Dehlavī,

= Mīrzā Shams al-Dīn Ḥabībāllāh "Maẓhar" (d. 1195/1781), an important Naqshbandi sheikh, founder of the Shamsīya branch of the order. According to the indication by Storey, I/2: 1033 n. 2, the work is an anthology of single lines and selected quatrains; Storey (*ibid.*) also gives reference to manuscripts (thus correcting the earlier mistaken attribution in the printed catalogues) and to editions (appended to the author's *Dīvān*), as well as details on his other works. The title is also listed by Naqavī among the *tadhkeras* "the copies of which are not known to exist today," and without mentioning the author's name; see Naqavī 1347sh./1968, 712, no. 4.[119]

(V.18) *Tārīkh-e ṣobḥ-e Ṣādeq*,

By Mīrzā Moḥammad-Ṣādeq "Ṣādeq(ī)" Eṣfahānī Āzādānī, who was a paternal uncle of Mīrzā Ṭāher Naṣrābādī (see IV.7); a historical and geographical account including many biographies, composed in 1048/1638–39; see Golchīn Ma'ānī 1363sh./1984, II: 665–68; Naqavī 1347sh./1968, 773; Storey, I/1: 125–26, no. 142.

(V.19) *Tārīkh-e Fereshta*,

By Moḥammad-Qāsem Hendūshāh Astarābādī, known as Fereshta; a chronicle also known as the *Tārīkh-e Nawras-nāma* and the *Golshān-e Ebrāhīmī*, composed for its main part in 1015/1606–07, for the ruler of Bijapur; see Golchīn Ma'ānī 1363sh./1984, II: 732–33; Storey, I/2: 442–50.

(V.20) *Tārīkh-e 'ālam-ārā-ye 'Abbāsī*,

By Eskandar Beg Torkemān Monshī; a chronicle composed *ca.* 1025/1616, and dedicated to the Safavid Shāh 'Abbās I; see Golchīn Ma'ānī 1363sh./1984, II: 681–81; Storey/Bregel, II: 874–81.

(V.21) *Tārīkh-e Badā'ūnī*,

= *Montakhab al-tavārīkh* of 'Abd al-Qāder Badā'ūnī, written *ca.* 1004/1595–96; see Golchīn Ma'ānī 1363sh./1984, II: 792–98; Storey/Bregel, I: 417–22; Storey, I/2: 439, no. 614.

(V.22) *Tārīkh-e Akbarī*,

Probably the *Tārīkh-e Akbarī* by Mīr 'Arīf Qandahārī of Akbar's court is meant here, which was written *ca.* 981/1573 (see Storey, I: 541, no. 707); but also, the well-known *Ā'īn-e Akbarī*, by Abū-l-Faḍl 'Allāmī, composed in 1006/1597–98, might be meant (see Golchīn Ma'ānī 1363sh./1984, II: 432–38; Storey, I: 549–51, no. 709(2).

119. Apparently the name appears only in the Tashkent manuscript, which was not available to Naqavī.

(V.23) "All four volumes (*jeld*)" of the *Akhbār al-akhyār* by Shaykh ʿAbd al-Ḥaqq Dehlavī,

= *Akhbār al-akhyār fī asrār al-abrār*, by ʿAbd al-Ḥaqq Dehlavī Bokhārī; a *tadhkera* of Indian Sufis and saints, compiled before 996/1588, and revised and completed in 999/1590–91; see Naqavī 1347sh./1968, 743; Storey, I/2: 978–79, no. 1298(1).

(V.24) *Tārīkh-e Jahāngīrī*,

= *Noskha-ye zībā-ye Jahāngīr* by Moṭrebī Samarqandī, completed in or after 1037/1627–28 in Balkh; see Golchīn Maʿānī 1363sh./1984, II: 526; Naqavī 1347sh./1968, 186.

(V.25) "All three volumes (*jeld*)" of the *Tārīkh-e Shāh-Jahān-nāma*,

The information regarding the number of volumes suggests that the author is referring to the *Pādshāh-nāma* or *Shāh-Jahān-nāma* by ʿAbd al-Ḥamīd Lāhūrī (d. 1065/1654–55), structured in three *daftar*s, each devoted to a period of ten years of Shāh-Jahān's reign; the third *daftar* was completed by the author's disciple, Moḥammad Vāreth (d. 1091/1680), and revised by ʿAlāʾ al-Molk Tūnī (d. 1073/1663);[120] see Golchīn Maʿānī 1363sh./1984, II: 490–92; Storey, I: 574–577.

(V.26) *Tārīkh-e ʿĀlamgīrī*,

= A history of Awrangzeb. Neither of the two texts known under this precise title, by ʿAbd al-Ḥayy and Aḥmad Qolī Ṣafavī, appears to have been very popular; see Storey I/2, no. 755/ 11 and 12, where only one manuscript for each of these texts is recorded. Rather than the *ʿĀlamgīr-nāma* by Moḥammad Kāẓem (d. 1092/1681), probably the *Maʾāther-e ʿĀlamgīrī* by Moḥammad Sāqī Mostaʿedd Khān (d. 1136/1724) is intended here, since it includes the whole reign of Awrangzeb and is considered the main reference for the period.

(V.27) *Tārīkh-e Nāderī*,

Since the title appears among other Mughal texts, it is most probably the *Bayān-e vāqeʿ*, also named *Tārīkh-e Nāderī*, by ʿAbd al-Karīm Kashmīrī, composed in *ca.* 1198/1784 (see Storey/Bregel, II: 926–27, no. 781); however, it might also refer to the *Tārīkh-e Jahān-goshā-ye Nāderī*, a chronicle of Nāder-Shāh Afshār, by Mīrzā Mahdī Khān Astarābādī, *ca.* 1160/1747 (see Storey/Bregel, II: 905–11).

(V.28) *Tārīkh-e Merʾāt-e āftāb-nemā*,

A short chronicle with a special part on biographies of poets and learned men, by Navvāb ʿAbd al-Raḥmān Shāh-Navāz Khān Hāshemī Dehlavī, completed in 1218/1803–04; see Golchīn Maʿānī 1363sh./198, II: 774–75;

120. Some Persianate authors refer separately to these *daftar*s as if they were distinct *Shāh-Jahān-nāmas*; see for example the *Sarv-e Āzād* by Mīr Gholām ʿAlī Āzād (see above, V.7), who lists the *Shāh-Jahān-nāma* by ʿAbd al-Ḥamīd Lāhūrī and the *Shāh-Jahān-nāma* by ʿAlāʾ al-Molk Tūnī among the sources of his work (cf. Naqavī 1347sh./1968, 384).

Storey, I/1: 146, no. 175; it is also listed by Naqavī 1347sh./1968, 778, no. 13, among historical works that contain biographies.

(V.29) *Safīnat al-awliyā'*,
A *tadhkera* by Moḥammad Dārā-Shokūh "Qāderī," son of Shāh-Jahān, completed in Ramadan 1049/January 1640; see Naqavī 1347sh./1968, 745, no. 23; Storey, I/2: 992–98, no. 1321(1).

(V.30) *Cherāgh-e hedāyat*,
A dictionary of Persian words used in poetry after Jāmī, by Serāj al-Dīn ʿAlī Khān "Ārezū" (see above, V.13), composed in 1147/1734–35; see Naqavī 1347sh./1968, 332–33.

(V.31) *Farhang-e Rashīdī*,
By ʿAbd al-Rashīd b. ʿAbd al-Ghaffūr Ḥosaynī Madanī Tatavī, a dictionary of Persian language composed in 1064/1654.

(V.32) *Farhang-e Jahāngīrī*,
By Jamāl al-Dīn Ḥosayn b. Fakhr al-Dīn Ḥasan Īnjū (d. 1035/1625–26); see SVR, I, no. 458.

References

Abbreviations

GAL: Carl Brockelmann (1898–1902), *Geschichte der arabischen Litteratur*, 2 vols., Berlin.

GAL SB: Carl Brockelmann (1937–42), *Geschichte der arabischen Litteratur. Supplement-Bände*, 3 vols., Berlin.

Rieu: Charles Rieu (1879–83), *Catalogue of Persian Manuscripts in the British Museum*, 3 vols., London; (1885), *Supplement*, 1 vol., London.

Storey: Storey, C. A. (1927–53), *Persian Literature. A Bio-Bibliographical Survey*, I/1–2: *Qur'ānic Literature; History and Biography*, London: Luzac and Co.

Storey/Bregel: *Stori, C. A.: Persidskaja literatura. Bio-bibliograficheskiï obzor (Koranicheskaja literatura; Istorija)*, translated into Russian and augmented by Yuri Bregel [Iuriï Bregel'], 3 vols., Moscow: Nauka.

SVR: A. A. Semënov *et al.*, eds. (1953–87), *Sobranie vostochnykh rukopiseï Instituta vostokovedenija Akademii Nauk uzbekskoï SSR*, 11 vols., Tashkent: Fan.

I. *Primary sources*

ʿAbdallāh [Khvāja] Kābolī, *Tadhkerat al-tavārīkh*, "Biruni" Oriental Institute, Uzbek Academy of Sciences, Tashkent, MS. 2093.

ʿĀsheq, Ḥasan-Qolī Khān ʿAẓīmābādī, *Neshtar-e ʿeshq*, "Biruni" Oriental Institute, Uzbek Academy of Sciences, Tashkent, MS. 2096. (Non-critical edition: Ḥasan-Qolī Khān ʿAẓīmābādī ʿĀsheq, *Neshtar-e ʿeshq*, ed. Aṣghar Jānfedā [Asġar Jonfido], ʿAlā-khān Afsaḥzād [Alokhon Afsakhzod] and Jābolqā Dādʿalīshāyef [Dzhobulko Dodalishoev] (gen. eds.), 5 vols., Dushanbe: Donish, 1981–88.)

Bābur (Pādshāh Ghāzī), Ẓahīruʾd-Dīn Muḥammad, *Bābur-nāma (Memoirs of Bābur)*, transl./comm. Annette S. Beveridge, London: Luzac, 1922 (reprint: New Delhi: Oriental Reprint, 1979).

Elāhī, Mīr Emād al-Dīn Maḥmūd Ḥoseynī, *Khazīna-ye ganj-e Elāhī*, Königliche Bibliothek zu Berlin, MS. 626.

Fakhrī Heravī, Solṭān-Moḥammad b. Amīrī, *Tadhkira Rowdhatal-Salatin and Jawaharal-Ajaib (with Divan Fakhri Harvi)*, ed. S.H. Rashdi, Hyderabad: Sindhi Adabi Board, 1968.

Kāmī Qazvīnī, ʿAlāʾ al-Dawla b. Yaḥyā, *Nafāyes al-moʾāther*, "Biruni" Oriental Institute, Uzbek Academy of Sciences, Tashkent, MS. 1858/I.

Loṭf-ʿAlī Beg b. Āghā Khān Begdalī Shāmlū "Ādhar," *Āteshkada*, ed. Ḥasan Sādāt Nāṣerī, 3 vols., Tehran: Amīr Kabīr, 1337–40sh./1958–61.

Maḥmūd b. Amīr Valī, *Baḥr al-asrār fī manāqib al-akhyār*, "Biruni" Oriental Institute, Uzbek Academy of Sciences, Tashkent, MS. 2372. India Office Library and Records (London), MS. 575. (Russian partial transl.: *More taĭn otnositelʾno doblesteĭ blagorodnykh (geografija)*, transl. Bori A. Akhmedov, Tachkent: Fan, 1977.)

Malīḥā Samarqandī, [Moḥammad-Badīʿ], *Tadhkerat Modhakker al-aṣḥāb*, "Biruni" Oriental Institute, Uzbek Academy of Sciences, Tashkent, MS. 4270.

Malīḥā Samarqandī, Moḥammad-Badīʿ b. Moḥammad-Sharīf, *Tadhkerat Modhakker al-aṣḥāb yā tadhkerat al-shoʿarā-ye Malīḥā-ye Samarqandī (sadda-ye 11 hejrī-ye qamarī /17 mīlādī)*, ed. Kamāl al-Dīn Ṣadr al-Dīn-zāda-ye ʿAynī, Sefārat-e Jomhūrī-ye Eslāmī-ye Īrān dar Tājīkestān, Dushanbe: Enteshārāt-e Peyvand, 1385sh./2006.

Moṭrebī Samarqandī, *Noskha-ye zībā-ye Jahāngīr*, ed. Esmāʿīl Bīkjānūf and Seyyed ʿAlī Mawjānī, Qom: Ketābkhāna-ye Marʿashī Najafī, 1377sh./1998. (English partial transl.: "Mutribi" al-Asamm of Samarqand, *Conversations with Emperor Jahangir*, transl. Richard C. Foltz, Costa Mesa: Mazda Publishers, 1998.)

Moṭrebī Samarqandī, Solṭān-Moḥammad, *Tadhkerat al-Sho'arā'*, ed. Aṣghar Jānvafā and 'Alī-Rafī'ī 'Alā' Marvdashtī, Tehran: Āyina-ye Mīrāth, 1377sh./1998.

Navā'ī, Mīr 'Alī-Shīr, *Tadhkera-ye Majāles al-nafāyes*, ed. 'Alī-Aṣghar Ḥekmat, Tehran: Ketābkhāna-ye Manūchehrī, 1363sh./1984.

Nethārī Bokhārī, Khvāja Ḥasan, *Tadhkera-ye Modhakker al-aḥbāb*, ed. Najīb Māyel-Heravī, Tehran: Markaz, 1377sh./1998. (Uzbek translation [in Cyrillic script]: Ḥasankhozha Nisoriĭ, *Muzakkiri aḥbob: Dustlar ednomasi*, transl. Ismoil Bekzhon, Tashkent: Abdulla Qodiriĭ nomidagi khalq merosi nashrieti, 1993.)

Sām Mīrzā Ṣafavī, *Tadhkera-ye Toḥfa-ye Sāmī*, ed. Rokn al-Dīn Homāyūn Nafarrokh, Tehran: 'Alī-Akbar 'Elmī, n.d.

Taqī Awḥadī, [Taqī b. Mo'īn al-Dīn b. Sa'd al-Dīn Awḥadī Eṣfahānī], *'Arafāt al-'āsheqīn va-'araṣāt al-'ārefīn*, India Office Library and Records, London, MS. 3654 (the copy ends with the letter *qāf*).

Vāṣefī, Zayn al-Dīn Maḥmūd, *Badāye' al-vaqāye'*, ed. A. N. Boldyrev, Moscow: Vostochnaja Literatura, 1961 (2nd edition Tehran: Bonyād-e Farhang-e Īrān, 1970).

II. *Secondary literature*

Abiad, Malak (1979[1980]), "Origine et développement des dictionnaires biographiques arabes," *Bulletin d'Études Orientales* 31: 7–15.

Afshar, Iraj (1997), " *'Arż* عرض dans la tradition bibliothéconomique irano-indienne," in: François Déroche and Francis Richard (eds.), *Scribes et manuscrits du Moyen-Orient*, Paris: Bibliothèque nationale de France, 1997: 334–43.

Akhmedov, Bori A. (1977), "Vvedenie [Introduction]," to: Makhmud Ibn Vali, *More taĭn otnositel'no doblesteĭ blagorodnykh (geografija)*, transl. into Russian by Bori A. Akhmedov, Tashkent: Fan, 3–12.

—— (1985), *Istoriko-geograficheskaja literatura Srednej Azii XVI–XVIII vv. (pis'mennye pamjatniki)*, Tashkent: Fan.

Alam, Muzaffar, and Sanjay Subrahmanyam (2004), "The Making of a Munshi," *Comparative Studies of South Asia, Africa and the Middle East* 24/2: 61–72.

Berkey, Jonathan (1992), *The Transmission of Knowledge in Medieval Cairo: A Social History of Islamic Education*, Princeton: Princeton University Press.

Bernardini, Michele (2003), "Ottoman 'Timuridism': Lāmi'i Çelebi and his *şehrengiz* of Bursa," in: Éva M. Jeremiás (ed.), *Irano-Turkic Cultural Contacts in the 11th–17th Centuries*, Acta et Studia I, Piliscsaba: The Avicenna Institute of Middle Eastern Studies, [2002] 2003: 1–16.

—— (2006), "A propos du *vaṭan* timouride," in: M. Bernardini, M. Haneda and M. Szuppe (eds.), *Liber Amicorum. Études sur l'Iran médiéval et moderne offertes à Jean Calmard*, special issue of *Eurasian Studies* 5/1–2: 55–67.

Boldyrev, A. N. (1957), *Zaïnaddin Vasifi, tadzhikskiï pisatel' XVI veka (opyt tvorcheskoï biografii)*, Stalinabad.

Browne, Edward G. (1928), *A Literary History of Persia*, III: *The Tartar Dominion (1265-1502)*, Cambridge: Cambridge University Press.

de Bruijn, J. T. P. (2000), "Tadhkira. 2. In Persian literature," in: *Encyclopaedia of Islam*[2], Leiden: E. J. Brill, X: 53–4.

Cooperson, Michael (2000), *Classical Arabic Biography*, Cambridge: Cambridge University Press.

Daniel, Elton L. (2004), "Historiography. iii. Early Islamic Period," in: *Encyclopaedia Iranica*, E. Yarshater (gen.ed.), Center for Iranian Studies, Columbia University, New York, XII: 330–48.

Davidson, Olga M. (2001), "La 'publication' des textes arabes sous forme de lectures publiques dans les mosquées," in: Luce Giard and Christian Jacob (eds.), *Des Alexandries*, I: *Du livre au texte*, Paris: Bibliothèque nationale de France, 401–10.

Erkinov, Aftandil (1999), "La querelle sur l'ancien et le nouveau dans les formes littéraires traditionnelles. Remarques sur les positions de Jâmi et de Navâ'i," *Annali* 59/1–4 (Istituto Universitario Orientale, Napoli): 18–37.

Fazlullah, Muhammad (1975), "Some Persian Poets of Transoxiana (beyond the Oxus) who Migrated to India during the Early Mughal Period (10th c.H./16th c.AD)," in: R. N. Dandekar *et al.* (eds.), *Sanskrit and Indological Studies. Dr. V. Raghavan Felicitation Volume*, Delhi - Patna - Varanasi: Motilal Banarsidass, 113–26.

Foltz, Richard C. (1996), "Two Seventeenth-Century Central Asian Travellers to Mughal India," *Journal of the Royal Asiatic Society*, 3rd Series, 6/3: 367–77.

——, transl. (1998a), *Conversations with Emperor Jahangir by "Mutribi" al-Asamm of Samarqand*, Mazda: Costa Mesa.

—— (1998b), *Mughal India and Central Asia*, New York: Oxford University Press.

Fragner, Bert G. (1999), *"Die Persophonie": Regionalität, Identität und Sprachkontakt in der Geschichte Asiens*, ANOR 5, Berlin - Halle: Das Arabische Buch.

—— (2001), "The Concept of Regionalism in Historical Research on Central Asia and Iran (a Macro-Historical Interpretation)," in: Devin DeWeese (ed.), *Studies on Central Asian History in Honor of Yuri Bregel*, Bloomington,

In.: Indiana University, Research Institute for Inner Asian Studies, 341–55.

Golchīn Maʾānī, Aḥmad (1363sh./1984), *Tārīkh-e tadhkerahā-ye fārsī*, 2 vols., [Tehran]: Enteshārāt-e Ketābkhāna-ye Senānī (2nd edition).

Gibb, H. A. R. (1962), "Islamic Biographical Literature," in: B. Lewis and P. M. Holt (eds.), *Historians of the Middle East*, London-New York: Oxford University Press, 54–8.

Gilliot, Cl. (2000), "Ṭabaḳāt," in: *Encyclopaedia of Islam*², Leiden: E. J. Brill, X: 7–10.

Gruendler, Beatrice, and Louise Marlow, eds. (2004), *Writers and Rulers. Perspectives on Their Relationship from Abbasid to Safavid Times*, Wiesbaden: Dr Ludwig Reichert Verlag.

Haneda, Masashi (1997), "Emigration of Iranian Elites to India during the 16th–18th Centuries," *Cahiers d'Asie Centrale*, 3–4: *L'Héritage timouride: Iran - Asie centrale - Inde, XVe-XVIIIe siècles*, Maria Szuppe (volume ed.), Tashkent: IFÉAC - Aix-en-Provence: Édisud, 129–43.

Heffening, W. (1936) "Ṭabaḳāt," in: *Encyclopaedia of Islam*¹, Leiden: E. J. Brill, Supplement: IX: 214–15.

Humphreys, R. S. (1998), "Taʾrīkh. II. Historical Writing. I: In the Arabic World, a, b" in: *Encyclopaedia of Islam*², Leiden: E. J. Brill, X: 271–80.

Lambton, Ann K. S. (1962), "Persian Biographical Literature," in: B. Lewis and P. M. Holt (eds.), *Historians of the Middle East*, London-New York: Oxford University Press, 141–51.

—— (1998), "Taʾrīkh. II. Historical Writing. II. In Persian," in: *Encyclopaedia of Islam*², Leiden: E. J. Brill, X: 286–90.

Makdisi, George (1981), *The Rise of Colleges: Institutions of Learning in Islam and the West*, Edinburgh: Edinburgh University Press.

McChesney, Robert D. (1990), "The Anthology of Poets: *Muzakkir al-Ashab* as a Source for the History of Seventeenth-Century Central Asia," in: Michel M. Mazzaoui and Vera B. Moreen (eds.), *Intellectual Studies on Islam. Essays Written in Honor of Martin B. Dickson*, Salt Lake City: The University of Utah Press, 57–84.

Meisami, Julie Scott (1999), *Persian Historiography to the End of the Twelfth Century*, Edinburgh: Edinburgh University Press.

Melville, Charles (2001; 2007), "From Adam to Abaqa: Qāḍī Baydāwī's Rearrangement of History," Part 1 *Studia Iranica* 30/1: 67–86; Part 2 *Studia Iranica* 36/1: 7–64.

Naqavī, Dr. Seyyed ʿAlī-Reḍā (1347sh./1968), *Tadhkera-nevīsī-ye fārsī dar Hend va Pākestān*, Tehran: ʿAlī Akbar ʿElmī.

Nūr al-Dīnūf, Shams al-Dīn [=Nuriddinov, Shamsuddin] (1365sh./1986), *Tadhkerat al-tavārīkh-e ʿAbdallāh-e Kābolī*, Kabul: Mūnūtāyp-e Maṭbaʿe-ye Dowlatī.

Paul, Jürgen (1993), "The Histories of Samarqand," *Studia Iranica* 22/1: 69–92.

—— (1998), *Doctrine and Organization: The Khwājagān/Naqshbandīya in the First Generation after Bahāʾuddīn*, ANOR 1, Halle-Berlin: Das Arabische Buch.

al-Qadi, Wadad (1995), "Biographical Dictionaries: Inner Structure and Cultural Significance," in: George N. Atiyeh (ed.), *The Book in the Islamic World: The Written Word and Communication in the Middle East*, Albany: State University of New York Press, 93–122.

—— (2006), "Biographical Dictionaries as the Scholars' Alternative History of the Muslim Community," in: Gerhard Endress (ed.), *Organizing Knowledge: Encyclopædic Activities in the Pre-Eighteenth Century Islamic World*, Leiden-Boston: Brill, 23–75.

Richard, Francis (1997), *Splendeurs persanes. Manuscrits du XIIe au XVIIe siècle*, Bibliothèque nationale de France, Paris.

Robinson, Chase F. (2003), *Islamic Historiography*, Cambridge: Cambridge University Press.

Roded, Ruth (1994), *Women in Islamic Biographical Collections*, Boulder-London: Lynne Rienner Publishers.

Rosenthal, Franz (1968), *A History of Muslim Historiography*, Leiden: Brill (2nd revised edition).

Rota, Giorgio (1996), "Vāṣefi e i suoi tempi: uno sguardo alle *Badāyeʿ oʾl-vaqāyeʿ*," in: Michele Bernardini (ed.), *La civiltà timuride come fenomeno internazionale*, 2 vols., special issue of *Oriente Moderno*, N.S. XV (LXXVI/2), I: 139–64.

Schoeler, Gregor (2002), *Écrire et transmettre dans les débuts de l'islam*, Collection "Islamiques," Paris: Presses Universitaires de France.

Simidchieva, Marta (2004), "Kingship and Legitimacy in Niẓām al-Mulk's *Siyāsatnāma*, Fifth/Eleventh Century," in: Beatrice Gruendler and Louise Marlow (eds.), *Writers and Rulers. Perspectives on Their Relationship from Abbasid to Safavid Times*, Wiesbaden: Dr Ludwig Reichert Verlag, 97–131.

Sprenger, A. (1854), *Catalogue of the Arabic, Persian and Hindùstàny Manuscripts in the Libraries of the King of Oudh*, I: *Persian and Hindùstàny Poetry*, Calcutta, 1854.

Subtelny, Maria E. (1984), "Scenes from the Literary Life of Tīmūrid Herāt," in: Roger M. Savory and Dionisius A. Agius (eds.), *Logos Islamikos: Studia Islamica in Honorem Georgii Michaelis Wickens*, Papers in Mediaeval Studies 6, Toronto: Pontifical Institute of Mediaeval Studies, 137–55.

—— (1994), "The Symbiosis of Turk and Tajik," in: Beatrice F. Manz (ed.), *Central Asia in Historical Perspective*, Boulder - San Francisco - Oxford: Westview Press, 45–61.

Subtelny, Maria Eva and Anas B. Khalidov (1995), "The Curriculum of Islamic Higher Learning in Timurid Iran in Light of the Sunni Revival under Shāh-Rukh," *Journal of the American Oriental Society* 115/2: 210–36.

Szuppe, Maria (1996), "The Jewels of Wonder: The Female Intellectual Milieu in Timurid and Post-Timurid Herat: Faxri Heravi's Biography of Poetesses, *Javāher al-ʿajāyeb*," in: Michele Bernardini (ed.), *La civiltà timuride come fenomeno internazionale*, 2 vols., special issue of *Oriente Moderno*, N.S. XV (LXXVI/2), I: 119–37.

—— (1999), "Lettrés, patrons, libraires: l'apport des recueils biographiques sur le rôle du livre en Asie centrale aux XVIe et XVIIe siècles," *Cahiers d'Asie Centrale*, 7: *Patrimoine manuscrit et vie intellectuelle de l'Asie centrale islamique*, A. Muminov, F. Richard and M. Szuppe (volume eds.), Tashkent: IFÉAC - Aix-en-Provence: Édisud, 99–115.

—— (2004), "Circulation des lettrés et cercles littéraires entre l'Asie centrale, Iran et Inde du Nord (XVe–XVIIIe siècles)," *Annales. Histoire, sciences sociales* 59/5–6: 997–1018.

—— (2006), "Notes sur l'historiographie indo-persane: une 'chronique' en chronogrammes de ʿAbdallāh Kābolī (*ca.* 990/1582)," in: M. Bernardini, M. Haneda and M. Szuppe (eds.), *Liber Amicorum. Études sur l'Iran médiéval et moderne offertes à Jean Calmard*, special issue of *Eurasian Studies* 5/1–2: 333–56.

Touati, Houari (2000a), *Islam et voyage au Moyen Âge. Histoire et anthropologie d'une pratique lettrée*, Paris: Le Seuil.

—— (2000b), "La dédicace des livres dans l'Islam médiéval," *Annales. Histoire, sciences sociales* 55/2: 325–53.

Vajda, Georges (1983), *La Transmission du savoir en Islam (VIIe–XVIIIe siècles)*, Nicole Cottart (ed.), London: Variorum Reprints.

Verzeichniss der persischen Handschriften der Königlichen Bibliothek zu Berlin (1888), ed. Wilhelm Pertsch, Berlin.

Wright, O. (1994; 1995), " ʿAbd al-Qādir al-Marāghī and ʿAlī b. Muḥammad Bināʾī: Two Fifteenth-Century Examples of Notation," Parts 1 and 2, *Bulletin of the School of Oriental and African Studies* 57/3: 475–515, and 58/1: 17–35.

Autobiography and Biography: The Turco-Mongol Case: Bābur, Ḥaydar Mīrzā, Gulbadan Begim and Jahāngīr

Stephen Dale

One of the distinguishing features of the pre-modern historiography of the Islamic world is the lack of biographies that convey individuality or at least the humanity of Muslims. Few authors attempt to reconstruct the life of a complex individual, an individual in the Aristotelian sense of a unique person, or even persuasively to depict their subjects' deeply felt and universally recognizable human emotions. Pre-modern biographies of Muslims tend to be narratives of political, religious or literary stereotypes, whose personality traits and emotionally charged struggles can only be surmised. Therefore, while biographies represent a major genre of Islamic literature, by and large the subjects of biographies remain two-dimensional portraits with little human appeal. Most lives, whether written as a *tārīkh*, a narrative history, or a *tazkira*, a biographical notice, are unable to offer readers an evocative sense of self and a genuine feeling of contingent, unpredictable events in a life history.[1] Given the constraints of biographical literature the natural place to search for the individuality and human emotion that could enliven biographies is in autobiographies, but most pre-modern Muslim autobiographies, such as Ibn Sīnā's famous account of his religious, philosophical and religious education, are similarly lacking these human qualities and represent little more than "extended *curriculum vitae*."[2] There are, however, significant exceptions to this general rule. Among the most notable are four autobiographies and/or memoirs written, in turn, by the founder of the Timurid-Mughal Empire of India and by his cousin, daughter and great-grandson. These authors are, respectively, Ẓahīr al-Dīn Muḥammad Bābur (888–937/1483–1530, r. 932–7/1526–30), his cousin, the Mongol or Mughul, Ḥaydar Mīrzā Dūghlāt (1499–1551), Bābur's daughter, Gulbadan Begim (ca. 929–1011/1523–1603) and his great-grandson, the emperor Jahāngīr (977–1037/1569–1628). Their texts are linked to each other in that Bābur's autobiography probably stimulated the composition of the

1. For a recent discussion of Islamic biographical literature, see Tucker 2001.
2. Young 1990, 183. For Ibn Sīnā's work see Gutas 1988, 23–30, 194–8.

memoir of his cousin and the autobiography of his great-grandson, while his daughter's memoir was written at the request of Bābur's grandson, the emperor Akbar (r. 963–1014/1556–1605) to commemorate the life of her father and his grandfather. Together these works constitute a compelling group of texts that illumine the aspirations, emotions and sometimes even the individuality of four important Timurid-Mughals and their Mongol relations, while also offering uniquely rich material for understanding their societies.

Although little known in the West, autobiographies were a well-developed literary form in the Islamic world, even if most such works, like most European autobiographies or memoirs of the pre-romantic era, were not devoted to the analysis of the growth of individual personality: the modern ideal.[3] For the purposes of this essay, autobiography is defined in the most general terms simply as a retrospective account of a life. In fact, most pre-modern autobiographies in Islamic as well as Christian, Jewish and even Chinese society tended to be "professional" memoirs, self-statements by monarchs or clerics, artists or writers. This characterization applies, for example, of Benvenuto Cellini's late-sixteenth century *Vita*, a work sometimes seen as the first modern autobiography, a title that should probably go to Rousseau's *Confessions*. However, the autobiographies or memoirs of military and political leaders are often far more revealing than those of religious figures, for whom autobiography was often seen as a profane enterprise – in both the West and the Islamic world.[4] This greater degree of openness characterizes the four related works of Bābur, his Mongol cousin, his daughter and great-grandson. While their texts are certainly not "modern" autobiographies, in that these individuals are not preoccupied or even concerned with the growth of personality, each one tells a human story in a compelling manner that reveals, in varying ways, individuals and aspects of their social and cultural milieu that can scarcely be imagined in most pre-modern literature of the Islamic world.

Three of these individuals, Bābur, Ḥaydar Mīrzā and Jahāngīr, composed readily recognizable genres, narrations or histories of events that were decorated and given literary legitimacy by quotations of apposite verse from prestigious classical Persian-language poets. Such quotations were a typical literary device of court historians, and in citing such verses all three

3. For an important recent discussion of Arabic-language autobiographical tradition see Reynolds 2001. An early, classic study of the autobiographical genre by one of the few authors to mention Bābur in connection with European and American authors is Pascal 1960.

4. Christian and Muslim clerics both condemned egotism and many poets who wrote devotional verse strongly echoed these sentiments. See, for example, Khalidi 1994, 11 and De Bruijn 1997, 29–50. Two important autobiographies of military-political figures who were not shy about displaying their egotism are available in Tibi 1986 and Hitti 1987.

men demonstrated they had literary as well as political ambitions, or rather literary ambitions which were an integral part of their sovereign presumptions, wishing to be seen as cultured individuals, one of the recognized attributes of kingship in the Islamic world and beyond. They did not see themselves as literary pioneers who were introducing a new genre to the Islamic world, and the reception of their texts implicitly demonstrates that their descendants treated these works as typical narrative histories, largely ignoring the elements that attract European and American scholars eager to reconstruct the motivations and personality traits of individuals. Bābur wrote in his native Turki, or Chaghatay Turkish, while Ḥaydar Mīrzā, also a native Chaghatay speaker, chose the prestigious lingua franca, Persian, over Turki or, if he knew it, Mongol. Jahāngīr also wrote in Persian, which by his reign had become the established literary and bureaucratic language of the Timurid-Mughal court. He claimed to know Turki but probably did not feel comfortable writing in that language. Gulbadan Begim's late sixteenth-century memoir is also in Persian, although it is not clear if it was composed or dictated in that language or originally in Turki, which for her as for Bābur, was her native tongue. Her memoir is distinctly different from the other three works in that she wrote simply and directly, even by the relatively unadorned standards of her father's prose. It does not contain the wealth of literary aphorisms that implicitly declared the literary and sovereign ambitions of her relatives and descendants.

Ẓahīr al-Dīn Muḥammad Bābur wrote the foundational text of this group of four personal accounts, a work he described as a *Vaqā'i'*, literally a history of events.[5] His is also the only one of these works that has a sense of "contingency" and "unpredictability," a characteristic that some Western scholars identify as a distinguishing feature of the most dramatically compelling life histories. Bābur never, apparently, wrote an introduction explaining his reason for composing what is, by almost any standard, a remarkable autobiographical memoir.[6] Nonetheless he makes it implicitly clear throughout the work that he wrote principally to commemorate his tumultuous and ultimately successful attempt to create a viable Timurid successor kingdom to the fragmented city states that fourth and fifth-generation Timurids had ruled in late-fifteenth century Central Asia and Afghanistan. His self-pro-

5. The definitive critical edition of Bābur's autobiography is Eiji Mano's splendid work, the *Bābur-nāma (Vaqāyi')* (Kyoto: Syokado, 1995); see also his accompanying volume *Concordance and Classified Indexes* (Kyoto: Syokado, 1996). Afterwards cited as Mano 1995, 1996. For a recent bibliography of Bābur utilizing Mano's texts, see Dale 2004.

6. Scholars have not generally been precise about distinguishing the terms "autobiography" and "memoir" but Karl Joachim Weintraub usefully suggests that the difference lies in the practice of introspection that characterizes autobiography. See Weintraub 1975, 821–48.

claimed *mulkgirliq*, that is "kingdom-seizing" or imperialist ambition is the leitmotif of the work. Bābur seems to have written most of the text in Agra between 1527 and 1530, following his Indian victories over Muslim Afghans and Hindu Rajputs that established the nascent Timurid-Mughal Empire, although he probably used a diary when composing the work, which, indeed, in its later pages, has almost the quality of a daily, unrevised record of events. Bābur was not a simple man and his text is not a one-dimensional work, but functions in several different ways — as a political self-statement, a culturally legitimizing memoir illustrating Bābur's literary and religious ideals, a mirror for Timurid princes and a gazetteer of the three principal regions where Bābur pursued his imperial ambitions: Central Asia, Afghanistan and India. However, what has attracted Europeans to the *Vaqāʾiʿ* after they discovered it in the eighteenth century was its autobiographical character, equal in significance, as the Anglo-Indian scholar Henry Beveridge wrote, to St. Augustine's *Confessions*.[7]

Beveridge and others who have since admired the work and sometimes identified it as the first Muslim autobiography, did not mean that Bābur wrote an introspective work preoccupied with personal development and family relations like those of modern European and American autobiographers.[8] Instead, Bābur wrote about himself like Cellini, powerfully demonstrating his own ambition, egotism, self-pity and self congratulation — all traits of other autobiographers. He does not examine his own actions and character traits with the same critical and even astringent eye that he uses when composing his often unsparing accounts of his own relations, never mind his contemptuous sketches of his Afghan and Uzbek enemies. He did not manifest a modern man's preoccupation with his own unique emotional history and consequent personality. However, he was able to engage his readers' sympathies. His often emotionally charged tales of his Herculean struggles, personal betrayals and ultimately spectacular successes continue to draw readers to his side, so much so that most have accepted what he says about himself and others largely at face value, becoming his posthumous friends and partisans.

Bābur is particularly skilful in depicting his feelings, and he does so in both prose and his own poetry. He included some of these verses in the *Vaqāʾiʿ*, but most have remained unexamined in his *dīvān*, or collection of verse. Bābur is most effective in describing his fragile and confused emotions at two periods of his life, youth and old age. They are on display, first,

7. Quoted by Lane-Poole 1909, 12. Henry Beveridge was the husband of Annette S. Beveridge, who made the first complete English translation from the Turki text.

8. Thackston 1996a, 9.

when he describes his youthful years in Central Asia, after he inherited his father's small appanage in the Ferghana valley, far east of Samarqand in 1494. When relating how he felt at the accidental death of a Mongol friend he reports begin overwhelmed with grief, crying for nine successive days. On another occasion, a moment of political crisis, he recounts, "Since I had known myself (*ta ozümni bilip idim*), I never knew such pain and grief.... It was very hard on me. I wept uncontrollably."[9] Then, when recounting his first marriage and nearly simultaneous but distant infatuation with a boy in the fortress of his Andijan appanage in eastern Ferghana, he evokes an adolescent emotional turmoil in both prose and verse that seems both heartfelt and instantly recognizable as the emotional response of an overwrought adolescent. His juvenile Persian verse vividly evokes this recollection.

> May no person be as ravaged, lovesick and humiliated as I,
> May no lover be as pitiless and unconcerned as thou.[10]

It is no wonder that Westerners have been attracted to a work in which a Muslim and a conqueror recalls emotions that are rarely if ever the stuff of traditional court histories or biographical dictionaries of scholars or clerics. It is difficult to find genuinely affecting accounts of individuals in most pre-modern historical or biographical literature in the Islamic world — or, it should be added, in any culture! And while Bābur writes mostly — and in sometimes stupefying detail — about his military and political struggles, he also is able to convey a sense of his emotional and political maturation. Perhaps more affecting than any other aspect of his writings, are poems composed in India that convey with an existential power the depression and isolation Bābur felt there, even as a successful conqueror.

Thus at almost the very moment of his stunning military successes, he expressed his loathing for India — apart from its wealth — a reaction shared by many of his most intimate companions. Some of this is related in the *Vaqāʾiʿ*, especially his Augustine-like repentance for his dissolute life during his Kabul days from 1504 to 1525, when he drank and wrote ribald, not to say obscene poetry with great abandon. The poems Bābur wrote in 1527 and 1528 are, however, far more powerful expressions of his emotional state at this period of his greatest triumph. In them he evokes the theme of *ghurbat* or exile, a trope no doubt, of Islamic and other poetic traditions, but which Bābur invokes to describe his complex feelings of alienation and depression, as illness and old age overtook him amidst the heat and dust of the exotic but alien and repulsive Indian environment.

9. Mano 1995, 81 (fs. 54a–b).
10. Mano 1995, 111–12 (f. 75b).

> In exile (*ghurbat*) this month of abstinence (Ramadan) ages me.
> Separated from friends exile (*ghurbat)* has affected me.[11]

In Islamic culture verse has usually been the preferred and respectable genre for expressing individual emotion, and Bābur adheres to this custom, but with far more emotional power and immediacy than was commonly the case. It is also important that in his *dīvān* his poems are organized chronologically, rather than according to poetic criteria. This means that it is often possible to judge when they were written and possible, therefore, to associate them with specific events of his life — a rare opportunity in Islamic history and literature. While he quotes classical Persian poets such as Ferdowsī and Saʿdī for literary effect, he usually cites his own verse to illustrate an emotion or mood. There is, indeed, an organic relationship between the *Vaqāʾiʿ* and his verse, for he quotes fragments of some poems in his prose text while he wrote others preserved only in his *dīvān* that, from their content, he meant to include in that text, but died before he could do so. In one such poem, he informs readers how he intended both prose and poetry to serve his autobiographical purpose:

> Everyone whose reads these Events [*Vaqāʾiʿ*] will know
> What grief and what sorrow and what difficulties I have seen.[12]

Taken together Bābur's dramatic narrative with its compelling flashes of affecting emotion and his highly self-referential verse represent what may be the single most emotive body of autobiographical literature in the pre-modern world. If Bābur does not engage in the often self-indulgent introspection of later Western writers, he still offers more of himself than any other pre-modern ruler. The magnitude of Bābur's achievement may partly be measured by the nature of the three texts that are linked to his, for none of them is as comparably dramatic and affecting as his work. Still they are remarkable enough given the period in which they were composed. Two of them in fact, have a relatively small emotional content and even fewer revelations of individuality. These are the *Tārīkh-i Rashīdī* of his cousin, Muḥammad Ḥaydar or Ḥaydar Mīrzā Dūghlāt, and the *Aḥvāl-i Humāyūn Pādshāh* of his daughter, Gulbadan Banu Begim. However, the last of these texts in Timurid-Mughul history is as exceptional as Bābur's, if in a different way. This is the *Tūzuk-i Jahāngīrī*, the autobiography of Bābur's great-grandson, Jahāngīr. While not as ambitious or as artistically compelling as that of his ancestor, Jahāngīr's text offers some tantalizing insights into the psychology of its author.

Muḥammad Ḥaydar, son of Muḥammad Ḥusayn Gurkan, was Bābur's

11. Yücel, *Bâbür Dîvânı* 1995: 190, no. 124.
12. Ẓahīr al-Dīn Muḥammad Bābur, *The Rampur Diwan*, Agra, December 1528.

maternal cousin and thus a Mughul or Mongol — Bābur's mother was a descendant of the Mongol, Yunas Khan, who was an important figure in mid-fifteenth-century Central Asia. Ḥaydar Mīrzā, as he calls himself, was a Dūghlāt, one of the most prestigious Mongol tribes of Mughulistan or eastern Turkistan (now Xinjiang), the last center of Mongol power that lay east of Bābur's Ferghana homeland. He wrote his book between 1541 and 1547, following his successful occupation of the Kashmir valley in November 1540, which he later ruled as a Timurid-Mughul governor. The second half was finished first, in 1541, while the shorter first half was completed in 1547.[13] It is impossible to prove that he was moved to write because of Bābur's example, and he may not have been. However, Ḥaydar Mīrzā's life was often closely entwined both with Bābur's and Humāyūn's, Bābur's son, and when he wrote he was familiar with Bābur's writings — the *Vaqāʾiʿ* and the *dīvān*, as well as his cousin's other works on Islamic law and Turkic prosody. He specifically mentions that he included some material from the *Vaqāʾiʿ* in his own history.

As the title of his work indicates, Ḥaydar Mīrzā wrote a history, an account of his Mongol forbears who, as he observes, had not been able to accomplish this themselves.[14] Ḥaydar Mīrzā wrote in Persian, an interesting choice, as Turki was his native language as well as Bābur's, and it is doubtful that he knew Persian any better than his cousin, given his own tumultuous life largely in Central Asia, where native Persian-speakers were relatively scarce outside the major cities. He may have chosen Persian because when he decided to write a history, the only examples he knew were some of the enormous corpus of Persian-language works that were models for Muslim historians in India and the Ottoman Empire in this era. Ḥaydar Mīrzā explicitly states in the Introduction that he was writing a traditional dynastic or, as he expresses it, a "royal history" of his ancestors, the Mongol Khaqans, and that he was doing so in order that they would not be forgotten. With engaging frankness he states that due to his own lack of literary training in the florid style of traditional Perso-Islamic histories, he decided to begin his work by simply quoting the introduction of such a work, Sharaf al-Dīn ʿAlī Yazdī's history of Tīmūr, the *Ẓafarnāma* or *Book of Victory*.[15] Yet, Ḥaydar Mīrzā himself raises questions about his professed inability to write in this style, when he prefaces Part II of his History with an elaborately composed Introduction written by one "driven by the whirlwind of pride and the waves of

13. W. M. Thackston recently edited Ḥaydar Mīrzā's Persian text, including the poetry he quotes, and also published a new English translation; see Thackston 1996b. The first English translation is more fully annotated, although it omits most of Ḥaydar Mīrzā's verse quotations; see Elias and Ross 1972.

14. Elias and Ross 1972, I: 2 (Introduction).

15. Yazdī died in 1454.

ignorance and intoxication."[16] In his desire to emulate Persianate historical writing Ḥaydar Mīrzā sprinkles his account with relevant quotations from the Qurʾan and aphorisms from Persian literature. His open acknowledgement of his wholesale borrowing from Yazdī and explicit references later on to other sources, such as Bābur's *Vaqāʾiʿ* that he utilized for his account, hint at the charm of a man who is genuinely modest and self-conscious about his lack of experience as an historian, although he was proud of his other cultured accomplishments, pointedly remarking: "In the arts of calligraphy, reading, making verses, epistolary style [*inshá*] painting and illuminating I became not only distinguished, but a past-master."[17]

In some respects Ḥaydar Mīrzā's account resembles Bābur's and, as suggested above, may have been partly inspired by his cousin's text. In particular he includes character sketches of his relatives and compatriots, although these generally seem less frank or balanced than Bābur's. A typical example and one understandably positive is his characterization of his protector, his uncle Sulṭān Saʿīd Khān who was, writes Ḥaydar Mīrzā:

> ... a noble, happy, and prosperous prince, and was adorned with acquirements and good qualities .... His conduct of life was irreproachable. His conversation was both graceful and eloquent, whether in Turki or in Persian, and when he showed favour to any one, he used to blush before speaking. He was always gay, open-hearted, generous and affectionate.[18]

Ḥaydar Mīrzā devotes the second part of his work to the history of the Mongols during his lifetime, that is the first half of the sixteenth century. This section is, therefore, part memoir, and in this much larger part of the work he occasionally recalls his own feelings, such as his moving description of his situation in 1508–09, a particularly disastrous period for the Chaghatay Mongol line and associated tribes in western Central Asia. Speaking of the conquests of the Uzbek, Shaybānī Khān, who by 1504 had either expelled or killed most of the Timurids and Chaghatay Chingizids who had previously ruled Transoxiana, Ḥaydar Mīrzā writes:

> This king, who could commit such atrocities and practise such violence, was resolved on my death, at a time when I had only just passed the half of my childhood, and I did not know my right hand from my left, nor good from evil; nor had I the ability to use my own strength — nay, I had not enough intelligence to execute my own wishes. I had become an orphan, without father or mother, my paternal uncles were scattered and my

16. Elias and Ross 1972, II: 150.
17. Elias and Ross 1972, I: 3–4 (Translation). See also II: 151, 256.
18. Ibid., I: 137.

maternal uncles slain. I had not [even] an elder brother who could share in my grief; no friend or relation to comfort me.[19]

Yet not only are such evocative passages extremely rare in the hundreds of pages of Ḥaydar Mīrzā's narration, but they have a stylized, rhetorical quality and, in consequence, little of the impact that Bābur is able to convey with his emotion-laden narrative. Unlike Bābur, whose Turki prose is relatively spare, direct and particular, Ḥaydar Mīrzā attempts whenever possible to "elevate" his narration, even his account of personal emotional crises, with expressions of metaphorical Persian prose. He adopted the Persian literary or scholarly style he believed was necessary to write a respectable history. In another contrast with Bābur, Ḥaydar Mīrzā does not cite his own verse in the text, and, indeed, if he composed a poetical *dīvān* like that of his cousin, full of existential angst and *cris de coeur*, it has not survived. His history is extraordinarily useful as an account of a young Mongol trying to navigate the treacherous waters of sixteenth-century Central Asian politics, and, while far more personal than any court history of the time, as an autobiography it is only a pale reflection of his cousin's *Vaqāʾiʿ*. As N. Elias notes in his Introduction to the Ross translation of Ḥaydar Mīrzā's work, "Baber ... was a better autobiographer than Mirza Haidar.... But, on the other hand, his cousin may be fairly acknowledged the better historian."[20]

Bābur's daughter, Gulbadan Banu Begim wrote the third of these linked autobiographies or memoirs sometime after 1587.[21] As already mentioned, she either wrote or dictated her work in Turki, which for her as for Bābur and Ḥaydar Mīrzā, was her native tongue, or composed them in Persian, which by that time was established as the official administrative and literary language of the Timurid-Mughal court. Her autobiographical memoir, the *Aḥvāl-i Humāyūn Pādshāh* is as remarkable in its own way as Bābur's. First, Gulbadan Begim's Persian prose — or speech — is remarkably simple. Unlike Ḥaydar Mīrzā, who sought public recognition as an historian, she had no obvious literary ambitions and responded, as simply and directly as possible, to Akbar's request to commemorate Bābur, and by the evidence of the text, composed just a memoir. Her modest intention is suggested not only by the lack of rhetorical flourishes but also by the absence, apart from a few minor examples, of poetic citations. A reader might wonder whether her tumultuous life had allowed her to receive anything beyond a smattering of a religious or literary education, but references in her writing suggest she

19. Ibid., II: 210.

20. Elias and Ross 1972, I: 3 (Introduction).

21. Gul-Badan Begam, *The History of Humāyūn (Humāyūn-nāma)* (hereafter *HN*). See also the extended discussion of this work in Lal 2005, 50–68.

was capable of making sophisticated literary allusions. Several later Timurid-Mughul princesses, writing no doubt in calmer, more prosperous times, were accomplished poets.[22] Apart from its exceptionally simple style, Gulbadan Begim's work is unique in that it provides a sympathetic insight into the world of Timurid-Mughal women, a view that, until recently, was largely neglected by scholars of the early modern Islamic world.

Gulbadan's work is divided into two parts. In the first, brief section she narrates a truncated account of her father's life, and much of this material is taken from Bābur's *Vaqāʾiʿ*. She devotes the remainder of her autobiographical memoir to the reign of her brother, Humāyūn. Gulbadan, like Bābur and Ḥaydar Mīrzā, is not trying to offer an intimate self-portrait. Nor is she trying to emulate Bābur's ambitious account of his life. Still, she records occasional and touching insights into her own emotions and also an affecting account of her father's last days. Thus in 1527 at the age of five, she describes being reunited with her father Bābur outside Agra, having travelled there with many other Timurid women from their secure base at Kabul, and again she recalls how she felt in 1533, "lonely and abandoned" and would "weep, grieve and mourn" after the death of her foster mother.[23] Her account of the last year and a half of Bābur's life is the only contemporary record of this time that is not covered in his own memoirs. It must have been an account reconstructed from the stories of her female relatives, as Gulbadan was too young to have witnessed all the events she describes or to have heard all the comments she quotes. However she acquired this information, she offers an affecting description of her father's decline and death. In particular her rendition of Bābur's deathbed scene seems authentic, not a trope, in its portrait of a conqueror, now merely a terminally ill man, exhibiting a self-absorbed, irritable preoccupation with his own mortality, longing for his son Hind-al to arrive from Afghanistan and angrily upbraiding one of his amirs, Mīr Bardī Beg, for selfishly detaining Hind-al at Mīr Bardī Beg's marriage in Kabul.[24] It is the very particular quality of this report that makes it seem a valid account of the actual scene.

While Gulbadan describes only a few recollections of her own deeply felt emotions, these are exceptional enough in pre-modern Islamic literature, where women's voices, if they are heard at all, are usually confined to the respectable medium of poetry, even more so than in the case of her father, Bābur. What makes her memoir even more memorable is that she provides an account of the lives of Timurid-Mughal women. Particularly memorable are the contrasting accounts of these women's joys, as they first

22. Several later Mughal princesses wrote poetry using the pen name *Makhfī*, "secluded."
23. *HN* (Persian Text) 30 (f. 23b).
24. *HN* (Persian Text) 21–2 (ff. 17a–b).

revelled in their lavish Agra accommodations and then later, their trials and sorrows as they suffered and some died when, in 1540, Gulbadan's brother Humāyūn was driven from India by the Afghans, whom Bābur had defeated to win Hindustan in 1526. If Gulbadan had done nothing more than to list the more than eighty women who attended the so-called "Mystic Feast" in 1533, her memoirs would constitute a remarkable document.[25] However, in her subsequent narrative of Humāyūn's brief reign in India, his flight to Afghanistan and Iran and then return to Kabul in 1545 she also discusses, although usually in a matter of fact tone, the marriages, children and situation of other women. Thus in a way virtually unheard of in other literature of the pre-modern Islamic world and especially striking in view of the largely pallid extant accounts of Safavid and Ottoman women, Gulbadan reveals Timurid-Mughal women not as Orientalists would depict them — as passive, reclusive haram captives — but as vibrant, politically influential individuals, who frequently partied together in Kabul's entrancing gardens. Writing of one such gathering with Humāyūn near Kabul in 1548 Gulbadan recalls:

> He [Humāyūn] took up his residence in the "Heart Expanding Garden"... Quli Beg's house where the Begims were was close by and overlooked it .... It was a moonlight night. We talked and told stories, and Mīr and Khānish *āghācha*, and Ẓarīf the reciter, and Sarū-sahī and Shāham sang softly, softly. [Afterwards] up to our time of reaching Laghman neither the royal tents nor the pavilions of the *begims* had arrived, but the *mihr-āmīz* tent had come. We all, his majesty and all of us, and Ḥamīda Bānū Begim, sat in that tent until three hours past midnight and then we went to sleep where we were, in company with that altar of truth [Humāyūn].[26]

Nor did such occasions cease when, three-quarters of a century later Humāyūn's grandson Jahāngīr travelled, hunted and camped with his favourite wife, Nūr Jahān. In the latter era, however, Nūr Jahān has no posthumous voice, although she did, as is well known, wield enormous influence over her husband and the Empire. Indeed, her role can be better imagined after a reading of Gulbadan's memoirs.

Jahāngīr (r. 1014–37/1605–28), who praises Nūr Jahān's marksmanship when she shoots a lion on one of these expeditions, wrote the last of these four Timurid-Mughal autobiographical-memoirs.[27] While he does not explain his reason for writing, it seems quite likely he was inspired by Bābur's

25. Annette S. Beveridge discusses this gathering, whose title may have had an astrological significance. See especially *HN* 114 n. 1, 118, n. 1.

26. *HN* (Persian Text) 85–6 (ff. 73a–73b).

27. *The Tūzuk-i-Jahāngīrī or Memoirs of Jahāngīr* (= Beveridge 1978) (hereafter *TJ*). For a more fluent and beautifully illustrated translation, see Thackston 1999. For the Persian text, see the edition of Mohammad Hashim (*Jahāngīrnāma* = *Tūzuk-i Jahāngīrī*). See also Balabanlilar 2007.

example. Like Ḥaydar Mīrzā and Gulbadan, Jahāngīr had read the *Vaqā'i'*, and asserts, indeed, when visiting Bābur's tomb in Kabul, that he could read it in the original Turki.[28] Whether he read it in Turki or Persian, it is doubtful that he could have comfortably composed his own *Tūzuk-i Jahāngīrī* in that language, which had fallen into disuse at the Timurid-Mughal court by the time of his reign. Jahāngīr wrote, as Bābur did, a yearly narrative of events, and like Bābur, he intersperses the text with both his own verses and those of such Persian-language poets as Ḥāfiẓ, Sa'dī, Jāmī and Amīr Khusraw Dihlavī; these function either as aphorisms or illustrations for his narrative. Like Bābur, he also exhibits the same fascination for the exotica of India, and he appears to have possessed the same innate scepticism of the fantastic and fabulous that defied common sense. He also indicates that, like Bābur, he partly intended the work to be a kind of "mirror for princes," not only for his son, the future Shāh Jahān, but for neighbouring rulers, most probably the Safavid Shahs of Iran. Like Bābur he distributed parts of his text to his closest amirs.[29] However, he does not seem to have inherited either Bābur's literary ambition or Bābur's and his father Akbar's imperialist instincts, and overall his autobiographical memoir is less intellectually expansive and far less dramatically compelling than the *Vaqā'i'*. Nonetheless, Jahāngīr's *Tūzuk* is as exceptional a royal memoir for the seventeenth century as is Bābur's for the sixteenth, but for different reasons: Jahāngīr's persistent concern with his ideal of kingship and his ingenuous revelations of his fragile psychology.

Jahāngīr no more engages in introspection than do Bābur or Ḥaydar Mīrzā, and in fact he is never as openly critical of himself as Bābur, who openly acknowledges how he lost several early battles due to poor planning. Nonetheless, the overall personal impression that emerges from Jahāngīr's *Tūzuk* is that of a psychologically frail individual who felt inadequate in the face of his father's monumental achievements, even while he fervently desired to be revered as a prototypical "just sultan." Indeed, his first act, he tells his readers, most particularly his son, was to erect a "Chain of Justice" that hung down from the wall of Agra fort.[30] Speaking later in his reign about a visit to Ahmadabad in Gujerat, whose climate he despised, Jahāngīr writes about his devotion to his sense of justice and compassion.

> I, from the date on which I entered the city, notwithstanding the heat of the air, every day, after completing the midday prayer, went and sat in the *Jharoka* ...... For the sake of administering justice, I sate [*sic*] there for two

28. *TJ* I: 109.

29. *TJ* II: 37, where he mentions distributing two copies of the *Jahāngīr-nāma*, giving one to his father-in-law.

30. *TJ* I: 7.

> or three sidereal hours and listened to the cries of redress, and ordered punishments on the oppressors according to their faults and crimes. Even in the time of weakness [throughout his reign] I have gone every day to the *jharoka*, though in great pain and sorrow, according to my fixed custom, and have looked on ease of body as something unlawful (*ḥarām*) for me.[31]

It was usual, he continues, again emphasizing his royal sense of duty, that he slept only three hours each night. And throughout his text he repeatedly recounts his compassion for the peasantry, the poor and sick, his opposition to disfiguring punishment and his respect for private property and, of course, his reverence for Islamic law and "the army of prayer."

Jahāngīr's days were filled, as he describes them, with the minutiae of administration: the awards of positions and land, reception of ambassadors and dispatch of envoys, the appointment of commanders to armies of punishment or conquest, periodic hunts — he reports killing a total of 17,167 animals from his twelfth year (1580) to the eleventh year of his reign — and entertainments, particularly the elaborate Nowruz or New Year's feasts. At no time does he describe leading an army into battle or even accompanying a major campaign. In contrast to Bābur's exhausting marches, disastrous campaigns and near-death military experiences, Jahāngīr's greatest physical exertion seems to have occurred during a visit to Kabul. In typical self-assured and relatively unadorned prose he mentions giving a wine party for some unnamed boon companions.

> .... I gave a wine entertainment to my intimates, and on account of hilarity and excitement ordered those who were of equal age to myself and had been my playfellows to jump over the stream that flowed through the middle of the garden and was about four gaz in width. Most of them could not jump it, and fell on the bank or into the stream. Although I jumped it, yet now that I was 40 years of age I could not jump it with the activity that I had shown in the presence of my revered father when I was 30. On this day I perambulated seven of the famous gardens of Kabul. I do not think that I ever walked so far before.[32]

Jahāngīr's off-hand remark about his garden tour reveals the degree to which Bābur and Humāyūn's peripatetic state had evolved, under Akbar's tireless efforts and constant campaigns, to become the firmly established, and, for its rulers, the sedentary Timurid-Mughal Empire. Although his open admission to alcohol and opium addiction have led many readers to conclude

31. *TJ* II: 14.
32. *TJ* I: 105–6.

that he was an inattentive monarch, it seems clear from his memoirs — and his evident pride in them — that Jahāngīr was a conscientious ruler, even, evidently, when suffering from an alcoholic or opium hangover! After all alcoholism and opium addiction — not to speak of other intoxicants — was a signature trait of earlier and later Turco-Mongol rulers!

Nonetheless, the contrasts between Jahāngīr and Akbar, or Jahāngīr and Bābur, or Jahāngīr and Ḥaydar Mīrzā *suggest* a profound psychological distance between Jahāngīr and his predecessors. The contrast may derive from Jahāngīr's sense of being overshadowed by a dynamic, domineering father. Thus, his public attachment to his mature wife, Nūr Jahān and his recognition of her late in his reign as almost a vice-regent for whom "drums and [the] orchestra should be sounded after those of the king," might reflect Jahāngīr's dependant personality.[33] Or these contrasts might also be due to a combination of this common-enough phenomenon with the social psychology described by the fourteenth-century Arab historian, Ibn Khaldūn (732–84/1332–1406) when he analyzed the social, political and psychological distance that separated founders of empires from their descendants. Ibn Khaldūn argued that in dynastic histories the original qualities of conquerors atrophied and their descendants had no memory or understanding of their ancestors' struggle and achievements. If Jahāngīr's place in the Timurid-Mughal succession does not precisely correlate with Ibn Khaldūn's model, his actions and mentality do. He had no evident taste for battle or even monumental architecture, however much he might admire his ancestors for their conquests or architectural patronage. While Bābur could speak casually of the slaughter of prisoners, Jahāngīr expresses his revulsion for torture and sensitivity for the emotional suffering of others. Apart from his evidently genuine concern for responsible rule, he was principally interested in art — not artillery, not fortress construction and certainly not universal empire. Jahāngīr enjoyed being king, which for him involved constant attention but not physical exertion! In many respects he seems to have shared the attitude to kingship which Ibn Buluggīn (r. 465–483/1073–1090), the eleventh-century amir of Granada expressed in *his* autobiography when he wrote, after describing the pleasures — and dangers — of wine: "is not kingship or wealth intended for enjoyment and adornment?"[34]

Jahāngīr's *Tūzuk* and the three earlier memoirs and autobiographies of Gulbadan Begim, Ḥaydar Mīrzā and Bābur, together comprise a most remarkable group of personal texts in the history of the Islamic world. Reading them it is possible to imagine the composition of Islamic biographies be-

33. *TJ* II: 228.
34. Tibi 1986, 192.

coming something more than dry narrations of military and political events or stereotypical portraits of scholars or writers. This is particularly true in the case of Bābur and Jahāngīr, who reveal more than enough to humanize themselves, even if most of their emotional lives remain forever hidden. It is even possible to imagine composing a meaningful life of Ḥaydar Mīrzā, despite the limitations of his formal style of historical writing. Much can be inferred from his narration about the life of a young Mongol boy caught up in the murderous, chaotic political situation of post-Timurid Central Asia, especially when his account is informed by a knowledge of Bābur's *Vaqāʾiʿ* and other historical sources for this epoch. It is more difficult to imagine a separate biography of Gulbadan, but it is very easy to see how scholars might combine her unique information about the social, political and emotional lives of herself, her female relations and companions with later, fragmentary information about such women as Nūr Jahān to reconstruct a meaningful picture of elite Timurid-Mughal women. Such an effort might yield particularly compelling results if the religious and literary scholarship of the women of Shāh Jahān's and Awrangzeb's reigns were studied and translated. Their *makhfī dīvāns* might render these women's lives a good deal less "hidden," just as Bābur reserves for poetry expressions of his rawest emotions.

The question of individuality still remains a problem, even for biographers of these individuals, because, as has been noted, for all their openness they are still more effective at characterizing others than revealing themselves. It is easier to make inferences about Jahāngīr's emotional life than for the others, but lacking the personal insights of contemporaries — the kind of information available to biographers of Benjamin Franklin — it is difficult to reconstruct lives of these individuals or even to understand how their emotional personalities differed from one another. However, biographers can at least identify what might be called the cultural personalities of Bābur, Ḥaydar Mīrzā, Gulbadan Begim and Jahāngīr, individuals who were all, to varying degrees the legatees of Turco-Mongol history and society and Perso-Islamic culture of the Timurid and Timurid-Mughal era. Indeed, it might be rewarding to compile an integrated group of biographical sketches locating all four personalities on a spectrum of Turco-Mongol military and social influence and Perso-Islamic culture. "Eminent Turco-Mongols" might lack the cachet of Lytton Strachey's famous work *Eminent Victorians* (1918), but Bābur, his contemporaries and descendants could ride faster and further, shoot more accurately, drink more heavily, speak more languages, cry more openly and perhaps even compose better poetry than Strachey's English subjects.

Bibliography of Works Cited

Bābur, *Vaqā'i'*, see Mano 1995.

Bābur, *Bāburnāma*, see Thackston 1996a.

Balabanlilar, Lisa (2007), "Lords of the Auspicious Conjunction: Turco-Mongol Imperial Identity on the Subcontinent," *Journal of World History* 18: 1–39.

Beveridge, Henry (ed.) (1978), *The Tūzuk-i-Jahāngīrī or Memoirs of Jahāngīr*, Translated by Alexander Rogers and Edited by Henry Beveridge, 3rd ed., New Delhi: Munshiram Manoharlal.

De Bruijn, J. T. P. (1997), *Persian Sufi Poetry: An Introduction to the Mystical Use of Classical Poems*, Richmond, Surrey: Curzon Press.

Dale, S. F. (2004), *The Garden of the Eight Paradises: Babur and the Culture of Empire in Central Asia, Afghanistan and India* (1483–1530), Leiden: E. J. Brill.

Dūghlāt, Mīrzā Ḥaydar, see Thackston 1996b.

Elias, N. and E. Denison Ross (1972), *A History of the Moghuls of Central Asia, Being the Tarikh-i-Rashidi of Mirza Muhammad Haidar, Dughlát*, An English Version Edited, with Commentary, Notes, and Map by N. Elias, The Translation by E. Denison Ross, London: Curzon Press [first published 1895].

Gul-Badan Begam (1901, repr. 1972), *The History of Humāyūn (Humāyūn-nāma). Translated, with Introduction, Notes, Illustrations and Biographical Appendix; and reproduced in the Persian from the only known MS. of the British Museum* by Annette S. Beveridge, Delhi: Idarah-i Adabiyāt-i Delli.

Gutas, Dimitri (1988), *Avicenna and the Aristotelian Tradition: Introduction to Reading Avicenna's Philosophical Works*, Leiden: E. J. Brill.

Hitti, Phillip K (1987, repr. 2000) (trans.), *An Arab-Syrian Gentleman and Warrior in the Period of the Crusades, Memoirs of Usāmah Ibn-Munqidh*, Princeton: Princeton University Press; repr. New York: Columbia University Press.

Jahāngīr (1980), *Jahāngīrnāma = Tūzuk-i Jahāngīrī*, ed. M. Hashim, Tehran: Bunyād-i Farhang [Persian].

Khalidi, Tarif (1994), *Arabic Historical Thought in the Classical Period*, Cambridge: Cambridge University Press.

Lal, Ruby (2005), *Domesticity and Power in the Early Mughal World*, Cambridge: Cambridge University Press.

Lane-Poole, Stanley (1909), *Bábar*, Oxford: Clarendon Press.

Mano, Eiji (1995), *Bābur-nāma (Vaqāyi'): Critical Edition Based on Four Chaghatay Texts with Introduction and Notes*, Kyoto: Syokado.

—— (1996), *Bābur-nāma (Vaqāyi'): Concordance and Classified Indexes*, Kyoto: Syokado.

Pascal, Roy (1960), *Design and Truth in Autobiography*, London: Routledge and Kegan Paul; Cambridge, Mass.: Harvard University Press.

Reynolds, Dwight (2001), *Interpreting the Self: Autobiography in the Arabic Literary Tradition*, Berkeley: University of California Press.

Thackston, Wheeler M. (1996a), *The Baburnama: Memoirs of Babur, Prince and*

Emperor. Translated, edited, and annotated, New York: Oxford University Press.
—— (1996b), *Mirza Haydar Dughlat's Tarikh-i-Rashidi: A History of the Khans of Moghulistan*, Persian Text and English Translation and Annotation, Cambridge, Mass.: Harvard University Department of Near Eastern Languages and Civilizations, Sources of Oriental Languages and Literatures 37, 38.
—— (1999), *The Jahangirnama: Memoirs of Jahangir, Emperor of India*, Translated, edited, and annotated by Wheeler M. Thackston, Washington, D. C.: Smithsonian Institution.
Tibi, Amin T. (1986), *The Tibyān: Memoirs of ʿAbd Allāh b. Buluggīn, Last Zīrid Amīr of Granada*, Translated from the Emended Arabic Text and Provided with Introduction, Notes and Comments, Leiden: E. J. Brill.
Tucker, Judith E. (2001), "Biography as History: The Exemplary Life of Khayr al-Din al-Ramli," in: *Auto/Biography and the Construction of Identity and Community in the Middle East*, ed. Mary Ann Fay, New York: Palgrave, 9–17.
Usāma b. Munqidh, see Hitti.
Weintraub, Karl J. (1975), "Autobiography and Historical Consciousness," *Critical Inquiry* 1: 821–48.
Young, M. L. J. (1990), "Arabic Biographical Writing," in: *Religion, Learning and Science in the ʿAbbasid Period*, ed. M. L. J. Young, J. D. Latham and R. B. Serjeant, *The Cambridge History of Arabic Literature*, Cambridge: Cambridge University Press, 168–87.
Yücel Bilâl (1995), *Bâbür Dîvânı*, Ankara: Atatürk Kültür Merkezi.

Women's Biographies in Islamic Societies: Mīrzā ʿAbd Allāh al-Iṣfahānī's *Riyāḍ al-ʿulamāʾ*

Devin Stewart

It has been recognized for some time now that Islamic biographical literature devotes a great deal of attention to women, and that the large and variegated genre of the biographical dictionary is one of the main sources available for the study of women in pre-modern Islamic societies. Hamilton A. R. Gibb observed in 1962, "The biographical dictionaries also supply almost the sole materials for the social activities and status of women in Muslim communities."[1] Gibb overstated the case, neglecting legal documents, court chronicles, marriage manuals, and other sources, but nevertheless correctly emphasized the importance of women's biographies. His statement must be seen against a dearth of attention in the field to women's biographies in general. For example, the section on biographical literature in Franz Rosenthal's large and erudite study of Islamic historiography includes not one mention of women.[2] R. Stephen Humphreys' manual for historians of the Middle East treats biographical dictionaries entirely within the topic of *ʿulamāʾ* or scholars and does not mention women once in this regard.[3] In a recent survey of Islamic biographical literature, women are devoted one short paragraph.[4] Relatively few studies using material derived from biographical dictionaries for the investigation of women have been published to date; the main work in this area is a sweeping survey of biographical collections undertaken by Ruth Roded that provides significant results, countering views that the seclusion of women prevented them from acquiring an education or participating in Islamic society.[5] The present study aims primarily to supplement Roded's findings, particularly with regard to women scholars, by focusing on the women's biographies in one major work she did not consult, *Riyāḍ al-ʿulamāʾ wa-ḥiyāḍ al-fuḍalāʾ* (Gardens of the Scholars and Pools of the Learned), by Mīrzā ʿAbd Allāh al-Iṣfahānī (d. ca. 1130/1718). This biographical dictionary, devoted to scholars in the Twelver Shiite tradition, was compiled at the

1. Gibb 1962, 54–8, here 58.
2. Rosenthal 1968, 100–6.
3. Humphreys 1991, 187–208.
4. Gilliot 2002, 1–49, esp. 49.
5. Roded 1994.

end of the seventeenth century in Safavid Iran. While the section Mīrzā ʿAbd Allāh devotes to women is quite short — only eight pages out of over two thousand in the entire work — it is quite interesting in comparison with the biographies of women in other better known works such as al-Sakhāwī's *al-Ḍawʾ al-lāmiʿ* and stands out in its revelation of the author's attitudes towards the women subjects about whom he writes.

In accord with the dictates of political mobilization, there has been a tendency in feminist scholarship to depict pre-modern women in the Islamic world — and elsewhere — as completely and utterly backward. To claim that women in pre-modern Islamic society (up until, or even especially, in the nineteenth century) were universally uneducated and had no access to higher culture is meant to bring out the stark contrast with the progressive, "modern" period, when women are being educated, entering the work force, and competing with men openly on a more equal footing. This point of view, seen in the works of feminist authors such as Fatima Mernissi and Nawal al-Saadawi, is skewed, over-generalizing, and more often than not simply undocumented, but serves an important polemical purpose, to claim that the liberation of women is a necessary part of the sloughing off of backwardness required by entrance into the modern era. Feminist writings focusing on the Middle East and North Africa in this vein have many shortcomings. A particularly striking defect, and one shared by many other studies of modern Middle Eastern history in general, is the monolithic, undifferentiated portrayal of the period before "modern" times, usually set to begin in 1798, with Napoleon's invasion of Egypt. This has produced such oddities as an essay in a volume devoted to women in Middle Eastern history with the audacious title, "Women in the Middle East 8,000 B.C.E.–C.E. 1800."[6] Even if a scholar had control of the languages and sources involved in researching such a topic — something very unlikely — the idea that one can make useful generalizations about such a vast period of time suggests the polemic purpose such an essay serves vis-à-vis the modern period more than anything concrete about the history of the Middle East over nearly seven millennia. Perhaps even more telling is the assumption that the two centuries after 1800 require as much — or more — attention that the ninety-eight preceding centuries.

Another shortcoming comes from a simplistic and undifferentiated understanding of patriarchy itself. Many studies tend to omit a full portrayal of the power politics that obtain in society, so that, for example, Fatima Mernissi speaks of the oppression of women when mothers-in-law abuse and lord it over their daughters-in-law.[7] Indeed it is oppression, but Mernissi

6. Nashat 1999, 5–72.
7. Mernissi 1987, 121–36.

apparently does not notice that mothers-in-law are actually women too, and her model does not explain why young wives count as women and mothers-in-law do not, or how exactly women fit into domestic or societal power structures. In portraying women as utterly oppressed, many studies tend to ignore the ways in which agents in a subordinate social position can and regularly do exercise power.[8] Each of these topics deserves focused treatment, but the main advances in understanding of the status of women in the pre-modern Middle East will come from the judicious use of sources that provide concrete information about them — and biographical dictionaries are some of the most important sources available.

The Arabo-Islamic genre of the biographical dictionary provides rich material for the study of the history of women, not only presented incidentally in accounts of the lives of men, but also as objects of attention themselves. The genre falls into two main categories: *ṭabaqāt* (literally, "classes"), which group entries by generation, and *tarājim*, which present entries in alphabetical order. As scholars have devoted attention to this material in the last few decades, certain results have been achieved. Some attention has been paid to the portrayal in biographical sources of exemplary women.[9] Marilyn Booth has discussed several biographical texts devoted to women from the nineteenth and twentieth centuries, emphasizing the adaptation of the traditional genres by early feminists in order to present contemporary women with accounts of exemplary role models from the Arabo-Islamic past. She has provided what is perhaps the best analysis to date of pre-modern women's biography in an Arabo-Islamic context.[10] Several studies have shown that women participated to a significant extent throughout the medieval period in Islamic education, especially in the science of hadith and the transmission of the canonical texts of the Islamic sciences. While women were certainly much less frequently educated than men, it is now clear that many women in the pre-modern Islamic world were indeed educated. They could read and write, and many participated broadly in the preservation of the patrimony of Islamic religious literature. A number of female scholars gained great renown in these fields, such as Shuhda bt. Abī Naṣr Aḥmad al-Ibarī (d. 574/1178), a very important transmitter of hadith, particularly al-Bukhārī's famous collection *al-Ṣaḥīḥ*. In the capacity of students, teachers, and transmitters of the Islamic patrimony, women often entered the public sphere, including religious institutions traditionally dominated by men such as the

8. For an example of those who are generally considered powerless exerting forms of power, see Scott 1985. A similar approach might be taken for the examination of women's power in the Middle East.

9. See, for example, Spellberg 1994.

10. Booth 1996, 133–7; 1997, 827–90; 2001, esp. 1–34.

mosque and the *madrasa*.[11] M. Z. Siddiqui even argues that the level of participation of Muslim women in the study, teaching, and transmission of *hadith* represents an outstanding feature of medieval Islamic society unmatched in other cultures of the period.[12] A few exceptional women became recognized as authors and leading scholars in their own right. Among the most brilliant female scholars was ʿĀʾisha bt. ʿAbd al-Hādī al-Bāʿūnīya (d. 922/1516), who excelled in Arabic grammar and rhetoric, Islamic law, theology, and mysticism. Her collection of poetry has survived, as well as a number of treatises on mysticism and a fragment of an autobiographical text.[13]

As suggested above, the most substantial work devoted to the biographical literature on women in the pre-modern Middle East to date is Ruth Roded's 1994 work *Women in Islamic Biographical Collections: From Ibn Saʿd to Who's Who*, which examines the treatment of women in representative works of the Islamic period, beginning in the early ninth century and ending in the twentieth century A.D., followed by a number of modern works of the *Who's Who* type. She surveys thirty-two pre-modern biographical collections, including a number of the largest and best known works in the biographical tradition, such as the *Ṭabaqāt* of Ibn Saʿd (d. 230/845), *Wafayāt al-aʿyān* of Ibn Khallikān (d. 681/1282), *al-Ḍawʾ al-lāmiʿ* of al-Sakhāwī, and others. She performs several basic statistical analyses using a database created from these works and finds that the number of entries devoted to women varies widely from work to work, ranging from 1 to 1,500 in number, or from less than 1 to 23 per cent of the total entries. In some cases, the compilers set aside a special section devoted to women, and in others the women's entries are interspersed among those of the men according to alphabetical order. Roded notes a decline in attention to women over time, especially a dramatic drop in the number and proportion of women treated from the sixteenth to the late nineteenth centuries: "But from the sixteenth century onward, women were rarely included in biographical dictionaries ... ."[14] Beyond the quantitative results, she presents a useful taxonomy of three main types of women portrayed in the biographical collections, providing a discussion of each category: 1) idealized women of the early Islamic period; 2) learned women and scholars; and 3) mystic women.[15]

Roded's pioneering effort, despite its successes, has some obvious limitations. Thirty-two large biographical dictionaries might seem like a great

11. Lutfi 1981, 104–24; Berkey 1991; 1992, 161–81.

12. Siddiqui 1993, 117–23: Appendix I "Women Scholars of Hadith."

13. Mukhliṣ 1941, 66–72; al-Dhahabī and al-Khiyamī 1981, 110–21; ʿAlawī 1994; Rabābiʿa 1997; Reynolds et al. 2001, 272; Homerin 2002, 191–3; Homerin 2003, 211–34.

14. Roded 1994, 11, 157.

15. Roded 1994, 15–114.

deal of material on which to base such a study, but it is still a tiny fraction of the extant biographical collections, one of medieval Islam's most popular and prolific genres. The biographical tradition itself is so broad and variegated that her collection of thirty-two works only begins to capture the complexity of the Islamic societies they represent, and does not even attempt to capture the geographical spread of Islamdom. Her selection of biographical collections concentrates on the central lands of the Middle East and leaves vast areas of the Islamic world unrepresented.[16] It bears keeping in mind that all the collections that Roded consulted were written in Arabic, omitting works in Persian, Turkish, Urdu, or other Islamic languages. Her sample does not include any works devoted to North Africa or al-Andalus, though quite a few exist; nor does she include any works from the Shiite traditions. The result is that a number of generalizing, and at times categorical, statements she makes about "women" at a particular era must be understood to be limited to the sources she has consulted. So, for example, when she states that the number of women scholars accorded biographical entries fell in the sixteenth century, and dwindled to next to nothing in the seventeenth and later centuries, this must be taken as a provisional statement based on a restricted collection of sources, however important or representative they are.

Roded's taxonomy of women leaves out an important group evident in many biographical collections such as al-Sakhāwī's *al-Ḍawʾ al-lāmiʿ*: that of women connected with the ruling elite or military class. A number of important works have been devoted to this group, including, in older scholarship, Nabia Abbott's *Two Queens of Baghdad: Mother and Wife of Harun al-Rashid*.[17] Recent works on women rulers include Fatima Mernissi's *The Forgotten Queens of Islam*, and Farhad Daftary's article on Sayyida Ḥurra, the Ṣulayḥid queen of Yemen.[18] A number of important studies have been devoted to women's roles and the exercise of power at court in Timurid Iran, Safavid Iran, the Ottoman Empire, and Moghul India.[19] This overlaps with consideration of women of the ruling classes as patrons of art and architecture, custodians of property, and founders of endowments.[20] The modern historian may, in fact, be able to learn the most about this particular group, because they figure most promi-

16. A general idea of the extent of the genre may be gained from Auchterlonie 1987. This bibliographical guide contains references to hundreds of published works in Arabic. It does not cover Persian, Turkish, Urdu, or other languages of the Islamic world. Furthermore, it does not include references to works published since 1987 or works that remain in manuscript.

17. Chicago: Chicago University Press, 1946.

18. Mernissi 1993; Daftary 1998.

19. Peirce 1993; Szuppe 1994, 1995, 1998; Soucek 1998; Golsorkhi 1995; Babayan 1998, esp. 351–7; Lal 2005.

20. Petry 1991; Blake 1998.

nently in conventional sources such as chronicles and endowment deeds. It is odd that Roded leaves them out, given the amount of information recorded about them in a number of biographical dictionaries.

In addition, the collections Roded analyzes vary widely in method and conventions, so that it is difficult to compare distinct members within this general class. In the attempt to perform a sweeping survey of the field, Roded has largely had to ignore the rhetorical strategies and conventions of individual works. For example, Roded compares the biographical work *Naẓm al-ʿiqyān* of Jalāl al-Dīn al-Suyūṭī (d. 911/1505) with *al-Ḍawʾ al-lāmiʿ* of al-Sakhāwī (d. 902/1497), noting that al-Suyūṭī has only five women out of 200 biographies, whereas al-Sakhāwī includes 1,075 entries on women in his work. She comments, "Thus it is difficult to understand why [al-Suyūṭī] found so few women worthy of inclusion in his centenary biographical collection and made no mention of some very prominent women whom al-Sakhawi included in his work."[21] Roded is comparing apples and oranges here and does not adequately understand the two authors' principles of inclusion. The two works in question, though both by Cairene scholars and both focused on the fifteenth century, do not belong to the same sub-genre within the larger genre of biographical collections. Al-Sakhāwī's work is a large — twelve volumes in the published edition — centenary biographical collection like his teacher Ibn Ḥajar's (d. 852/1449) work *al-Durar al-kāmina*, devoted to the eighth/fourteenth century. He aims to be comprehensive, including all people worthy of note from the ninth/fifteenth century, and is especially interested in any figure who has some demonstrated involvement in the transmission of hadith. Al-Suyūṭī's work, on the other hand, belongs to the sub-genre of biographical collection that focuses on scholars who have lived during the author's own lifetime — including in effect, "great scholars whom I have known or met during my own lifetime." Following the model of such works as al-Ṣafadī's (d. 764/1362) *Aʿwān al-naṣr fī aʿyān al-ʿaṣr*, al-Maqrīzī's (d. 845/1442) *al-Durar waʾl-ʿuqūd*, and Ibn Ḥajar al-ʿAsqalānī's *Inbāʾ al-ghumr bi-abnāʾ al-ʿumr*, al-Suyūṭī does not attempt to be comprehensive, and is limiting consideration to figures whom he considers the most noteworthy scholars of his day in various fields. The fact that he includes five women in this highly selective group is actually a tribute to their high level of scholarly competence, achievement, and status.

It is Roded's fourth chapter, devoted to learned women and scholars, which is of the most concern in the present study.[22] She makes a number of important points in this chapter, noting, like Berkey and Siddiqui, the

21. Roded 1994, 68.
22. "Transmitters of Knowledge, Learned Women, and Scholars," Roded 1994, 63–89.

substantial role women played in the transmission of knowledge, despite the widely touted seclusion of women in medieval Islamic societies. One element brought out by Roded's study is the importance of women in the field of hadith. Many pre-modern Islamic societies placed a high premium on the transmission of Islam's second scripture, the hadith, which consists of reports about what the Prophet said or did — or, for the Shiites, what the Imams as well as the Prophet said or did. Women were often in a position to assume a substantial role in the transmission of this body of material, which, by the late middle ages, consisted primarily of those hadith collected in "the six books": the *Ṣaḥīḥ* of al-Bukhārī (d. 256/870), the *Ṣaḥīḥ* of Muslim (d. 261/874), the *Sunan* of Abū Dāwūd (d. 275/888), the *Sunan* of Ibn Māja (d. 273/886), the *Sunan* of al-Nasāʾī (d. 303/915), and *al-Jāmiʿ al-ṣaḥīḥ* of al-Tirmidhī (d. 279/892), supplemented by several other frequently consulted collections such as the *Sunan* of al-Dārimī (d. 255/868), the *Musnad* of Aḥmad b. Ḥanbal (d. 241/855), and so on. A woman who lived to the age of ninety or one hundred years and who had been granted a certificate of transmission as a young girl by her father or one of her father's colleagues often ended up being one of the last living direct links to a famous scholar of a bygone generation, so that a certificate of transmission from her would be in high demand. Roded portrays a number of the most famous women transmitters, including Shuhda al-Ibariyya, Fāṭima al-Juzdāniyya (d. 524/1129), Zaynab bt. al-Shaʿrī (d. 615/1218), and others, showing not only that women indeed attained the ranks of the learned but also that they on occasion surpassed their male peers. She finds that many learned women had privileged access to learning because they were the daughters of scholars, and that most women learned from men, often family members. However, she also makes the important point that female networks of learning existed, so that the transmission of knowledge without the intervention of males was possible.

Something that work to date touches on but does not bring out sufficiently is the close link between biography and authority. Huda Lutfi emphasizes that the biographical collections are meant to serve the purpose of moral edification for the layman.[23] Marilyn Booth emphasizes exemplarity: the subjects of biography are held up as examples of excellence to be emulated by the intended readers, though she does note that this genre was used by elites to construct their own histories.[24] The attention to "exemplarity" must be tempered here. Other biographical genres are driven by "exemplarity" more clearly than the biographical dictionary. The *sīra* is a monograph biography of an exemplary individual, first and foremost the Prophet Muhammad, but

23. Lutfi 1981, 107; Khalidi 1973, 53–65, here 55–8.
24. Booth 2001, 7–8.

also caliphs, sultans, or other heroic figures. Another genre of work devoted to exemplary individuals is the hagiography, cultivated primarily in the Sufi tradition. The biographical dictionary, in contrast, is concerned primarily with establishing the authority of a professional group, such as Maliki jurists, Muʿtazili theologians, Arabic grammarians, or scholars of hadith, and only secondarily with portraying outstanding individuals.

The biographical tradition as a whole is intensely concerned with the authority of particular societal groups and with the rank of individuals within that group.[25] The mere act of inclusion of women's biographies in biographical collections reveals a great deal about the compilers' views on women, for it suggests that they are willing to hold up women as authority figures and to confer upon them the status implied by belonging to the group to which the biographical dictionary in question is devoted. Thus, for example, al-Sakhāwī's devotion of a considerable section of *al-Ḍawʾ al-lāmiʿ* to women's biographies represents a strong statement, on his part, that women have played an important role in the transmission of the Islamic sciences, and particularly hadith, in the course of the ninth Islamic century, and thus share in the authority enjoyed by Muslim scholars in general. These concerns have been for the most part overlooked in Roded's study.

Roded's work includes some errors having to do with the technical terminology of medieval Islamic education. For example, she takes the term *musnida* to mean "transmitter of a collection of traditions," evidently seeing in it a reference to the *musnad*, a collection of oral reports of the Prophet arranged according to transmitters.[26] In one passage she remarks, "Seven women studied the *Musnad* of Ahmad Ibn Hanbal, and 2 were styled *musnida*."[27] In another, she comments on an important transmitter of hadith, "Three women are cited as having received knowledge from Fatima al-Juzdaniyya (425–534/1033–1129) — a transmitter of compilations of traditions (*musnida*) — the last of whom died in 607/1210."[28] The term *musnida* does not refer to the *Musnad* of Aḥmad b. Ḥanbal or other famous *musnad* works. Rather, it denotes someone who provides a *sanad* or *isnād*, that is, a chain of authorities; it means that this woman scholar is an "anchor" or pivotal "support" who provides an important link for an entire generation of scholars in the chain back to earlier Muslim authorities.[29] The title does not mean that she transmits one specific work but rather indicates that she

25. See, for example, Makdisi 1993, 371–96; Stewart 1997; Cooperson 2000; Jaques 2006.

26. Roded 1994, 68.

27. Roded 1994, 69.

28. Roded 1994, 74.

29. See, for example, Siddiqui 1993, 119, where he translates *Musnidat Iṣfahān* as "the great *ḥadīth* authority of Isfahan."

plays a crucial role in the transmission of authoritative religious knowledge in general, probably as one of the last living direct links to the leading scholars of a bygone generation.

The Seventeenth-Century Biographical Dictionary Riyāḍ al-ʿulamāʾ

Mīrzā ʿAbd Allāh al-Iṣfahānī came from a prominent Turkish family who evidently originated in Azerbaijan but had lived in Isfahan for several generations and established important connections with the Safavid royal court. He reports that his grandfather Muḥammad Ṣāliḥ Beg was a courtier of Shah Abbas I (r. 996–1038/1587–1629), and that his great uncle served as overseer of the royal workshops (*nāẓir al-buyūtāt*) for Shah Abbas I, Shah Safi (r. 1038–52/1629–42), and Shah Abbas II (r. 1052–77/1642–66). His father, ʿĪsā Beg, was born ca. 1034/1624–25 and studied with the leading scholars of the capital, including Khalīfa Sulṭān Ḥusayn b. Rafīʿ al-Dīn Muḥammad (d. 1064/1653–54), Muḥammad Taqī al-Majlisī (d.1070/1659), Mīrzā Rafīʿ al-Dīn Muḥammad b. Ḥaydar al-Nāʾīnī, known as Mullā Rafīʿā (d. 1099/1688), and others. The family lived in the quarter of al-Shaykh Yūsuf Bannā, which lay outside the old city of Isfahan. ʿĪsā Beg inherited considerable wealth, yet his son reports that he was not concerned with wealth or social prestige, and he declined positions as judge and *shaykh al-islām* of Isfahan. He died in 1074/1663–64, in Isfahan. He left a great deal of property to his six sons, including land and about one thousand volumes of books.[30]

Mīrzā ʿAbd Allāh was born in Isfahan ca. 1067/1656–57 and lived there as a youth.[31] He lost both his parents when he was very young, his mother at the age of seven months and his father at the age of seven, and was subsequently raised by a maternal uncle and an older brother. He lived many years in Tabriz, apparently with his mother's relatives, and there, he married the daughter of one of them. At some point he returned to Isfahan, where the bulk of his studies were conducted with the leading scholars of the day, including al-Āqā Jamāl al-Dīn al-Khwānsārī (d. 1125/1712), al-Muḥaqqiq al-Sabzawārī (d. 1090/1679), and others. His most important teacher was Muḥammad Bāqir al-Majlisī (d. 1111/1699), a leading figure in Isfahan and eventually *shaykh al-islām* of the capital. Al-Iṣfahānī worked closely with al-Majlisī, helping, along with other students of the master, to put together

30. *Riyāḍ al-ʿulamāʾ*, IV: 306–9.

31. He does not provide this exact date, but provides two relevant pieces of information. First, he states that he was seven when his father died in 1074 (*Riyāḍ al-ʿulamāʾ*, IV: 307). Then, in his autobiographical entry, he states that he was writing in 1106, at the age of roughly forty (*Riyāḍ al-ʿulamāʾ*, III: 231).

the compendious encyclopedia of Shiite Islamic lore, *Biḥār al-anwār*. He traveled extensively inside and outside Iran, to Azerbaijan, Khurasan, Iraq, Fars, Syria, Egypt, and Anatolia. Writing when he was about forty, he reports that he had spent nearly half his life — that is, roughly twenty years — traveling. His first trip, to Kashan to visit relatives of his deceased mother, took place when he was only five. He boasts of having completed three pilgrimages to Mashhad, three pilgrimages to the shrines of the Imams in Iraq, and three pilgrimages to Mecca by middle age. Little is known about the details or exact dates of these travels, but he reports that he lost about one hundred books when he left Mecca after his first pilgrimage, including the works that he authored in his youth. He was apparently in Isfahan in 1106/1694–95, compiling *Riyāḍ al-ʿulamāʾ*.[32]

The main source for al-Iṣfahānī's life after this point is *al-Ijāza al-kabīra* by ʿAbd Allāh b. Nūr al-Dīn al-Shushtarī (d. 1173/1759–60), a grandson of Niʿmat Allāh al-Jazāʾirī (d. 1112/1701), a well-known scholar of law and hadith and one of Mīrzā ʿAbd Allāh's colleagues from Isfahan. When al-Shushtarī was very young, Mīrzā ʿAbd Allāh came to Shushtar, where he stayed for a while, holding learned discussions with Nūr al-Dīn, ʿAbd Allāh's father, and other local scholars, and examining books in the family's library. This must have been before ca. 1120/1709, since ʿAbd Allāh was born in 1112/1701. Al-Shushtarī reports that Mīrzā ʿAbd Allāh obtained his nickname al-Afandī from an incident involving an Ottoman Sultan — he does not specify which. On one of his pilgrimages, Mīrzā ʿAbd Allāh supposedly had an altercation with the Sharif of Mecca. Afterwards, he repaired to Istanbul, where he succeeded in getting that Sharif dismissed from office and replaced. The title al-Afandī was applied to him in recognition of his influence on the Sultan. Al-Shushtarī reports that he died in "the decade of the thirties" (*ʿashr al-thalāthīn*), by which he apparently intends between 1130/1717 and 1139/1727.[33]

Mīrzā ʿAbd Allāh's most famous work, the biographical dictionary *Riyāḍ al-ʿulamāʾ wa-ḥiyāḍ al-fuḍalāʾ* (Gardens of Scholars and Pools of Learned Men) is an indispensable source for the biographies of scholars in the Twelver Shiite tradition, particularly of the sixteenth and seventeenth centuries. Like many other works of the period devoted to the religious sciences, it is written in Arabic though the author, a speaker of Persian and probably Turkish, was writing in Iran. Al-Iṣfahānī drew on the standard early works from the Twelver Shiite biographical tradition, as well as a number of contemporary works, such as *Amal al-āmil*, by Muḥammad al-Ḥurr al-ʿĀmilī (d. 1099/1688),

32. *Riyāḍ al-ʿulamāʾ*, III: 230–34.

33. al-Tustarī [or al-Shushtarī], *al-Ijāza al-kabīra*, 146–7. See al-Amīn, *Aʿyān al-Shīʿa*, VIII: 64–5.

which was completed in 1097/1686. He also drew a great deal of information from notes and colopha written on manuscripts in libraries throughout Iran, perhaps gathered in connection with his work for his teacher Muḥammad Bāqir al-Majlisī, to whom he refers as *al-Ustād al-Istinād* "(Our) Professor and (Our) Reliance" throughout *Riyāḍ al-ʿulamāʾ*. Mīrzā ʿAbd Allāh was compiling the work in 1106/1694–95.[34] The book shows signs that it remained incomplete, a work in progress, including missing death dates left blank to be filled in later and other blanks left for more substantial information. For example, at the end of the section translated below, al-Iṣfahānī completes a quotation from Ibn Khallikān's biographical dictionary, then begins to give his own comments with the phrase, "and I say," but there the text breaks off.

The work as a whole is quite large, five volumes of over two thousand pages in all in the modern edition. Because of the spacious typesetting, this makes it something like one quarter the size of al-Sakhāwī's famous twelve-volume biographical dictionary, *al-Ḍawʾ al-lāmiʿ*, but slightly larger than al-Ghazzī's (d. 1061/1651) *al-Kawākib al-sāʾira*, and roughly equivalent in size to the biographical dictionary of his Syrian contemporary al-Muḥibbī (d. 1111/1699), *Khulāṣat al-athar*, which, incidentally, does not include any notices on women. *Riyāḍ al-ʿulamāʾ* is devoted to Shiite scholars from the early Islamic period until the day of the author, the late seventeenth century. Al-Iṣfahānī does not exclude from his compilation scholars who are important but still alive, as some compilers do. He obviously benefited from the collections of materials belonging to Twelver tradition that had been acquired and gathered in Isfahan by scholars such as his teacher, Muḥammad Bāqir al-Majlisī, and from the private collections of other prominent scholars in Iran. He also used *Amal al-āmil* as a major source, and drew as well on a *rijāl* work — a work devoted to biographies of hadith transmitters — by Faraj Allāh al-Jazāʾirī (d. 1060–69/1650–59). The work includes a total of 2,491 entries, though this number may include some duplicates because of alternative names.

Like fourteen of the thirty-two pre-modern works Roded examined, al-Iṣfahānī devotes a separate section of his work to biographical entries on women and, as in many of those works, it is placed at the end of the work (but before a final section that lists scholars known by their *kunya*s rather than their given names). The section on women in *Riyāḍ al-ʿulamāʾ* includes nineteen figures in seventeen entries, since two pairs of daughters are included. Of these, one figure is in Mīrzā ʿAbd Allāh's estimation a literary fiction and perhaps not an actual woman. The earliest of the figures described is Sukayna (d. 117/735), daughter of Ḥusayn, the Prophet's grandson, and the

34. *Riyāḍ al-ʿulamāʾ*, II: 54; III: 231.

latest are still alive as al-Iṣfahānī is writing. Nineteen, or eighteen, out of 2,491 represents less than one per cent of the total number of biographies, and one wonders why al-Iṣfahānī includes so few notices on women, when he obviously took a sympathetic view of women scholars. One reason may be that this section of the work is made up of incomplete notes. The last entry breaks off abruptly, and the notices are in no discernible order — neither alphabetical order by name, nor chronological order. Al-Iṣfahānī does not include famous Companions or women of the early Islamic period who are held up as role models in the Shiite tradition, such as Fāṭima, Zaynab, or many other "saintly" women of *ahl al-bayt*. Rather, he seems to be limiting his scope to women of earlier periods who have left documented evidence of individual learning, such as works they authored, commentaries they wrote, works they copied, *ijāza*s they granted, or *ijāza*s granted to them by others, or to women of his own day of whose learning he has other direct or reliable evidence.

An idea of the chronological spread of the subjects in al-Iṣfahānī's section on women, as well as the lack of either chronological or alphabetical order, can be gained from the following outline:

1. Umm Ayman, contemporary of the fifth Imam al-Bāqir, 8th century
2. Fāṭima, daughter of al-Shahīd al-Awwal, 14th century
3. Umm ʿAlī, wife of al-Shahīd al-Awwal, 14th century
4. Ḥamīda bt. Muḥammad Sharīf al-Ruwaydashtī, 17th century
5. Fāṭima, daughter of Ḥamīda, 17th century
6. Fāṭima, daughter of Muḥammad al-ʿUkbarī, 13th century
7. Ḥusniyya, contemporary of Hārūn al-Rashīd, 8th–9th century
8. Daughter of al-Shaykh ʿAlī al-Minshār, 16th–17th century
9. Āmina Khwātūn, daughter of Muḥammad Taqī al-Majlisī, 17th century
10. Daughter of al-Masʿūd al-Warrām, 11th or 13th century

11, 12. Daughters of Raḍī al-Dīn Ibn Ṭāwūs, 13th century

13. Mother of Ibn Ṭāwūs, 12th–13th century
14. Daughter of al-Sharīf al-Murtaḍā, 11th century

15, 16. Daughters of al-Shaykh al-Ṭusī, 11th century

17. Copyist of Ibn Mītham al-Baḥrānī's *Sharḥ Nahj al-balāgha*, fl. after 13th century
18. Sister of Raḥīm al-Iṣfahānī, 17th century
19. Sukayna [Sakīna], daughter of the third Imam, Ḥusayn b. ʿAlī, 7th–8th century

Of these women, five, a significant proportion, are from the Safavid period, and all lived in Isfahan in the seventeenth century. Mīrzā knows four of them directly; the fifth, the daughter of ʿAlī al-Minshār (d. 984/1576) and wife of Bahāʾ al-Dīn al-ʿĀmilī (d. 1030/1621), had died before his time.

The biographical notices devoted to women in *Riyāḍ al-ʿulamāʾ* show that there is at least one exception to the claim that interest in women plummeted in the sixteenth century in the Islamic biographical tradition. They also confirm many of Roded's general statements while providing additional evidence. Women were certainly involved in the transmission of Islamic knowledge. Many of the women al-Iṣfahānī portrays gained access to learning through male family members, as daughters, sisters, and wives of established scholars. As Roded finds, it is clear that the majority of the women in al-Iṣfahānī's work gained their education first and foremost from their fathers, who were scholars, and in some cases also possibly from brothers. She notes, for example, that of the women noted as having studied with men in al-Sakhāwī's *al-Ḍawʾ al-lāmiʿ*, 20% studied with family members.[35] In al-Iṣfahānī's case, this percentage would appear to be higher; though the entries do not always specify that the learned daughters studied with their fathers, one assumes this to be the case. In one case, that of Fāṭima, daughter of Ḥamīda Ruwaydashtī, a woman clearly has her education from her mother, for al-Iṣfahānī pointedly remarks that her father was utterly ignorant. Roded notes similar examples in her material, though she finds that the female family members most likely to serve as teachers are paternal and maternal grandmothers, and females appear decidedly less frequently than males. Al-Iṣfahānī mentions a woman scholar who is the sister of Mullā Raḥīm Iṣfahānī without mentioning her father. He may mean to imply that her learning derives from her brother, though this is not explicit. Note that he makes a similar omission in the case of Fāṭima, daughter of Ḥamīda, where the message is clearly that her father had nothing to do with her education, something emphasized by the fact that he refers to him simply as "the husband of her mother," which ordinarily means "stepfather" in Arabic and Persian but here may simply serve as an expression of deprecation for the man. This suggests that segregation of the sexes played an important role in shaping the educational opportunities for women and that women who had access to male scholars within the family were most likely to become accomplished. It should be recognized, though, that males who were born into scholarly families also had privileged access to learning, and certain families produced prominent scholars for many generations, though academic pursuits were not off limits to boys from other backgrounds.

35. Roded 1994, 76.

In addition, women served specific educational functions important for society. Al-Shahīd al-Awwal (d. 786/1384), for example, held up his wife as an authority for women to consult if they had questions about the legal obligations of women in particular. The point is that women would have had understandable difficulties approaching male legal authorities and discussing such things as menstruation and the detailed rulings regarding ritual purity and the performance of ablutions frankly and in detail, while a woman could convey information to them much more effectively.[36]

Several of the women described in *Riyāḍ al-ʿulamāʾ* clearly taught other women regularly. In one instance, al-Iṣfahānī specifies that these teaching sessions were being held in Isfahan in his day, in the home of the descendants of Khalīfa Sulṭān (d. 1064/1653–54), a famous vizier who had served under Shah Abbas I, Shah Safi, and Shah Abbas II and who had earned the epithet *Sulṭān al-ʿUlamāʾ* on account of his scholarly accomplishments.[37] This suggests that the women involved enjoyed the patronage of female members of that elite family, who were actually related to the Safavid dynasty, since Khalīfa Sulṭān had married a daughter of Shah Abbas I. Given their wealth and the probable size of their house in Isfahan, a fairly large audience may have been involved. As Roded notes, such female-female teaching practices meant that learning in pre-modern Islamic societies could be, and indeed occasionally was, freed from direct male domination or dependence on male authorities. Female networks of learning in fact existed, and though relatively little is known about them, they may have played an important role in the lives of many women in the pre-modern Middle East.[38]

The medieval biographical notice generally begins with a list of adjectives or substantives applied to the subject of the notice. These terms are often read over quickly by modern investigators as being relatively unimportant, empty prose, but are in fact of great importance for an interpretation of the notice as a whole. Like lists of positive adjectives in a letter of recommendation, they serve in a general fashion to establish the merit and authority of the subject. In a more specific fashion, they work to establish the relative rank of the subject within the authoritative class portrayed in the biographical dictionary through an internal calculus of the relative values of the various terms employed in each case. In addition, the adjectives serve to indicate the distinct, special qualifications of the subject, pointing out his or her areas of expertise as opposed to relative ability or status.

36. See also Berkey 1992, 168, 173.
37. See *Riyāḍ al-ʿulamāʾ*, II: 51–5.
38. Roded 1994, 72–5.

The main adjectival labels applied to the women discussed in *Riyāḍ al-ʿulamāʾ* merit consideration. A look at the adjectives applied to the women included in this section shows that the most common are *fāḍila* and *ʿālima*, which usually occur paired, in that order. They occur in this fashion with reference to thirteen of the eighteen women described. In one entry the term *fāḍila* appears unaccompanied by the pair *ʿālima*, and in one other entry the pair occurs with the order reversed: *ʿālima fāḍila*. Two entries use the (masculine) plural of *ʿālim*, stating that the woman in question is *min al-ʿulamāʾ* "one of the scholars" or *min ajillat al-ʿulamāʾ* "one of the exalted scholars" – high praise indeed. This last phrase perhaps conveys to us the intended sense of *jalīla*, "important, exalted, magnificent," which appears once, and appears to be elliptical for *jalīlat al-qadr* "of exalted standing." These are the feminine forms of *fāḍil* and *ʿālim*, which likewise occur frequently in the biographical notices of men, paired and in that order. They seem to bear the brunt of the argument for the inclusion of each individual in a work devoted to scholars in particular. The term *ʿālim/ʿālima*, I contend, refers specifically to learning in the Islamic religious sciences, such as law, hadith, Qurʾanic commentary; and *fāḍil* refers to learning in the "extra" sciences, including grammar, rhetoric, poetry, and the literary arts. Therefore, the combination *fāḍil-ʿālim* or *fāḍila-ʿālima* which appears so frequently means of well-rounded, broad education, or learned in two-thirds of the traditional divisions of the sciences, leaving out the sciences of the ancients: medicine, astronomy, arithmetic, geometry, and philosophy. In addition, the term *fāḍila* is used in contexts that suggest it stresses the ability of the subject to read and write at least well enough to copy works in the tradition, but does not necessarily imply the ability to compose commentaries or produce original texts.

Another set of adjectives applied to the women stresses their piety and devotion. The adjective *taqiyya* or *muttaqiya* "God-fearing" occurs in two entries, the near-synonym *wariʿa* once. Three women are described as *ʿābida* "devout", and five as *ṣāliḥa* "righteous, devout." Such adjectives occur in the biographical notices of men as well. In both cases, they appear, here, not to be justifications for inclusion in the work in the first place. One could not imagine that such qualities would be deemed sufficient, given al-Iṣfahānī's own definition of the parameters for inclusion. Clearly there were many devout yet uneducated men and women in every generation who would not merit inclusion in the work. They must serve a different purpose here. One is to stress a certain respect for the women, to draw attention away from their potential roles as sexual beings or objects of desire. Another may be to stress these figures' importance when al-Iṣfahānī has few other concrete pieces of information to provide.

Several adjectives describe particular sorts of expertise and indicate a fairly high level of accomplishment. The term *muḥadditha* "hadith expert" is to be expected, given the remarks of Siddiqui, Berkey, and Roded on the matter. What is perhaps surprising is that it occurs with reference to only one woman in the section, though another woman is referred to as *baṣīra bi'l-akhbār wa'l-āthār* "a perspicacious critic of traditions and reports." Mīrzā ʿAbd Allāh applies the designation *faqīha* "jurist" to no less than four women in the list. Berkey, in contrast, observes that few women in Mamluk Egypt excelled in law or theology, in contrast with the field of hadith, and that the term *faqīha* appears infrequently in the sources.[39] Roded's findings also suggest that this is a very large percentage in comparison with other data. In her entire corpus, covering thousands of entries and fourteen centuries, she finds only about a dozen cases of women who are noted as being learned in the law, and only four who acted as jurists.[40] It may be the case that legal knowledge was more highly valued in the Shiite tradition than in Sunni circles, particularly relative to knowledge of hadith. It would appear that the many opportunities to hear hadith recited that existed in Mamluk Egypt and Syria for example, where works such as al-Bukhārī's *Ṣaḥīḥ* were recited ceremonially during Ramaḍān and other occasions, did not exist for Shiites living as minorities, and even appear to be absent in Safavid Iran, an officially Shiite kingdom. This may explain the relative frequency of hadith study by women in Mamluk and other Sunni sources; in those contexts, hadith study was a frequent pietistic activity, like memorization of the Qur'an, and also served recognized social and ceremonial functions.[41] Interest in Shiite hadith in Iran greatly increased with the teaching of Ḥusayn b. ʿAbd al-Ṣamad al-ʿĀmilī (d. 984/1576) and his successors, and became particularly strong in the second half of the seventeenth century, when al-Iṣfahānī was writing, as a consequence of the Akhbārī movement.[42] This resurgence of interest in the main Shiite hadith collections is reflected in his notices on women, particularly in the case of Ḥamīda Ruwaydashtī, who studied the science of hadith transmitters intensively and wrote a commentary on one of the four canonical Twelver hadith collections, *al-Istibṣār* by al-Shaykh al-Ṭūsī (d. 460/1067). Even then, however, the transmission of hadith did not become a public community exercise as it had in Sunni environments.

The term *kātiba* "writer, scribe" might mean several things, but here

39. Berkey 1992, 175, 180.

40. Roded 1994, 80–4.

41. Berkey, for example, stresses the transmission of hadith as a community activity in Mamluk Egypt (Berkey 1992, 210–16).

42. For a brief overview of the Akhbārī movement, see Kohlberg 1985; Madelung 2004.

does not appear to mean that the woman in question is an author in her own right. Rather, it seems to mean that she in fact knows how to write as well as read, and to write well enough to copy a substantial work accurately. Al-Iṣfahānī's entry on the sister of Mullā Raḥīm al-Iṣfahānī shows that this adjective indicates a woman who has an excellent hand. He goes on to state that he has seen her handwriting (*khaṭṭ*), including an excellent copy of *Sharḥ al-Lumʿa* (a multi-volume legal work, the commentary of Zayn al-Dīn al-ʿĀmilī on *al-Lumʿa al-dimashqiyya* by al-Shahīd al-Awwal). He adds that she writes the *naskh* script as well as *naskh-taʿlīq* script. When he refers to the two daughters of Raḍī al-Dīn Ibn Ṭāwūs as *kātibatayn*, this must be what he means as well. The term *ḥāfiẓa*, which refers to two women in the list, probably indicates here a woman who has memorized the Qur'an but may also indicate that she has memorized a large body of hadith reports. The term *ʿārifa*, literally "knower," is applied to only one woman in the corpus. It is not exactly clear what it means from context, but it may indicate involvement with *ʿirfān*, mystical gnosis. Two women are described as *muʿallima* "teacher," showing that they taught in their own right, in each case other women.

Another term that al-Iṣfahānī uses on occasion is *shaykha*, the feminine of *shaykh*. Literally, "old man/old woman," the term *shaykh/shaykha* is used in biographical sources as the most basic term for a teacher, particularly an authority for the transmission of hadith. Thus, when it is reported that al-Shahīd al-Awwal's wife was known as *Sitt al-Mashāyikh* "the Mistress of (all) Shaykhs," this suggests that she was a prominent authority for the transmission of knowledge. Mīrzā ʿAbd Allāh refers to one thirteenth-century female scholar, the daughter of Muḥammad b. Aḥmad b. ʿAbd Allāh al-ʿUkbarī, as *al-Shaykha* Fāṭima. In both cases, the use of this term suggests prominence in the transmission of knowledge and membership in the predominantly male class of *shuyūkh*.

Among the prominent authority statements al-Iṣfahānī includes, in addition to the adjectives just described, are references to praise by other scholars, which appear several times, and indications that other scholars recommended them as authorities, which occur twice. As in the biographical notices of men, reports that established scholars lavished praise on the subjects in question serves as evidence of their having attained a certain level of authority. Thus, for example, when al-Iṣfahānī reports that al-Shahīd al-Awwal directed women to consult his wife on Islamic legal matters, he is not merely indicating that she served an important function, but also presenting an argument that she was quite learned, for an outstanding, recognized authority in the tradition had referred to her as such. Prominent among the other authority statements al-Iṣfahānī presents are reports of having copied important texts on law or hadith or having written commentaries on such texts. The emphasis on copying suggests that, in al-Iṣfahānī's understanding, the women involved could not have done the copying without understanding the text. He probably assumes that the fact that they copied the work meant that they had studied it with a master, as it was common practice for students to copy out works as they studied them.

A key question that Roded's study does not address is whether the biographical notices devoted to women belong to a distinct, separate genre from men's biographical notices, or whether they have any distinctive features. While it is difficult to make a definitive statement without further examination of the sources, al-Iṣfahānī's section on women allows some preliminary comparative statements. At this point it appears that biographical notices devoted to women do not so much form a separate genre as they do an important sub-category of the general genre of biographical notice (*tarjama*). They share many features and conventions of the standard *tarjama* devoted to a male subject in biographical collections arranged by "classes" or "generations" (*ṭabaqāt*) or arranged alphabetically (*kutub al-tarājim*), often differing only in degree. Berkey has noted one significant difference regarding women's biographical notices: they generally lack the technical terms *ṣāḥaba* and *lāzama*, which refer to lengthy and close study with a particular professor.[43] This omission in women's biographies may be due to the facts themselves — that women could not spend the many hours over lengthy periods necessary to establish the type of teacher-student relationship so described. It may be due in part as well to the inappropriate suggestions of intimacy created by these terms.

Several additional features may be cited as distinguishing women's biographical notices from men's biographical notices. First is the question of placement: in many biographical collections, women's biographical notices are placed in a special section at the end of the work. This placement implies both that women's biographies are somehow distinct from those of men and that men are more important or superior, for precedence generally indicates superiority or a higher level of reverence. Thus in references to "Moses and Aaron" in the Qur'an, Moses is held to come first naturally on account of his superiority and greater importance; the one case where the order is reversed requires an explanation.[44] We see this principle at work, for example, in biographical collections which place all the subjects named Muhammad first out of reverence for the Prophet, despite following strict alphabetical order in the remaining notices, as does al-Khaṭīb al-Baghdādī (d. 463/1071) in *Tārīkh Baghdād*, or Tāj al-Dīn al-Subkī (d. 771/1370), who places all of the subjects named Aḥmad — also understood to be a name of the Prophet —

43. Berkey 1992, 179.
44. al-Bāqillānī, *I'jāz al-Qur'ān*, 83.

and Muḥammad first in each class, before presenting the remaining subjects in alphabetical order in his biographical dictionary of Shāfiʿī jurists.[45]

A second difference regards dates. Al-Iṣfahānī's text reports death dates, generally a crucial feature of the biographical notice, for only two women out of nineteen. This is odd, given Rosenthal's statement about Islamic biography in general, "The one common element which can be expected to be found in all biographies except in the oldest times is the date of death of the subject of the biography."[46] While it occasionally occurs in men's biographical notices that the author has not been able to find a death date and so does not mention one, it is rare that such a concentration of notices without death dates should occur, and a similar cluster does not occur anywhere else in *Riyāḍ al-ʿulamāʾ*. In fact, an author of a biographical collection who has not found a death date for a particular notice often includes the phrase *wa-tuwuffiya ...* "and he died" and then leaves a blank space to be filled in when he finds the information in another source. But even this does not occur here. This is thus a distinct feature that sets the women's biographical notices apart from the men's notices in al-Iṣfahānī's collection. The reason does not seem to be that he is not interested in such information with regard to women, for he in fact includes a death date in two of the notices, but rather that the information is unavailable, suggesting, perhaps, that such information is less likely to be preserved with regard to women than it is with regard to men. This is certainly not the case in all biographical collections; al-Sakhāwī gives many dates of death of female subjects.

A third distinctive feature is the fact that the women's given names and *kunyas* are in many cases actually absent, something that occurs rarely in men's biographical notices. For example, al-Iṣfahānī includes entries on an unnamed daughter of al-Sharīf al-Murtaḍā (d. 436/1044), two unnamed daughters of al-Shaykh al-Ṭūsī (d. 460/1067), and an unnamed daughter of al-Masʿūd Warrām (d. 605/1208). He devotes an entry to the two daughters of Raḍī al-Dīn Ibn Ṭāwūs (d. 664/1266), only one of whose names appears in the notice. Likewise, the mother of Raḍī al-Dīn Ibn Ṭāwūs is unnamed. Al-Iṣfahānī includes a notice on a learned woman who completed a copy of Ibn Mītham al-Baḥrānī's (d. 679/1280–81) commentary on *Nahj al-balāgha* that he saw in the shrine of ʿAbd al-ʿAẓīm in Rayy, though he apparently remembers nothing else about her, and does not provide any part of her name. He devotes an entry to an unnamed sister of Mullā Raḥīm al-Iṣfahānī, a contemporary living in Isfahan. This represents a quite large percentage of the

45. al-Khaṭīb al-Baghdādī, *Tārīkh Baghdād aw Madīnat al-Salām*; Tāj al-Dīn al-Subkī, *Ṭabaqāt al-shāfiʿīya al-kubrā*.
46. Rosenthal 1968, 102

total number of women to whom al-Iṣfahānī devotes biographical notices. Even though this may not be said to be typical of all women's biographical notices — al-Sakhāwī, for example, is very good about providing women's given names — the lack of given names in so large a proportion of the notices would be inconceivable in biographical notices devoted to men.

A fourth distinctive feature of the women's notices is that their husbands are mentioned with relatively high frequency, while the converse is not true. The wives of male scholars are not frequently mentioned, though they do appear occasionally, sometimes in the course of anecdotes. Other times, a daughter is mentioned because a promising male student marries the daughter of his teacher, or when the grandson of a famous scholar through his daughter becomes a scholar of some repute — like Sibṭ Ibn al-Jawzī (d. 654/1257). Even in these cases, though, the woman's name is often left out — she is simply the daughter of So-and-so, the great master. The frequent mention of husbands stands out as a feature of women's biographical notices that is not paralleled in those of men.

In the end, these differences are for the most part differences in degree rather than radical distinctions that constitute a distinct set of generic conventions. The biographical notice is originally and predominantly the project and province of a male elite. Even the female subject in a biographical collection remains in certain senses an object, and all information about her has had to pass through the filter of the male elite point of view.[47] The information in women's biographies is more fragmentary on average than it is in the case of males, a function not only of less studied attention to their accomplishments in the tradition but also of the social strictures placed upon them. Thus al-Iṣfahānī omits the given name of one woman scholar, a contemporary living in Isfahan about whom he had considerable information and whom he had probably met; he nevertheless refers to her only as the sister of Mullā Raḥīm al-Iṣfahānī. In all likelihood he actually knew her given name. We must assume that he omits it because Mullā Raḥīm had somehow indicated to him that he preferred to limit the public exposure of the women in his family.

Two points stand out in al-Iṣfahānī's presentation, setting his biographical dictionary apart from many others: his frank recognition of the tension inherent in the project of female education, and his sympathy with women's social plight. A number of his anecdotes and comments poke fun at the transgression of boundaries set by traditional gender roles. Thus, for example, he mentions one scholar who jocularly calls his learned daughter *ʿallāmata*, inventing an entirely new grammatical form with two feminine endings. As he

47. Booth 2001, 13.

explains, one *-a* ending is for hyperbole, as in ordinary *ʿallāma* "an extremely learned man," and the other, for the natural feminine. This same scholar would pun that his daughter had a strong interest in "men" (*rijāl*), meaning that she intently studied the biographies of hadith transmitters (*ʿilm al-rijāl*), but flirting with the suggestion that she was strongly attracted to members of the opposite sex. In another example, al-Iṣfahānī points out the irony that the great scholar Muḥammad Ṣāliḥ al-Māzandarānī (d. 1086/1675–76), one of his own teachers, would have to ask his wife, Āmina Khwātūn, daughter of Muḥammad Taqī al-Majlisī (d. 1070/1659), how to construe certain phrases in the famous legal text *Qawāʿid al-aḥkām* by al-ʿAllāma al-Ḥillī (d. 676/1277). He stresses the irony in this relationship by referring to their marriage pointedly by stating that she was "under" (*taḥt*) al-Māzandarānī. In other words, she who was apparently "under" this male authority figure was actually *above* her husband by virtue of her superior knowledge of Arabic and legal texts.

Al-Iṣfahānī is not unique among authors of biographical collections in showing sympathy for a number of his women subjects. Many other authors, including al-Sakhāwī, show great respect and sympathy for their subjects, but usually as pious old women, saintly motherly figures, generous donors and patronesses of charitable institutions, and even as devotees of learning. Yet rarely do we see concern for women as peers come through. In several of the notices concerning women that al-Iṣfahānī knew personally, he takes a particular interest in their social fate. He is full of praise for the local female scholar Ḥamīda Ruwaydashtī, who was very learned in the science of hadith, taught women in Isfahan, and had written a commentary on the *Istibṣār* of al-Shaykh al-Ṭūsī. His father, he reports, even copied her notes and commentaries. Despite her accomplishments, and despite the fact that her father was a scholar as well, a student of Bahāʾ al-Dīn al-ʿĀmilī, "... she married, in order to please her mother, an ignorant and foolish man, one of the inhabitants of that village from among her relatives." A similar fate befell her daughter, Fāṭima, also learned and a teacher of women. He reports, "They married her off to a villager who is worse than a Bedouin, like a greengrocer (*bāqil*) in his understanding, and in his stupidity just like her mother's husband, who is not even a rational being." It becomes clear that Mīrzā ʿAbd Allāh has in his mind a particular rule: accomplished women scholars had a right to marry men who were their intellectual equals and could appreciate and encourage their talents.

One may read something of Mīrzā ʿAbd Allāh's personal experience into these portrayals of women scholars. One senses that he would like to have had a learned wife who would be more of a partner to him in scholarship. In his autobiographical entry, he reports that he married the daughter of an influential relative and suffered because of it. He writes, slipping into rhyming prose for dramatic effect, "... I resided in Azerbaijan in the city of Tabriz many years. There I married a person of wealth and status among my relatives, and that was the cause of my increased affliction, falling into perils, and suffering" (*tazawwajtu bi-baʿḍi arbāb al-dunyā min aqribāʾī* wa-kāna dhālika huwa 's-sababu li-mazīdi balāʾī* wa-wuqūʿī fī 'l-mahāliki wa-ʿanāʾī**).[48] He does not specify what these afflictions were exactly, but there is no doubt that they bothered him, and one senses that he regrets his choice of spouse. When juxtaposed with his disparaging remarks about scholarly women's moronic and ugly husbands, one senses on the one hand that he found these women scholars attractive and on the other that he is expressing regret that his own wife was not a scholar, but rather someone who came from a mercantile background or the landed aristocracy and was not a satisfactory intellectual partner. The difference in his attitudes towards women's roles from those common in contemporary Syria or Egypt during the same period may be due to general cultural ideas in Safavid court circles, with which Mīrzā ʿAbd Allāh had important family connections. As Kathryn Babayan suggests, the Safavid synthesis of Turko-Mongol traditions with Irano-Islamic ones included a conception of shared power among the entire dynastic house, including both male and female members, so that women customarily assumed an active role in political and cultural life at court.[49]

An overall assessment of al-Iṣfahānī's biographical notices on women scholars in the Twelver tradition does not bring any startling evidence that the patriarchy crumbled or was overturned, but it does suggest that some women were being well educated in the Safavid capital in the late seventeenth century and were teaching other women in much larger numbers. Roded's claim that the numbers of learned women had dropped off rapidly in the sixteenth century is suspect and probably, I would hazard, a function of the erratic coverage of the various biographical dictionaries themselves or the fact that the main intellectual centers in the Middle East were no longer Cairo and Damascus but Istanbul and Isfahan. It further suggests that some male scholars looked upon these learned women as peers entitled to a dignified station in life befitting the learned, and were pained by the societal pressures that forced talented women into lousy marriages with men who were their inferiors by far. In the end, it is al-Iṣfahānī's remarks on contemporary women in seventeenth-century Isfahan that are most interesting. While his several entries on these women only provide a glimpse at the life of women in that context, one may combine his material with other sources, such as the burlesque creed *ʿAqāʾid al-nisāʾ* analyzed by Babayan, or the trav-

48. *Riyāḍ al-ʿulamāʾ*, III: 231.
49. Babayan 1998, 351–3.

eler's accounts used by Ronald Ferrier, to gain a fuller picture of women's roles in Iranian society of the period.[50]

Many more biographical dictionaries remain unplumbed for information about women, not only in entries devoted to women subjects, but also incidentally in entries devoted to men. The number of such works excluded from Roded's study is quite large and, as mentioned above, includes many from areas of the Islamic world that Roded's survey did not cover. In addition, the number of biographical collections that remain in manuscript is also considerable. Investigators of this material, however, must pay close attention to the conventions and rhetorical strategies of the genre, which have not been investigated or explained in detail to date, as well as to the technical terms related to education in the Islamic sciences. They must also take into account the various sub-genres of biographical collection, as well as the idiosyncratic conventions and rhetorical strategies of individual authors. Further investigation will undoubtedly provide a great deal of data and provide new insights, particularly regarding women scholars, whose activities are among those most likely to be recorded.

Biographical Notices Devoted to Women in Riyāḍ al-ʿulamāʾ

[5: 403] Section on the names of women of the Imāmī scholars, whether they are known by their given names or their patronymics.

[No. 1] Umm Ayman

> As best I can recall, it is transmitted in *al-Kāfī*[51] or some other work on the authority of al-Bāqir[52] — peace be upon him — as a commentary on the verse "The oppressed ones (*al-mustaḍʿafīn*), whether men, women, and children ..." (Q 4:98) from the Chapter on Women that he was asked, "Who are they?" He answered, "Your women and your children." Then he asked, "Have you seen Umm Ayman? I testify that she is among the Inhabitants of Paradise, yet she has not known what you have suffered (*mā antum ʿalayhi*)."

[No.2] Umm al-Ḥasan Fāṭima, who is called *Sitt al-Mashāyikh* "The Mistress of Teachers."

> She is the daughter of Our Master the Martyr, the famous Muḥammad b. Makkī al-ʿĀmilī al-Jizzīnī.[53] [404] Our contemporary Master [Muḥammad

50. Babayan 1998; Ferrier 1998.

51. The famous collection of Shiite hadith by Muḥammad b. Yaʿqūb al-Kulaynī (d. 329/941).

52. That is, the fifth Imam of the Twelver Shiites, Muḥammad al-Bāqir b. ʿAlī Zayn al-ʿĀbidīn (d. 120/740).

53. The famous fourteenth-century Shiite scholar known in the tradition as al-Shahīd al-

b. al-Ḥasan al-Ḥurr al-ʿĀmilī] stated in *Amal al-āmil*: She was learned in the religious and literary sciences, knowledgeable in the law, upright, and devout. I have heard from authorities praise and encomia of her. She transmits from her father and from Ibn Muʿayya,[54] her father's teacher, by certificate, as was mentioned above in the notice on her brother Muḥammad b. Muḥammad b. Makkī.[55] Her father used to praise her and command the women to emulate her and refer to her concerning the legal rulings on menstruation, prayer, and such things. End of quote. I say: *al-Sitt* ("Mistress, Ma'am") is a reduced form of Sayyida (Mistress, Lady), with assimilation of the *-d-* to the *-t-*. This is as when one says *Sittī* ("My Lady") and *Sittī Fāṭima* (My Lady Fāṭima) The situation in these two instances is the same: they are both *Sayyidatī* ("My Lady") in origin.

[No. 3] Umm ʿAlī, the wife of the Martyr — may God have mercy on him.[56]

Our contemporary Master stated in *Amal al-āmil*: She was learned in the literary sciences, God-fearing, knowledgeable of the law, and devout. The Martyr used to praise her and command women to consult her. End of quote.

[No. 4] Ḥamīda, the daughter of Our Persian Master Muḥammad Sharīf b. Shams al-Dīn Muḥammad al-Ruwaydashtī al-Iṣfahānī.

Al-Ruwaydasht is a locale that is one of the dependencies of Isfahan. She — may God have mercy on her — was learned in the religious and literary sciences, adept in mystical knowledge, teacher of the women of her time, perspicacious in the science of hadith transmitters (*rijāl*), pure of speech, the remnant of (a long line of) great scholars in the literary and religious sciences, and particularly distinguished as God-fearing among the people. She authored super-commentaries and intricate glosses on the books of hadith like *al-Istibṣār* by al-Shaykh [405] al-Ṭūsī[57] and other works that indicate the high level of her understanding, her precision, and her wide reading, especially with regard to the accurate establishment

---

Awwal, "the First Martyr," since he was executed by the Mamluk authorities in Damascus in 786/1384.

54. Ibn Muʿayya is Tāj al-Dīn Abū ʿAbd Allāh Muḥammad b. al-Qāsim al-Dībājī, a teacher of the First Martyr who died in Ḥilla in 776/1374 (Agha Buzurg al-Ṭihrānī, *al-Ḥaqāʾiq al-rāhina*, 197).

55. The son of the First Martyr became a scholar in his own right (*Riyāḍ al-ʿulamāʾ*, V: 179–80).

56. That is, again, the First Martyr, Muḥammad b. Makkī al-Jizzīnī.

57. *Al-Istibṣār fīmā ukhtulifa fīhā min al-akhbār*, one of the four canonical collections of Twelver Shiite hadith, by Abū Jaʿfar Muḥammad b. al-Ḥasan al-Ṭūsī (d. 460/1067), a famous Twelver jurist of Baghdad.

of the hadith transmitter's identity. I have seen a copy of *al-Istibṣār* on which were recorded her glosses until the very end of the book. I believe that they were in her hand — may God be pleased with her.

My father — may God sanctify his soul — would often copy from her glosses on the margins of the books of hadith, and he would write them with care and consider them excellent. We had a copy of *al-Istibṣār* on which were the glosses of the above-mentioned Ḥamīda in the script of my father until the final sections of the book on prayer, and they included excellent edifying points.

Her father was one of the disciples of al-Shaykh al-Bahāʾī,[58] and our Professor and Main Support[59] also studied with him by certificate, as he stated explicitly in the chain of authorities in some of his certificates of transmission.[60]

She — may God have mercy on her — studied with her father, and her father used to praise her and joke, saying that Ḥamīda had a very strong interest in "men" (*rijāl*), meaning that she was concerned with the science of hadith transmitters (*ʿilm al-rijāl*). He used to call her, jokingly, *ʿallāmata* "the consummate female scholar," with two final *tāʾ*s, claiming that one of the two was to indicate the feminine, and the other indicated the emphatic form.

Among the strange things that happened was that she married, in order to please her mother, an ignorant and foolish man, one of the inhabitants of that village from among her relatives.

I saw her father when I was young, during the life of my father.[61] Her father had reached a very old age. He used to refuse to accept his great age and would say that it was less as a joke. I think that his age reached one hundred years.

She died — may God be pleased with her — as best I can recall, after her father, in the year one thousand and eighty-seven, or near to that date. But God knows best.

[No. 5] Fāṭima, the daughter of Ḥamīda, the daughter of the Persian Master[62]

58. The famous Safavid jurist who served as *shaykh al-islām* of Isfahan for most of the reign of Shah Abbas I, Bahāʾ al-Dīn Muḥammad b. Ḥusayn al-ʿĀmilī (d. 1030/1621).

59. Throughout the *Riyāḍ al-ʿulamāʾ*, al-Iṣfahānī uses this term, *al-Ustād al-Istinād*, to refer to his main professor in the Islamic sciences, Muḥammad Bāqir al-Majlisī.

60. Al-Iṣfahānī gives his name as Sharīf al-Dīn Muḥammad al-Ruwaydashtī and mentions that he was a student of Bahāʾ al-Dīn al-ʿĀmilī in a very short notice, without providing a death date (*Riyāḍ al-ʿulamāʾ*, V: 104).

61. That is, before 1074/1663–64, the death-date of his father, when Mīrzā ʿAbd Allāh was seven years old.

62. This is how I have rendered the term *al-Mawlā* = *al-Mullā*, a title reserved for Persians.

Muḥammad Sharīf b. Shams al-Dīn Muḥammad al-Ruwaydashtī al-Iṣfahānī — may God's approval be upon both of them and upon their father. She was also learned in the literary and religious sciences, devout, and pious. I know of no work that she authored, but she is also a teacher of the women of her time. For the most part, she [406] is to be found in the house of the descendants of the late Vizier, Khalīfa Sulṭān, in Isfahan. She is living now, but they married her off to a villager who is worse than a Bedouin, like a greengrocer (*bāqil*) in his understanding, and in his stupidity just like her mother's husband, who is not even a rational being.

[No. 6] The Shaykha Fāṭima, the daughter of the Master Muḥammad b. Aḥmad b. ʿAbd Allāh b. Ḥāzim al-ʿUkbarī.[63]

She was learned in the literary and religious sciences and a legal expert. She was among the authorities of al-Sayyid Tāj al-Dīn Muḥammad b. Muʿayya al-Ḥusaynī, and al-Shaykh the Martyr transmits from her through the intermediary of the above-mentioned Ibn al-Muʿayya.

She is apparently one of the Imami [transmitters], so take note. Al-Shaykh ʿAbd al-Ṣamad b. Aḥmad b. ʿAbd al-Qādir b. Abī al-Jaysh[64] granted her a certificate of transmission, according to what I found in certain passages. So take note.

[No. 7] Ḥusniyya

She was a slave girl who had been taken captive and had adopted Islam in the time of Hārūn al-Rashīd.[65] She was learned in the literary arts and the religious sciences, an exacting scholar who had insight into hadith reports. The Persian treatise compiled by al-Shaykh Abū al-Futūḥ al-Rāzī, the author of the famous Persian commentary on the Qur'an,[66] that treats the story of her debate over the Imamate in the assembly of Hārūn al-Rashīd is famous. In this treatise, the very high level of learning and most exalted standing of Ḥusniyya is evident, to such an extent that it crosses the mind (*yakhtalij*) that this treatise which was recorded by the above-mentioned Shaykh Abū al-Futūḥ, and made and

63. See *Riyāḍ al-ʿulamāʾ*, III: 123.
64. See *Riyāḍ al-ʿulamāʾ*, III: 123.
65. The famous Abbasid Caliph who reigned between 170/786 and 193/809.
66. Jamāl al-Dīn al-Ḥusayn b. ʿAlī b. Muḥammad b. Aḥmad al-Khuzāʿī al-Nīsābūrī al-Rāzī (fl. 1087–1131), teacher of al-Shaykh Muntajab al-Dīn and scholar of the sixth/twelfth century, wrote a Persian *tafsīr* widely cited as *Tafsīr Abī al-Futūḥ al-Rāzī* (see *Riyāḍ al-ʿulamāʾ*, V: 488–9). His *tafsīr* has been published: *Rawḍ al-jinān wa-rūḥ al-janān fī tafsīr al-Qurʾān*, ed. Muḥammad Jaʿfar Yāḥaqqī and Muḥammad Mahdī Nāṣiḥ (Mashhad: Bunyād-i Pazhūhish-hā-yi Islāmī, 1986).

recorded by him, but that he attributed it to al-Ḥusniyya in order to make the doctrines of the Sunnis look bad, and thereby to vituperate against the scandal of their creed, as his peer Ibn Ṭāwūs,[67] the author of *al-Iqbāl*,[68] did in the well-known *Kitāb al-Ṭarāʾif*, for he said in it: "I am a man of the people of the Pact," and debated and discussed with the proponents of the four *madhhab*s until he completed the proof against them [407] and proved the doctrine of the Shiites, and then states that he converted to Islam.[69]

On account of the lack of knowledge about this, the situation has confused a group of learned men, even the great stallions among the scholars, and they have reckoned that *Kitāb al-Ṭarāʾif* was written by ʿAbd al-Maḥmūd the Dhimmī, when [Ibn Ṭāwūs] is actually the one who introduced the book with him as a *tawriya*.[70] But God knows best the true nature of things. This has been explained above in their biographical notices.[71]

[No. 8] The daughter of al-Shaykh ʿAlī al-Minshār.[72]

She was learned in the literary and religious sciences, a jurist, and a hadith expert. She was the wife of our Master al-Bahāʾī, and she had studied with her father. We have heard from a certain trustworthy long-lived person who had seen her in his youth that she used to teach law, hadith, and other things, and that women would study with her, and that she inherited from her father four thousand volumes of books. A certain

67. Raḍī al-Dīn Abū al-Qāsim ʿAlī b. Mūsā Ibn Ṭāwūs (d. 664/1266), a prominent sayyid and Twelver Shiite scholar of the thirteenth century from Ḥillah in southern Iraq. On this scholar, see Kohlberg 1992b.

68. Ibn Ṭāwūs, *al-Iqbāl bi'l-aʿmāl al-ḥasana* (Tehran, 1902; reprinted 1970, 1987). See Kohlberg 1992b, 37–9.

69. The work is published as Raḍī al-Dīn Ibn Ṭāwūs, *Kitāb al-Ṭarāʾif fī maʿrifat madhāhib al-ṭawāʾif* (Qum, 1979). See Kohlberg 1992b, 57–9; 1992a, 325–50.

70. *Tawriya* is a rhetorical term that has the general sense "amphibology" or "double-entendre." It is more specifically an instance where the speaker seeks to hide the truth or his intended meaning behind a more evident meaning understood by the interlocutor. Kohlberg confirms this interpretation of the *Kitāb al-Ṭarāʾif*: that Ibn Ṭāwūs invented the *dhimmī* narrator for reasons of *taqiyya* or dissimulation, in order to avoid problems in connection with his criticism of the Sunni legal schools. See Kohlberg 1992a; 1992 b, 57–9.

71. By this al-Iṣfahānī apparently means the biographical notices on Abū al-Futūḥ al-Rāzī and Ibn Ṭāwūs. See *Riyāḍ al-ʿulamāʾ*, II: 156–63, V: 488–9, esp. II: 159. The entry on Raḍī al-Dīn Ibn Ṭawūs, to which al-Iṣfahānī refers in this and other passages, is not to be found in the published edition of *Riyāḍ al-ʿulamāʾ*.

72. A native of Jabal ʿĀmil who immigrated to Iran in the mid-sixteenth century and became *shaykh al-islām* of Isfahan during the reign of Shah Tahmasb (930–84/1524–76). He died the same year as the Shah, 984/1576, and apparently left no male heirs. See *Riyāḍ al-ʿulamāʾ*, IV: 266–8, 283–5.

learned man stated to us that she had abundant knowledge and a great deal of learning, and also that she was still living after the death of al-Shaykh al-Bahāʾī.[73]

[No. 9] Āmina Khwātūn, the daughter of the Persian Master Muḥammad Taqī al-Majlisī.[74]

She was learned in the literary and religious sciences, upright, and God-fearing, and was married to the Persian master Muḥammad Ṣāliḥ al-Māzandarānī.[75] We have heard that her husband, despite his extreme learning, would question her regarding the construal of some expressions in the *Qawāʿid* of al-ʿAllāma.[76] She is the sister of *al-Ustād al-Istinād* [Muḥammad Bāqir al-Majlisī], may God prolong his shadow.

[No. 10] The daughter of al-Masʿūd al-Warrām.[77]

I have not found out her name. She was the grandmother of Ibn Idrīs al-Ḥillī on his mother's side. She was learned in the literary and religious sciences [408] and devout. It has been mentioned above in the notice on Ibn Idrīs[78] that the mother of Ibn Idrīs was the daughter of al-Shaykh al-Ṭūsī and that her mother was the daughter of al-Masʿūd b. Warrām. The mother of Ibn Idrīs was full of learning and devotion, and a number of scholars granted her and her sister certificates of transmission. If this is the case, the daughter of al-Shaykh al-Ṭūsī was the learned one, not the daughter of al-Masʿūd b. Warrām. So take note.[79]

73. That is, after 1030/1621.

74. Muḥammad Taqī al-Majlisī was father of al-Iṣfahānī's main professor, Muḥammad Bāqir al-Majlisī, and a prominent jurist in Isfahan in the mid-seventeenth century. He died in 1070/1659.

75. Ḥusām al-Dīn Muḥammad Ṣāliḥ b. Aḥmad al-Māzandarānī (d. 1086/1675–76). See *Riyāḍ al-ʿulamāʾ*, V: 110.

76. A standard legal text by al-Ḥasan b. Yūsuf Ibn al-Muṭahhar al-Ḥillī (d. 726/1325), known as al-ʿAllāma "the Consummate Scholar."

77. Abū al-Ḥusayn Warrām b. Abī Firās, a descendant of al-Ḥārith al-Ashtar al-Nakhaʿī, a Companion of ʿAlī b. Abī Ṭālib. See *Riyāḍ al-ʿulamāʾ*, V: 282–6, where al-Isfahānī states that al-Masʿūd is a name of al-Warrām himself and not the name of his father, as stated below in this notice on his daughter.

78. See *Riyāḍ al-ʿulamāʾ*, V: 31–3. He died in 598/1202.

79. This entry is confused. Al-Iṣfahānī's conflation of three women here, which he half corrects, is based on a confusion of Ibn Idrīs and Raḍī al-Dīn Ibn Ṭāwūs. Al-Warrām's daughter was actually the mother of Ibn Ṭāwūs. Given that al-Warrām was contemporary with Ibn Idrīs, his daughter could not have been Ibn Idrīs' grandmother. Ibn Idrīs and Ibn Ṭāwūs are both descendants of al-Shaykh al-Ṭūsī through a female line. Ibn Idrīs' mother was the daughter of al-Ṭūsī, and Ibn Ṭāwūs' paternal grandmother was the daughter or granddaughter of al-Ṭūsī. See Kohlberg 1992b, 3.

[Nos. 11, 12] The two daughters of al-Sayyid Raḍī al-Dīn ʿAlī b. Ṭāwūs[80]

They were also learned in the literary and religious sciences, authors, and devout. Ibn Ṭāwūs himself — may God sanctify his soul — stated in *Kitāb Kashf al-maḥajja*, addressing his son Muḥammad: "Know that I brought your sister Sharaf al-Ashrāf, shortly before she reached puberty, and explained to her that which her state enabled her to comprehend, and that God — may His magnificence be glorified — conferred honor upon her by announcing to her the obligation to serve Him — may His magnificence be glorified — in all things, great and small. I described this situation in *Kitāb al-Bahja li-thamarat al-muhja*. End of quote.[81]

They were granted certificates along with their brothers Muḥammad and ʿAlī[82] by their father al-Sayyid Ibn Ṭāwūs for the *Dictations*[83] by al-Shaykh al-Ṭūsī, as has been mentioned above in the notice on their father. He said in describing these two daughters of his: the two memorizers and writers. The remaining text has been lost from the copy from which this was copied, as mentioned above.

[No. 13] The mother of al-Sayyid Ibn Ṭāwūs

She was among the magnificent scholars. One of the students of al-Shaykh ʿAlī al-Karakī[84] said in his treatise which he wrote on the names of scholars: "Among them is the mother of al-Sayyid Ibn Ṭāwūs. ...[85] for all of his works and transmitted texts, and he used to praise her for her learning." End of quote.

I say: The copy is defective; perhaps some text has fallen out, or else this phrase is the continuation of the notice on Ibn Idrīs, and the word *minhum* was inserted (inadvertently). So take note.

[409] [No. 14] The daughter of al-Sayyid al-Murtaḍā

She was learned in the literary arts and magnificent, and transmits *Kitāb*

80. Raḍī al-Dīn Ibn Ṭāwūs actually had four daughters. The unnamed scholarly daughter here is probably Fāṭima; the names of the two remaining daughters are not known. See Kohlberg 1992b, 17.

81. On *Kitāb Kashf al-maḥajja* and *Kitāb al-Bahja li-thamarat al-muhja*, see Kohlberg 1992b, 41–2 and 28–9, respectively.

82. On Ibn Ṭāwūs' sons, Jamāl al-Dīn Muḥammad (d. 680/1281–82) and Abū al-Qāsim ʿAlī (d. 711/1312), see Kohlberg 1992b, 17–18.

83. Published as al-Shaykh al-Ṭūsī, *Amālī al-Shaykh al-Ṭūsī*, ed. Muḥammad Ṣādiq Baḥr al-ʿUlūm (Beirut: al-Maktaba al-Ahliyya, 1981).

84. ʿAlī al-Karakī (d. 940/1534), known as *al-Muḥaqqiq al-Thānī*, was a prominent jurist from Jabal ʿĀmil who became a leading authority in the Safavid Empire during the reigns of Shah Ismaʿil I (r. 907–30/1501–24) and Shah Tahmasb (r. 930–84/1524–76).

85. There is evidently a lacuna in the text here. The passage must have originally included a statement to the effect that "He granted her certificates."

Nahj al-balāgha from her paternal uncle al-Sayyid al-Raḍī.[86] Al-Shaykh ʿAbd al-Raḥīm al-Baghdādī, who is known as Ibn al-Ikhwah, transmits from her, according to what al-Quṭb al-Rāwandī quoted at the end of his commentary on *Nahj al-balāgha*, as has been mentioned above in the notices on al-Quṭb al-Rāwandī[87] and al-Shaykh Zayn al-Dīn Abū Jaʿfar Muḥammad b. ʿAbd al-Ḥamīd b. Muḥammad, who is called ...[88]

[Nos. 15, 16] The two daughters of al-Shaykh al-Ṭūsī.

They were learned in the literary and religious sciences, and one of them was the mother of Ibn Idrīs, as was mentioned above in his biographical notice. Her sister was [...]. A certain scholar granted them certificates of transmission. The one who granted the certificate may have been their brother, al-Shaykh Abū ʿAlī b. al-Shaykh al-Ṭūsī,[89] or their father, al-Shaykh al-Ṭūsī. So take note.

[No. 17]

I saw in the shrine of ʿAbd al-ʿAẓīm[90] a copy of the commentary on *Nahj al-balāgha* by Ibn Mītham al-Baḥrānī, and it was in the hand of a learned woman.

[No. 18]

Also now in Isfahan, the sister of the Persian master Raḥīm al-Iṣfahānī who resides in the Karrān quarter[91] is among the scholars and writers. I have seen her handwriting and some of her instructive notes, including a commentary on the *Lumʿa* in her handwriting, of superior quality. She writes in both the *naskh* script and the *naskh-taʿlīq* script, and she studied with her father and brother as well. So take note.

[410] [No. 19] al-Sayyida Sukayna [Sakīna] the daughter of Our Master al-Ḥusayn b. ʿAlī b. Abī Ṭālib — may God's blessings be upon them.

She — may God be pleased with her — was the mistress of all the women

86. Al-Sharīf al-Raḍī (d. 406/1015), brother of al-Sharīf al-Murtaḍā, was a renowned poet and compiler of the most important collection of speeches and sayings of ʿAlī b. Abī Ṭālib, which he gave the title *Nahj al-balāgha* (The Path of Eloquence).

87. Quṭb al-Dīn Abū al-Ḥusayn Saʿīd b. Hibat Allāh b. al-Ḥasan al-Rāwandī, a Shiite scholar of the tenth and eleventh centuries who studied with al-Shaykh al-Mufīd (d. 413/1022). See *Riyāḍ al-ʿulamāʾ*, II: 419–37. For his transmission of *Nahj al-balāgha*, see II: 430.

88. See *Riyāḍ al-ʿulamāʾ*, II: 430, in the entry on Quṭb al-Dīn al-Rāwandī, where the same lacuna occurs in his name.

89. Given name al-Ḥasan. His death date is not known, but he was still alive in 511/1117 (see *Riyāḍ al-ʿulamāʾ*, I: 334–7).

90. Famous shrine of an Imāmzādah or descendant of one of the twelve Imams, in Rayy, now in the south of Tehran.

91. Dihkhudā, *Lughatnāmeh*, Volume *Kāf* I: 413.

of her time, and among the most beautiful of women, the wittiest, and possessor of the most excellent temperament. Muṣʿab b. al-Zubayr married her, but died before she did, then ʿAbd Allāh b. ʿUthmān b. ʿAbd Allāh b. Ḥakīm b. Ḥizām, and she bore him a *qarīn*,[92] then al-Aṣbagh b. ʿAbd al-ʿAzīz b. Marwān married her, but left her before consummating the marriage, then Zayd b. ʿAmr b. ʿUthmān b. ʿAffān married her, and Sulaymān b. ʿAbd al-Malik[93] commanded him to divorce her, and he did so.

Other versions of the sequence of her marriages have been said.

The Sukayniyya brocade[94] is named after her, and she has anecdotes and witty tales with poets and others. Sukayna's death occurred in Medina on Thursday, the fifth of the month of Rabīʿ the First, in the year one hundred and seventeen — may God be pleased with her.[95]

Some say that her name is Āmina, others say Amīna, yet others Umayma. Sukayna is a nickname applied to her by her mother al-Rabāb bt. Imruʾ al-Qays b. Zayd. This is what Ibn Khallikān said in his history.[96] I say ...

Bibliography of Works Cited

Abbott, Nabia Abbott (1946), *Two Queens of Baghdad: Mother and Wife of Harun al-Rashid* (Chicago: Chicago University Press).

ʿAlawī, Fāris Aḥmad (1994), *ʿĀʾisha al-Bāʿūnīya al-Dimashqīya* (Damascus).

al-Amīn, Muḥsin, *Aʿyān al-Shīʿa*, 10 vols. (Beirut: Dār al-Taʿāruf lil-Maṭbūʿāt, 1984).

Auchterlonie, Paul (1987), *Arabic Biographical Dictionaries: A Summary Guide and Bibliography* (Durham: Middle East Libraries Committee).

Babayan, Kathryn (1998), "The ʿAqāʾid al-Nisāʾ: A Glimpse at Ṣafavid Women in Local Iṣfahānī Culture," in: *Women in the Medieval Islamic World: Power, Patronage, and Piety*, ed. Gavin R. G. Hambly (New York: St. Martin's Press), 350–81.

al-Bāqillānī, *Iʿjāz al-Qurʾān*, ed. ʿImād al-Dīn Aḥmad Ḥaydar (Beirut: Muʾassasat al-Kutub al-Thaqāfīya, 1991).

92. I am not sure of the intended meaning of this term. A *qarīn* is a "match" or "counterpart." It could be meant to indicate that she bore him a son who resembled him or perhaps had the same name, ʿUthmān.

93. The Umayyad Caliph who reigned from 96/715 until 99/717.

94. The term *ṭurra* denotes a decorative border on a cloth garment.

95. This corresponds to 4 February 735 C.E.

96. By this al-Iṣfahānī means the well-known biographical dictionary, *Wafayāt al-aʿyān* by Ibn Khallikān (d. 681/1282).

Berkey, Jonathan P. (1991), "Women and Islamic Education in the Mamluk Period," in: *Women in Middle Eastern History*, ed. Nikki R. Keddie and Beth Baron (New Haven: Yale University Press), 143–57.

—— (1992), *The Transmission of Knowledge in Medieval Cairo: A Social History of Islamic Education* (Princeton: Princeton University Press).

Blake, Stephen P. (1998), "Contributors to the Urban Landscape: Women Builders in Safavid Isfahan and Mughal Shahjahanabad," in: *Women in the Medieval Islamic World: Power, Patronage, and Piety*, ed. Gavin R. G. Hambly (New York: St. Martin's Press), 407–28.

Booth, Marilyn (1996), "Women's Biographies and Political Agendas: Who's Who in Islamic History," *Gender and History* 8: 133–7.

—— (1997), "May Her Likes Be Multiplied: 'Famous Women' Biography and Gendered Prescription in Egypt, 1892–1935," *Signs* 22: 827–90.

—— (2001), *May Her Likes Be Multiplied: Biography and Gender Politics in Egypt* (Berkeley: University of California Press).

Cooperson, Michael (2000), *Classical Arabic Biography: The Heirs to the Prophets in the Age of al-Maʾmūn* (Cambridge: Cambridge University Press).

Daftary, Farhad (1998), "Sayyida Ḥurra: The Ismāʿīlī Ṣulayḥid Queen of Yemen," in: *Women in the Medieval Islamic World: Power, Patronage, and Piety*, ed. Gavin R. G. Hambly (New York: St. Martin's Press), 117–30.

al-Dhahabī, Mājid and Ṣalāḥ al-Khiyamī (1981), "Dīwān ʿĀʾisha al-Bāʿūnīya," *al-Turāth al-ʿarabī* (Damascus) 4: 110–21.

Dihkhudā, ʿAlī Akbar (1993–4), *Lughatnāmeh*, 15 vols. (Tehran: Muʾassaseh-yi Intishārāt va-Chāp-i Dānishgāh-i Tehrān).

Ferrier, Ronald W. (1998), "Women in Ṣafavid Iran: The Evidence of European Travelers," in: *Women in the Medieval Islamic World: Power, Patronage, and Piety*, ed. Gavin R. G. Hambly (New York: St. Martin's Press), 383–406.

Gibb, Hamilton A. R. (1962), "Islamic Biographical Literature," in: *Historians of the Middle East*, ed. Bernard Lewis and P. M. Holt (London: Oxford University Press), 54–8.

Gilliot, Claude (2002), "Prosopography in Islam: An Essay of Classification," in: *Arab-Islamic Medieval Culture*, ed. Manuela Marín, special issue of *Medieval Prosopography* 23: 1–49.

Golsorkhi, Shohreh (1995), "Parī Khān Khānum: A Masterful Safavid Princess," *Iranian Studies* 28: 143–56.

Homerin, Emil Th. (2002), review of ʿAlawī, *ʿĀʾisha al-Bāʿūnīya al-Dimashqīya*, *Mamluk Studies Review* 6: 191–93.

—— (2003), "Living Love: The Mystical Writing of ʿĀʾishah al-Bāʿūnīyah (d. 922/1516)" *Mamluk Studies Review* 7: 211–34.

Humphreys, R. Stephen (1991), *Islamic History: A Framework for Inquiry*, revised ed. (Princeton: Princeton University Press).

Ibn Ṭāwūs, Raḍī al-Dīn, *al-Iqbāl bi'l-a'māl al-ḥasana* (Tehran, 1902; reprinted 1970, 1987).

——, *Kitāb al-Ṭarā'if fī ma'rifat madhāhib al-ṭawā'if* (Qum, 1979)

al-Iṣfahānī, Mīrzā 'Abd Allāh, *Riyāḍ al-'ulamā' wa-ḥiyāḍ al-fuḍalā'*, 6 vols., ed. al-Sayyid Aḥmad al-Ḥusaynī (Qum: Makatabat Āyat Allāh al-Mar'ashī al-'Āmma, 1981).

Jaques, R. Kevin (2006), *Authority, Conflict, and the Transmission of Diversity in Medieval Islamic Law* (Leiden: Brill).

Khalidi, Tarif (1973), "Islamic Biographical Dictionaries: A Preliminary Assessment," *Muslim World* 63: 53–65.

al-Khaṭīb al-Baghdādī, *Ta'rīkh Baghdād aw Madīnat al-Salām*, 14 vols. (Cairo: Maktabat al-Khānjī, 1931).

Kohlberg, Etan (1985), "Aḵbārīya," *EIr* I: 716–18.

—— (1992a), "'Alī b. Mūsā b. Ṭāwūs and His Polemic against Sunnism," in: *Religionsgespräche im Mittelalter*, ed. Bernard Lewis and Friedrich Niewöhner (Wiesbaden: Harrassowitz), 325–50.

—— (1992b) *A Medieval Muslim Scholar at Work: Ibn Ṭāwūs and His Library* (Leiden: E. J. Brill).

Lal, Ruby (2005), *Domesticity and Power in the Early Mughal World* (Cambridge: Cambridge University Press).

Lutfi, Huda (1981) "Al-Sakhāwī's *Kitāb al-Nisā'* as a Source for the Social and Economic History of Muslim Women during the Fifteenth Century A.D.," *Muslim World* 71: 104–24.

Madelung, Wilferd (2004), "al-Akhbāriyya," *EI*[2] Supplement, XII: 56–57.

Makdisi, George (1993), "Ṭabaqāt-Biography: Law and Orthodoxy in Classical Islam," *Islamic Studies* 32: 371–96.

Mernissi, Fatima (1987), *Beyond the Veil: Male-Female Dynamics in Modern Muslim Society*, revised ed. (Bloomington: Indiana University Press).

—— (1993), *The Forgotten Queens of Islam* (Minneapolis: University of Minnesota Press).

Mukhlis, 'Abd Allāh (1941), "'Ā'isha al-Bā'ūnīya," *Majallat al-majma' al-'ilmī* (Damascus) 16: 66–72.

Nashat, Guity (1999), "Part I: Women in the Middle East 8,000 B.C.E.–C.E. 1800," in: Guity Nashat and Judith E. Tucker, *Women in the Middle East and North Africa: Restoring Women to History* (Bloomington: Indiana University Press), 5–72.

Peirce, Lesley P. (1993), *The Imperial Harem: Women and Sovereignty in the Ottoman Empire* (Oxford: Oxford University Press).

Petry, Carl (1991), "Class Solidarity Versus Gender Gain: Women as Custodians of Property in Later Medieval Egypt," in: *Women in Middle Eastern History: Shifting Boundaries in Sex and Gender*, ed. Nikki R. Keddie and Beth Baron (New Haven: Yale University Press), 122–42.

Rabābiʿa, Ḥasan (1997), *ʿĀʾisha al-Bāʿūnīya: Shāʿira*, Irbid.
al-Rāzī, Jamāl al-Dīn al-Ḥusayn b. ʿAlī, *Rawḍ al-jinān wa-rūḥ al-janān fī tafsīr al-Qurʾān*, ed. Muḥammad Jaʿfar Yāḥaqqī and Muḥammad Mahdī Nāṣiḥ (Mashhad: Bunyād-i Pazhūhish-hā-yi Islāmī, 1986).
Reynolds, Dwight F. et al. (2001), *Interpreting the Self: Autobiography in the Arabic Literary Tradition* (Berkeley: University of California Press).
Roded, Ruth (1994), *Women in Islamic Biographical Collections: From Ibn Saʿd to Who's Who* (Boulder, Colorado: Lynne Rienner Publishers).
Rosenthal, Franz (1968) *A History of Muslim Historiography*, second revised ed. (Leiden: Brill), 100–6.
Scott, James C. (1985), *Weapons of the Weak: Everyday Forms of Peasant Resistance* (New Haven: Yale University Press).
Siddiqui, Muhammad Zubayr (1993), *Hadith Literature: Its Origin, Development and Special Features*, revised ed. (Cambridge: Islamic Texts Society).
Soucek, Priscilla P. (1998), "Timurid Women: A Cultural Perspective," in: *Women in the Medieval Islamic World: Power, Patronage, and Piety*, ed. Gavin R. G. Hambly (New York: St. Martin's Press), 199–226.
Spellberg, Denise (1994), *Politics, Gender, and the Islamic Past: The Legacy of ʿAʾisha bint Abi Bakr* (New York: Columbia University Press).
Stewart, Devin J. (1997), "Capital, Accumulation, and the Islamic Academic Biography," *Edebiyat* 7: 345–62.
al-Subkī, Tāj al-Dīn, *Ṭabaqāt al-shāfiʿīya al-kubrā*, 10 vols., ed. ʿAbd al-Fattāḥ al-Ḥilw and Maḥmūd Muḥammad al-Ṭanāḥī (Cairo: Hajr, 1992).
Szuppe, Maria (1994, 1995), "La participation des femmes de la famille royale à l'exercise du pouvoir en Iran," *Studia Iranica* 23: 211–58 and 24: 1–58.
—— (1998), "'The Jewels of Wonder': Learned Ladies and Princess Politicians in the Provinces of Early Safavid Iran," in: *Women in the Medieval Islamic World: Power, Patronage, and Piety*, ed. Gavin R. G. Hambly (New York: St. Martin's Press), 325–47.
al-Ṭihrānī, Agha Buzurg, *al-Ḥaqāʾiq al-rāhina* = Juzʾ 5, *Ṭabaqāt aʿyān al-shīʿa*, 17 vols. (Beirut: Dār Iḥyāʾ al-Turāth al-ʿArabī, 2009).
al-Shaykh al-Ṭūsī, *Amālī al-Shaykh al-Ṭūsī*, ed. Muḥammad Ṣādiq Baḥr al-ʿUlūm (Beirut: al-Maktaba al-Ahliyya, 1981).
al-Tustarī [or al-Shushtarī], al-Sayyid ʿAbd Allāh al-Mūsawī al-Jazāʾirī, *al-Ijāza al-kabīra*, ed. Muḥammad al-Simāmī al-Ḥāʾirī (Qum: Maktabat Āyat Allāh al-Marʿashī al-Najafī, 1989).

Al-Maʾmūn and ʿAlī al-Riḍā (Emām Reza) on Iranian Television[1]

Michael Cooperson

Introduction

SOMETIME IN THE MID-1980'S, when I was an undergraduate taking my first courses in Middle Eastern history, I was struck by a passage from *A History of Medieval Islam* by J. J. Saunders. Speaking of al-Maʾmūn, the seventh caliph (r. 197–218/813–833) of the Abbasid dynasty, and ʿAlī al-Riḍā (d. 202 or 203/817, 818, or 819), the eighth imam of the Twelver Shiʿah, Saunders writes: "Maʾmun, who had much sympathy with the Shiʿa, endeavored to win over the Alids by recognizing Ali al-Rida, a descendant of the martyred Husain, as his heir but the opposition to his plan was so violent that he was obliged to abandon it."[2] I remember wondering about this heroic attempt — or so it seemed — to settle the feud between the Alids and the Abbasids. Some years later, I encountered the caliph and the Imam again. In the course of my graduate work, I had the good fortune to study with Prof. Aḥmad Mahdavī Dāmghānī, a scholar of unmatched expertise in both Arabic and Persian literature. When I asked him what the Shiite sources had to say about the nomination of their imam as heir apparent, he directed me to the massive biography of al-Riḍā by Ibn Bābawayh al-Qummī (d. 381/991). Twelver historians, it turns out, claim that the caliph forced the Imam to accept the heir apparency and then poisoned him when the arrangement became inconvenient. This unexpected discovery, along with others of a similar kind, led me to devote my dissertation[3] to the question of how a single life is represented from different points of view.

Seven years ago, one of my students at UCLA, Ms. Pari Iranmanesh, told me that Iranian television had aired a miniseries about al-Riḍā. After I expressed an interest in seeing it, she kindly brought me a boxed set of DVDs containing the entire production. Written and directed by Mehdi

1. I would like to thank the Ilex Foundation for its generous invitation to present a draft of this paper at the Fifth Biennial Conference on Iranian Studies. I would also like to thank Prof. Afsaneh Najmabadi for reading and commenting on a draft of this paper.

2. Saunders 1965, 112.

3. Later published as Cooperson 2000.

Fakhīmzādeh, the ten-part series, entitled *Velāyat-e ʿEshgh* (The Rule of Love), dramatizes the events of 193–203/809–18, during which al-Maʾmūn deposed his brother al-Amīn, nominated ʿAlī al-Riḍā as heir apparent, and then — according to Twelver tradition — poisoned him.[4] When she first brought the series to my attention, Ms. Iranmanesh told me that I would appreciate it because it was historically accurate. I later found out why she thought so: the closing credits contain a list of historical sources, including Ibn Bābawayh's biography of the Imam as well as the *Taʾrīkh* of al-Ṭabarī (d. 314/923) and the *Murūj al-dhahab* of al-Masʿūdī (d. 345/956). The basic sequence of events and many of the lines spoken by the characters indeed come from the Arabic historiography of the ninth and tenth centuries. Of course, such gestures toward documentary authenticity only emphasize the extent to which the series cannot possibly be accurate by any definition of the term.

In the most banal sense, the series is inaccurate in the same way a modern written history might be: that is, it narrates events differently than they are believed to have occurred. For example, the chronicles report that the caliph al-Amīn was killed after swimming away from a sinking riverboat (Ṭabarī 8: 484–5). In the series, he is simply stabbed to death in his palace, a scene easier and cheaper to produce than a river battle would have been. Other misrepresentations appear to respond to the need for narrative or expository economy. For example, the Twelver sources report that the Imam's companion and biographer, Abū al-Ṣalt al-Harawī, first joined him in Nishapur (Ibn Bābawayh 2: 132–7). In the series, the acquaintance is pushed back to an earlier period, a manipulation that gives Abū al-Ṣalt more time to serve as the Imam's confidant. Many discrepancies, finally, seem to be the result of ignorance or indifference. A contemporary poem informs us that al-Maʾmūn's general Ṭāhir b. al-Ḥusayn had only one eye (al-Masʿūdī 3: 424); in the series, he has two, evidently because the filmmakers happen not to have read the poem in question, or thought the matter insignificant. Such divergences are par for the course in historical fiction films, and generally pass unnoticed by viewers unless those viewers happen to be historians.

Less trivially, the fundamental inaccuracies in *Velāyat-e ʿEshgh* are those inseparable from the nature of its medium. Like any visual representation of the past, the series must invent many elements regarding which the sources are silent.[5] In print, I can limit myself to a single statement that is true or false: "In the year 201/817, ʿAlī b. Mūsā arrived at the court of al-Maʾmūn to assume the position of heir apparent." To make the same statement visually, Fakhīmzādeh is forced to add that the ceremony took place indoors, with

4. As of this writing, the series is available in its entirety on YouTube under the title "Serial Imam Reza A.S."

5. See Rosenstone 1995, 28; and 2002, 141–2.

the Abbasid dignitaries standing in rows facing the caliph's throne, and that the heir apparent was wearing an ankle-length white robe and the caliph a sort of headgear equipped with ear flaps. Any of these visual statements may be true or false. Unfortunately, we have no way to know which is which. Historians can (and customarily do) avoid the issue by saying nothing about costumes and scenery. But Fakhīmzādeh has no choice, and so the number of possibly false statements he makes per second is practically infinite.

The conventions of visual narrative set the series apart from written history in other ways as well. The visual media do not lend themselves to the presentation of conflicting interpretations, nor do they contain a convenient space for footnotes.[6] Regarding al-Riḍā's death, for example, there was (and still is) a controversy over whether al-Maʾmūn was indeed responsible for it. *Velāyat-e ʿEshgh* follows the story line familiar to present-day Shiites and shows the caliph poisoning the Imam. It does not point out that several prominent Twelver authorities expressed their doubts about this version of the story. Moreover, even if the filmmakers had wished to draw attention to the existence of variant accounts, there would have been no self-evident way to do so without shifting the focus of their work to the controversy itself (as happens, for example, in Kurosawa's *Rashomon*, 1950). All historians, of course, choose among interpretations and frequently collapse a profusion of events into a linear narrative. But the technology of print allows them to specify the nature and extent of these manipulations. The sequential character of the visual medium, on the other hand, cannot offer parallel or alternative accounts without foregrounding or displacing them.

Even as they acknowledge that the historical fiction film is a genre condemned by its very nature to violate or ignore the protocols of written historiography, several critics have wondered whether "film might have its own way of telling the past."[7] In one sense, *Velāyat-e ʿEshgh* adds little to the written tradition. Its basic contention — that the caliph deceived and poisoned the Imam — is the same as that argued in the fourth/tenth century by Ibn Bābawayh. In another sense, however, the film adds a great deal. Precisely because of its need for visual and narrative saturation, it suggests a more elaborate and dramatically plausible set of explanations for al-Maʾmūn's behavior than any of its models provide. In this respect, the series functions as a kind of visual historiography: that is, as a new and thought-provoking interpretation of the past it retells.

The first parts of this essay will accordingly be devoted to a comparison of the series with the accounts presented in the chronicles. Such an under-

6. See further Rosenstone 1995, 37–44, and Davis 2000, 131–6.
7. Rosenstone 2002, 136–7, and references cited; Davis 2000, *passim*.

taking requires a discussion of three elements: what the chronicles say, what modern historians have concluded on the basis of the chronicles, and what *Velāyat-e ʿEshgh* presents as real. In what follows, I have combined the first two into a single account.

For practical reasons, my account excludes a set of materials likely to have played some role in bridging the gap between the chronicles and the series: poetic lamentations (*rozeh, noḥeh*) of the deaths of the imams, and "passion plays" (*taʿziyeh*) performed in honor of the Imam Ḥusayn. As far as I know, there is no passion play about the death of al-Riḍā. Nevertheless, to judge by the offerings on YouTube, there exists in Arabic, Persian, and other languages a genre of sung or chanted lamentations as well as exhortations to visit his tomb. Moreover, several colleagues, notably Hassan Hussein, have reported to me that in Mashhad, processions take place in which historical figures, including the caliph al-Maʾmūn, are represented. As I lack both the opportunity to attend such events and the expertise necessary to study them, I am unable to judge the extent to which they may have served as mediators between written history and modern television.

In the course of describing *Velāyat-e ʿEshgh*, I will be making judgments about what is accurate, plausible, implausible, or simply wrong. Satisfying as such labels may be to historians, they tell us practically nothing about viewers' responses to the series (unless those viewers happen to be historians). On two separate occasions, I watched the series with an Iranian friend who wept at the scene of the imam's death. One friend had already had an earful from me about the many inaccuracies in the series but wept nevertheless. Such a response is perhaps unremarkable: after all, the passionate mourning that accompanies the *taʿziyeh* is in no way attenuated by the fact that the performers hardly resemble the historical figures they represent. To all appearances, then, judgments about historical accuracy are separate from the perception that a reality of some sort is being depicted or invoked. To the extent anyone pays attention to it, the listing of sources in the final credits of *Velāyat-e ʿEshgh* merely affirms the appropriateness of the response elicited by the series itself. In the last part of this essay, accordingly, I will address the function of historical representation in religious drama. For many Iranian viewers, I will argue, the series constitutes a form of visual historiography, but only in a limited sense. Instead of reconstructing or even reinterpreting the past, it presents something one might call "parallel reality," a term I have borrowed from science fiction.

First, some acknowledgements and admissions. I am an Arabist with a limited working knowledge of Persian. Without the kind assistance of Ms. Mahsa Maleki, who repeated much of the dialogue for me and translated the parts I did not understand, I would have made little sense of the series.[8] I am also indebted to Ms. Maleki for drawing my attention to the interview with Shahreyār Boḥrānī. Besides this interview, I was unable to obtain any firsthand testimony from producers of religious programming, nor do I have any information about the production or reception of the series in Iran. I am, furthermore, not a scholar of film or television. Much of what I have been able to learn is thanks to Mohsen Ashtiyani, who first directed me to Robert Rosenstone's work in filmic history. Suffering as it does from many inadequacies, this essay cannot purport to do justice to the series from a cultural-historical or media-studies perspective. All I can hope to do is to offer a reading of the series from the point of view of an Arabist long immersed in studying the events it purports to depict. Such a preliminary study will, I hope, stimulate further investigations on the part of scholars better qualified than myself to address the complex phenomenon of historical television and film production in present-day Iran. Finally, let me emphasize that I alone am responsible for the opinions here expressed.

The Chroniclers' Accounts of al-Riḍā and al-Maʾmūn

In the year 193/809, the Abbasid caliph al-Rashīd died and was succeeded by his son al-Amīn. In accordance with the succession arrangement established by al-Rashīd, another of his sons, al-Maʾmūn, assumed the governorship of Khurasan.[9] But many of the troops that had been ordered to remain with al-Maʾmūn decided to return to their families in Baghdad. The new governor was thus left without an army. On the advice of his vizier, al-Faḍl b. Sahl, he recruited new troops by making alliances with local Iranian and Turkic chiefs. In Baghdad, meanwhile, al-Amīn's advisors were urging the new caliph to exclude his brother from the succession. After demanding certain fiscal and territorial concessions, all of which al-Maʾmūn — reportedly on the advice of al-Faḍl — refused to grant, al-Amīn eventually dropped his brother's name from the Friday sermon and named his own son as heir apparent. In response, al-Maʾmūn declared himself *imām al-hudā*, that is, "rightly guided and rightly guiding leader."[10] He was now in open rebellion

8. Since this paper was written, an Arabic-dubbed version, titled *Gharīb Ṭūs*, has been produced. As of this writing it may be viewed online at AnwarNet (the search term is *Gharīb Ṭūs* in Arabic script). I have watched several of the important scenes again in Arabic, and admit that al-Maʾmūn seems to me more straightforwardly villainous in the Arabic version than in the original.

9. The impression that al-Rashīd granted al-Maʾmūn virtual autonomy has been dispelled by Tayeb El-Hibri, who argues that the succession agreement as preserved by the chroniclers reflects *ex post facto* tampering by partisans of al-Maʾmūn (El-Hibri 1992). For an earlier view see Kimber 1986.

10. See further Arazi and El'ad 1987 and 1988, *passim*; Nagel 1975, 140–4.

against the Abbasid regime. Defeating a series of armies sent from Baghdad, his forces laid siege to the capital. After a destructive fourteen-month siege, al-Amīn was killed trying to escape the city, and al-Maʾmūn was generally acknowledged as caliph (198/813). Rather than return to Iraq, however, he chose to remain in the Khurasani capital of Marv. In the absence of a central authority, the empire lapsed into anarchy. In Kufa, Mecca, and the Yemen, members of the house of ʿAlī b. Abī Ṭālib declared themselves to be imams; one even took the title of caliph. Though these uprisings were defeated, it was clear that al-Maʾmūn had little effective authority outside Khurasan.[11]

In 201/817, al-Maʾmūn astonished his contemporaries by naming ʿAlī b. Mūsā, a prominent member of the house of ʿAlī, as his heir apparent. The announcement of the designation declares that the caliph "wearied his body, caused his eye to be sleepless, and gave prolonged thought" to the question of succession. After examining the members of the Abbasid and Alid houses, he found no one more virtuous, scrupulous, and learned than ʿAlī b. Mūsā, a prominent member of the house of ʿAlī. He therefore declares him heir apparent and confers upon him the title of al-Riḍā.[12] Never before had a caliph willingly promised to transfer power to a member of another house.

Modern scholars, following the precedent established by the sources, have offered various explanations for the appointment. Taking the caliph at his word, one might well argue that he chose al-Riḍā on the basis of personal merit, as he was later to name his brother al-Muʿtaṣim over his own son al-ʿAbbās as heir apparent.[13] One might also note that the nomination represented a return to the principle that had brought the Abbasids to power in the first place: that the community should be led by *al-Riḍā min āl Muḥammad*, "a member of the Prophet's family acceptable to all." Hence the heir apparent's title, which — Twelver claims (Ibn Bābawayh 1: 13–14) notwithstanding — seems to have been invented by the caliph.[14]

Whatever its theoretical justification, the nomination may also have been a short-term measure calculated to pacify the Alids. The massive uprising of Abū al-Sarāyā in Kufa had been suppressed, but the Yemen was still in the hands of Alid rebels. As it happens, the leader of the rebellion in Mecca was al-Riḍā's uncle, and the rebel in the Yemen was his brother. Al-Riḍā himself did not join the insurrections; reportedly, he had even called upon

11. The fundamental primary source for these events is al-Ṭabarī, *Taʾrīkh*, 8: 275–86 and 365–545, most recently summarized in Cooperson 2005, 39–56; for discussion and further references see El-Hibri 1994, 1–87.

12. The text of the announcement appears in Ibn al-Jawzī 10: 93–9 and is translated in Crone and Hinds 1986, 133–9. See also al-Ṭabarī, *Taʾrīkh*, 8: 554–5.

13. Bayhom-Daou 2008, 11.

14. Crone 1989; Cooperson 2000, 29–31.

his brother to surrender.[15] By naming al-Riḍā his heir apparent, al-Maʾmūn may have been hoping to discourage further acts of rebellion. The nomination may even have amounted to an acknowledgement of the claims of the Alids. Conversely, it may have been an attempt to subvert and undermine those claims.[16] Among Twelver chroniclers, it is interpreted as an attempt to acquire those rights by association. This interpretation may contain some element of truth, although the Twelver presentation of it, insisting as it does on the caliph's malevolent cynicism, seems off the mark. Indicative, perhaps, of the caliph's good faith is his pledge of one of his daughters in marriage to al-Riḍā and of another to al-Riḍā's son.[17]

At the time of the designation, al-Riḍā was fifteen or twenty years older than al-Maʾmūn. This circumstance among others has provoked a lively debate over whether the caliph was more concerned with making a premillennial act of contrition than with providing a viable heir. On the basis of a letter purportedly written by the caliph to his relatives in Baghdad, Wilferd Madelung has suggested that al-Maʾmūn believed, on the basis of an obscure prophecy, that the Abbasid dynasty would end with him, and that he nominated al-Riḍā to atone for the ill treatment the Abbasids had visited upon the Alids.[18] In a rebuttal to Madelung, Tamima Bayhom-Daou has convincingly argued that the connection is not explicit but rather "merely a possible inference"; and more critically that the relevant portion of the letter was added by a later transmitter, Ibn Ṭāwūs (d. 664/1266), and therefore cannot be taken as an explanation for the caliph's motives.[19] Hayrettin Yücesoy, though also skeptical of the letter's authenticity, nevertheless maintains that the advent of the year 200 AH, al-Maʾmūn's rank as the seventh of the Abbasids, and the overthrow of al-Amīn would have been more than enough to stoke the caliph's millennial anxieties.[20]

Other scholars, finally, have taken a different tack, arguing that the decisions al-Maʾmūn made in the early part of his reign, including this one, were made under the influence of his vizier al-Faḍl. The chronicles are divided on this point, some saying that the vizier suggested the nomination and others insisting that he opposed it.[21] Whatever the case, there is no question

15. Al-Iṣfahānī, *Maqātil*, 360. Cf. Strothmann 1911, 78 (*anna l-Maʾmūna kallafa baʿḍa l-ʿAlawiyyīna an yatawassaṭa baynahu wa-bayna l-Qāsim*); I thank Ryan Schaffner for this reference.

16. Madelung 1965, 75; Nagel 1975, 414–24.

17. Sourdel 1962, 38.

18. Madelung 1981.

19. Bayhom-Daou 2008, 7, n. 25; and 16ff.

20. Yücesoy 2009.

21. Gabrieli 1929, 32ff.; Sourdel 1959–60, 2: 207–8; Madelung 1981, 348; and most recently, Tor 2001.

that opponents perceived the nomination of al-Riḍā as an attempt to revive specifically Iranian forms of government and religion. In both Marv and Baghdad, representatives of the old regime responded to the news by accusing al-Faḍl, a recent convert to Islam, of plotting to restore Zoroastrianism and Sasanid rule (al-Yaʿqūbī 2: 546; al-Jahshiyārī 312–14). This impression may reflect an attempt on the part of al-Maʾmūn's regime to appeal to non-Arab Muslims who, as has recently been argued, had a special attachment even at this early date to the family of the Prophet.[22]

A final point to be noted in this connection is that the caliph's announcement makes no mention of al-Riḍā's claim to the imamate. By the early third/ninth century, the Shiite theory of the imamate appears to have taken on many of its classical features, including the idea of privileged knowledge (*ʿilm*) and designation by a predecessor (*naṣṣ*).[23] Yet it is also clear that the Shiite communities of this period continued to disagree on many fundamental points, including the question of whether there was still a living imam, and if so, who he was. The only substantial evidence for al-Riḍā's position during this period comes from later Twelver sources, which present him in light of their own doctrinal certainties.[24] Even these sources, however, acknowledge that his imamate was a matter of dispute. Some of his father's followers refused to acknowledge him, reportedly because they wanted to retain control of his father's property. Others, reportedly, withheld their recognition because he had so far failed to produce an heir.[25] Only with the crystallization of Imami doctrine some hundred years later do we find al-Riḍā listed as the eighth of the twelve imams.[26] In all likelihood, he claimed to be the imam during his lifetime; but it is difficult to know precisely what that claim entailed at the time.[27] In any event, his understanding of the imamate did not prevent him from accepting the position of heir apparent to al-Maʾmūn, a problem which the Twelver sources explain away using a variety of narrative devices.

For the Abbasids in Baghdad, the nomination of al-Riḍā was the last straw. Blaming the appointment on "the plots of the Magians" (Yaʿqūbī 2: 546), they threw off their allegiance to al-Maʾmūn and swore fealty to his uncle, the famous singer Ibrāhīm b. al-Mahdī.[28] At that point, it would again

22. Crone 2004, 84–6.

23. For an overview see Jafri 1979, Momen 1985, Modarressi 1993, and most recently Crone 2004, 70–124.

24. The *locus classicus* is Ibn Bābawayh. For a compilation of later materials see Amīn, *Aʿyān*, 5: 3: 77–274 and ʿUṭāridī, *Musnad*. On the biographical process itself, Cooperson 2000, 77–106.

25. Ibn Bābawayh 1: 106, 112–14 and 2: 209–10; and further Modarressi 1993, 62–3, n. 38.

26. Kohlberg 1979.

27. Kohlberg 1988.

28. Menard 1869.

have been reasonable for al-Maʾmūn to return to Baghdad and reassert his authority. But al-Faḍl, who was hated in Iraq, knew that a return to the former Abbasid capital meant the end of his power. Reportedly, he therefore kept the caliph in the dark about what was happening in Baghdad. Reportedly, too, it was al-Riḍā who finally broke the news of the disorder in Iraq, prompting the caliph to set off on the long-deferred journey to Baghdad. Fearful for his own safety, al-Faḍl sought and obtained from al-Maʾmūn a written pledge to the effect that he (al-Faḍl) was free to renounce his duties as vizier.[29] He was nevertheless murdered during the journey back to Baghdad, reportedly by men acting on the caliph's orders (Ṭabarī 8: 555–6).

In Ṣafar 203/September 818 (according to some accounts, at any rate), during a stopover in a town called Sanabadh in the region of Tus, al-Riḍā fell ill and died. Al-Maʾmūn is said to have marched bareheaded in the funeral procession, crying out: "Whom will I turn to now?" (Yaʿqūbī 2: 550–1). He ordered the body interred beside that of his father al-Rashīd, who had perished in Tus a decade earlier while campaigning against rebels in Khurasan.[30]

Given his relatively advanced age and the rigors of the journey from Marv, al-Riḍā may have died a natural death,[31] although it is certainly odd that he happened to die in the very place where al-Rashīd was buried.[32] According to Sunni chroniclers, al-Riḍā perished from a surfeit of grapes (Ṭabarī 8: 568). Later Shiite sources, however, insist that he was murdered, and many modern historians are inclined to agree. As one contemporary poet noted, the death came at a suspiciously convenient moment for al-Maʾmūn.[33] The caliph had made up his mind to return to Baghdad, where it would be necessary to make peace with his Abbasid relatives. Given their strenuous objections to al-Faḍl and al-Riḍā, it stands to reason that he might attempt to reverse his pro-Khurasan and pro-Alid policy by ridding himself of both. This proposal makes even more sense if one accepts the argument that the nomination had been al-Faḍl's idea in the first place.

On the other hand, there is a good deal of circumstantial evidence for

29. Madelung 1981.

30. I have not been able to confirm reports that a part of al-Riḍā's tomb complex is currently identified as the place where al-Rashīd is buried. There is also a tomb popularly identified as al-Rashīd's, but it stands outside Mashhad altogether, near Ferdowsī's tomb in the modern town of Tus (I thank Ali Anooshahr for this information; see further Akbarpur 2004–5, 88–9). From older times comes a report evidently constructed to rile Shiite pilgrims: "Al-Rashīd is in the tomb people know as al-Riḍā's, thanks to a trick played by al-Maʾmūn. The two tombs are near each other, under one dome, and the people of the town [Sanābādh] are Shiites who have gone to great lengths to adorn the tomb they think belongs to al-Riḍā but which [actually] belongs to al-Rashīd" (al-Qazwīnī 392, *s.v.* Sanābādh). I thank ʿAmikam Elʾad for this reference.

31. Tor 2001, 112, n. 46.

32. Nawas 1996.

33. Diʿbil b. ʿAlī, quoted in al-Iṣfahānī, *Maqātil*, 268.

the caliph's innocence. According to one report, he immediately sought to recruit another Alid as heir apparent.[34] He also continued to use the green banners and uniforms he had adopted after al-Riḍā's nomination, abandoning them only after considerable persuasion.[35] He is also said to have written a letter to his Abbasid relatives defending his nomination of al-Riḍā and blaming them for the civil war.[36] During the remainder of his reign, he continued to express partiality to Alid causes. His later policies included the public proclamation that 'Alī was superior to Mu'āwiya, the institution of the fourfold *takbīr* (instead of the threefold one, normally shouted by the army), the restoration of the grove of Fadak to the descendants of 'Alī, and the proposal to legalize short-term marriage (a *sunna* associated with 'Alī).[37]

Most strikingly, several early chroniclers and compilers who normally accuse caliphs of murdering Alids say nothing to imply that they suspect al-Ma'mūn of doing away with his heir apparent. Al-Kulaynī (or al-Kulīnī, d. 328/939–40 or 329/940–41), for example, says merely that al-Riḍā died, not that he was poisoned (Kulaynī 1: 486). Abū al-Faraj al-Iṣfahānī (d. c. 363/972) provides two reports that blame al-Ma'mūn, but his citations from the eyewitness testimony of Abū al-Ṣalt al-Harawī (d. 236/851) do not name the caliph as the culprit. (In one passage, Abū al-Ṣalt even quotes al-Riḍā himself to the effect that the caliph is innocent.)[38] Al-Ya'qūbī, who also describes the Imam's death as natural, mentions a rumor that al-Riḍā was poisoned by 'Alī b. Hishām, a general from Khurasan (al-Ya'qūbī 2: 550–1). The possibility that al-Riḍā was indeed murdered, though not by al-Ma'mūn, is striking, if only because it breaks with the usual dichotomous presentation of the possibilities. The *abnā' al-dawla*, the descendants of the original Abbasid partisans, opposed the nomination of an Alid heir. Al-Riḍā's bodyguard included members of the *abnā'*, and the estate where al-Rashīd was buried belonged to a prominent *banawī* family. The *abnā'* seem therefore to have been in a position to do away with al-Riḍā, with or without the caliph's knowledge or consent.[39]

It was only with the crystallization of Twelver Shiite theology in the

34. Al-Iṣfahānī, *Maqātil*, 416–17; but cf. Bayhom-Daou, who doubts the accuracy of the report (5, n. 18).

35. Ibn Abī Ṭāhir, *Kitāb Baghdād*, 1–2. The Abbasid uniform color was black and the characteristic color of Alid dress was white; the green may have been a millennial reference to paradise (van Ess 1991–7, 3: 154).

36. Madelung 1981.

37. See further Gabrieli 1929, 29ff, 60–2; Sourdel 1962, 35, 40–1; Nagel 1975, 414; Kennedy 1981, 157–58; Cooperson 2005, 73–4 and 113–15.

38. Al-Iṣfahānī, *Maqātil*, 374–80. The exculpatory passage nevertheless appears to be a later addition to the manuscript. See Cooperson 2000, 84–90.

39. Cooperson 2000, 193–6.

late ninth and early tenth century that al-Riḍā's imamate, which entailed among other things being murdered by al-Maʾmūn, became a matter of faith for many Shiites. The person responsible for this development (or at least for the documenting of it) is Ibn Bābawayh al-Qummī (d. 381/991), author of a massive biography of al-Riḍā. According to Ibn Bābawayh, all the imams have been or will be murdered (Ibn Bābawayh 2: 203–4, supposedly quoting al-Riḍā himself). In the case of al-Riḍā, he says, al-Maʾmūn nominated him in order to discredit him; but when the Imam proved his superior virtue, the caliph grew jealous and poisoned him. To support this account, Ibn Bābawayh cites reports that are clearly fabricated. One of his supposed eyewitnesses, Harthama b. Aʿyan, is known to have been dead at the time; and the other, Abū al-Ṣalt al-Harawī, has left testimony in an earlier source, and this testimony bears no resemblance to what Ibn Bābawayh reports him as saying.[40] Of course, none of this means that al-Maʾmūn was innocent. But it does mean that Ibn Bābawayh could find no acceptable evidence for his guilt.[41]

Ibn Bābawayh's account was not universally accepted, even among Twelver Shiites. Among those who disagreed with it are such luminaries as al-Shaykh al-Mufīd (d. 413/1032), who took issue with the doctrine that all imams must be murdered. What, he asked, does being killed have to do with one's qualifications for the imamate?[42] Accounts of the deaths of the imams, he says, "fall under the heading of divisive rumors, and are not susceptible to confirmation."[43] After reading the letter al-Maʾmūn reportedly sent to the Abbasids, another Twelver scholar, Raḍī al-Dīn b. Ṭāwūs (d. 664/1266), declared the caliph innocent.[44] This opinion was seconded by ʿAlī b. ʿĪsa al-Irbilī (d. 717/1317), who cites the caliph's "kindness to and affection for [al-Riḍā], and his appointment of him at the expense of his own relatives and children."[45] In response to these objections, Twelver scholars dropped some of Ibn Bābawayh's more fantastic claims from their account of the incident. Nevertheless, the belief that al-Maʾmūn was personally responsible for poisoning al-Riḍā became standard in Twelver Shiism, and remains so today.

40. In what seems to be a case of trickle-down from the written tradition, both of these figures are commemorated by tomb-shrines in the Mashhad region. Harthama, an Abbasid general who died in Marv, is commemorated under the name Khᵛājeh Morād (Akbarpur 2004–5, 47–8), apparently on the strength of the report spuriously attributed to him by Ibn Bābawayh. Abū al-Ṣalt, who according to his (Sunni) biographers died in Baghdad, is nevertheless commemorated at a shrine near Mashhad (ibid, 40–6).

41. For details see Cooperson 2000, 84–100.

42. Al-Mufīd, *ʿAqāʾid*, 76–7.

43. Al-Mufīd, *Awāʾil*, 217.

44. But cf. Bayhom-Daou 2008, 16ff., on his likely motives for doing so.

45. Al-Irbilī, *Kashf*, 3: 112–13 (also the source for Ibn Ṭāwūs).

As far as I know, the only modern Shiite author to express dissent from this consensus is Ḥasan al-Amīn.[46]

Velāyat-e 'Eshgh

In 2000, Mehdī Fakhīmzadeh's ten-part miniseries depicting the events of 193–203/809–18 was aired on Iranian television. The story begins with the accession of al-Amīn, who is played with great panache by the comic actor Rāmbod Javān. The Arabic chronicles depict al-Amīn as petulant, dissolute, and irresponsible — a portrait that, as Tayeb El-Hibri has argued, represents an attempt to justify his assassination.[47] *Velāyat-e 'Eshgh* embraces this tradition, giving us an Amīn who either slouches on his throne or flings himself around the room shrieking at his vizier, his mother, and his slave companion. The series also follows the chronicles in depicting the civil war as the fault of al-Amīn, who not only neglects the business of government but also allows himself to be led astray by his scheming vizier Ibn al-Rabī'.

The caliph al-Amīn portrayed by Rāmbod Javān in *Velāyat-e Eshgh*, dir. Mehdī Fakhīmzādeh (Soroush Multimedia Corporation, 1996–2000).

In the series, as in the Shiite chronicles, the debauchery of the Abbasid caliph serves as a counterpoint to the dignity and wisdom displayed by the Imam, who is shown in a sequence of crosscut scenes set in Medina. There, he urges his followers to forbear from rebellion and to spare the blood of

46. In his *Ḥayāh siyāsiyya*. See further Cooperson 2000, 100–4.
47. El-Hibri 1999, 59–94.

fellow Muslims. In the Twelver biographies, al-Riḍā comes off as an oddly unreal figure, not only because of the supernatural abilities ascribed to him, but also because he is almost always speaking rather than acting. The same is true in *Velāyat-e ʿEshgh*, where his head is obscured by a superimposed ball of light and the rest of his body covered by a flowing white robe. He speaks slowly and with an unusually deep voice, and the numinous experience of encountering him firsthand is conveyed by the use of a slowly rotating camera and a distinct musical theme.

The contrast between al-Amīn and al-Riḍā is complicated, at least at first, by the depiction of al-Maʾmūn as a sober and conscientious leader. In the chronicles, the caliph is depicted even by hostile sources as deeply learned and intellectually adventurous. *Velāyat-e ʿEshgh* embraces this tradition too. But it goes beyond it to offer thoughtfully elaborated readings of his opinions and actions. One striking example is his reaction to al-Amīn's death (Episode 5). After the end of the civil war, al-Maʾmūn was presented with his brother's severed head. The Arabic sources offer conflicting accounts of his reaction, some describing it as mournful (Ibn Abī Ṭāhir 16) and others as cynical (Ṭabarī 8: 507). In the series, the brief passages given in the chronicles are replaced with a dramatic monologue. Descending from his throne, al-Maʾmūn — played by a masterful Moḥammad Ṣādeghī — commands his servants to carry the cloth-draped head, which is resting on a litter, around the audience hall. He then exhorts the Abbasid grandees to bear witness to the sacrifice he has made for the sake of the Muslim community. He will mourn al-Amīn in solitude, he says, because "there is no one dearer than a brother." But the part of him that is caliph will feel no pity. It was, after all, his fate to succeed al-Rashīd, as predicted on the so-called "night of the three caliphs," when al-Hādī died, al-Rashīd ascended the throne, and he (al-Maʾmūn) was born.

This speech borrows two themes from classical Arabic historiography: the trope that kingship has no mercy[48] and the story of the three caliphs.[49] But it uses them in ways the chroniclers do not, and it provides a speculative account of al-Maʾmūn's feelings that goes beyond the terse remarks reported in the sources. This sort of supplementation is, of course, commonplace in historical films. It is also a recurrent phenomenon in Persian classical literature, where characters about whom Arabic sources have little to say become the heroes of extended narratives. In the series, the invention appears to create sympathy for al-Maʾmūn. We know that he will murder al-Riḍā, but it is already clear that he is not the sort of man who can make such

48. See, e.g., Ibn Bābawayh, *ʿUyūn*, 1: 88–93, where al-Rashīd uses it to explain his decision to poison al-Riḍā's father, the imam al-Qāʾim.

49. Al-Jahshiyārī, *al-Wuzarāʾ*, 175.

a decision lightly. Even more pathetically, he may have no choice: just as he was fated to kill his own brother, so too may he be fated to kill the Imam. In that case, he becomes a tragic hero rather than a villain. If, on the other hand, the viewer is meant to understand the speech as a feigned display of grief, it serves another purpose: namely, to show how persuasive a figure the caliph was. At best, the speech performs both functions, leaving the viewer in the same state of uncertainty about the caliph's motives as many observers in the third/ninth century seem to have been.

Al-Maʾmūn (Moḥammad Ṣādeghī) addresses the severed head of his brother al-Amīn. From *Velāyat-e Eshgh*, dir. Mehdī Fakhīmzādeh (Soroush Multimedia Corporation (1996–2000).

In the scenes that immediately follow the caliph's speech, Fakhīmzādeh depicts the events that lead to ʿAlī al-Riḍā's appointment as heir apparent. From messengers who have arrived from the various provinces of the empire, al-Maʾmūn learns of the Alid insurrections in Kufa, Mecca, and the Yemen. He remarks to his vizier, al-Faḍl b. Sahl, that the family of ʿAlī has always commanded the loyalty of Muslims, a matter which al-Faḍl, being a recent convert, cannot be expected to understand. "If I were not the caliph," al-Maʾmūn adds, "I would be fighting under the banner of the Alids myself." Al-Faḍl, played with persuasive humility and craftiness by Akbar Zanjānpur, responds by wondering aloud what would happen if al-Riḍā[50] were to rise against the government. The story then cuts ahead to a scene between

50. The characters usually refer to the Imam as ʿAlī b. Mūsā, but to avoid unnecessary confusion I will continue to refer to him as al-Riḍā.

al-Faḍl and his wife. He explains to her that he has tricked the caliph into thinking that al-Riḍā is a threat and that the only way to deal with him is to bring him to Marv and put him under surveillance. Al-Riḍā, he says, will succeed in usurping al-Maʾmūn. Then, he says, the family of Sahl will dominate the empire, just as the Barmakī family of viziers did under al-Rashīd. This self-congratulatory monologue is interrupted by the sudden arrival of the caliph. Fearing that al-Maʾmūn has discovered his machinations, the vizier is gratified to learn that he has merely decided to their idea a step further. Bringing al-Riḍā to Marv is not enough, says the caliph; instead, the right thing to do is to make him heir apparent. As successor to the throne, al-Riḍā will be unable or unwilling to rebel; and the appointment will pacify the other Alids. When al-Faḍl points out that al-Riḍā is older than the caliph, the latter replies that his heir apparent need not ascend the throne; all he needs to do is accept the position of successor.

Al-Maʾmūn (Moḥammad Ṣādeghī, in the foreground) deliberates with his vizier al-Faḍl b. Sahl (Akbar Zanjānpur). From *Velāyat-e Eshgh*, dir. Mehdī Fakhīmzādeh (Soroush Multimedia Corporation, 1996–2000).

These imagined conversations take into account the known historical facts, including the Alid rebellions and ʿAlī al-Riḍā's seniority to al-Maʾmūn. Fakhīmzādeh's version, according to which al-Faḍl is responsible for bringing al-Riḍā to Marv and al-Maʾmūn is responsible for naming him heir apparent, is not attested in any source. Even so, it deftly integrates the conflicting reports of the chroniclers, some of whom hold the vizier responsible while others name the caliph as the instigator. Meanwhile, it also manages not to stray too far from the standard Twelver account, which claims that the nomination was never a sincere gesture of reconciliation but rather a calculated attempt to discredit the Imam. Nevertheless, Fakhīmzādeh's retelling maintains, even here — halfway through the series — its ambiguity about al-Maʾmūn's motives. The caliph claims with apparent sincerity that he would fight for the Alids himself if he could, but soon afterwards proposes a plan to undermine their resistance.

In *Velāyat-e ʿEshgh*, as in the classical biographies of al-Riḍā, the Imam is reluctant to accept the designation. Eventually, he agrees to do so in order to prevent further bloodshed. In conversation with his disciple Abū al-Ṣalt al-Harawī, he explains that his acceptance has been preordained. He adds that his followers are not to worry about him, as he has some time to live yet. When he dies, he will die in exile and be buried "beside one with the blood of Muslims on his hands," meaning al-Rashīd. In another scene he explains his acceptance by arguing that if Joseph could serve Pharaoh, then he (al-Riḍā) can serve al-Maʾmūn. All of these remarks appear in more or less the same form in Ibn Bābawayh's biography of the Imam (2: 138–40). Also based on the Twelver sources are the scenes in which al-Riḍā becomes the object of fervent devotion during his journey from Medina to Khurasan, as well as the episode in which he defeats Jews, Christians, and Sabeans in a debate organized by al-Maʾmūn in the hope of tripping him up (Ibn Bābawayh 1: 154–78).

Largely invented, on the other hand, is the scene in which God answers the imam's prayers for rain. The gift of *istijābat al-daʿwa* (having one's prayers answered) is attributed to the imams, including al-Riḍā; and there are reports in which he successfully predicts rainstorms (for this and other examples, see Ibn Bābawayh 2: 168–9). But Fakhīmzādeh's version, in which the entire population of Marv gathers in the desert to await the result of the imam's devotion, appears to be the product of the director's imagination. As a piece of invention, it is well calculated: without it, there would be no material proof that al-Riḍā is the man best qualified to lead the community. Less well calculated, however, are the intermittent episodes involving certain followers of the Imam who reject his decision to accept the heir apparency and conspire to assassinate him. There were indeed sectarians who refused to grant al-Riḍā the title of imam, but none, as far as I know, who attempted to do away with him.

In *Velāyat-e ʿEshgh* as in the chronicles, al-Maʾmūn discovers that the Abbasids of Baghdad have established their own caliphate. Blaming his vizier for hiding the truth from him, he orders his court to depart for Baghdad. Along the way, he gives orders for al-Faḍl's assassination. None of the chronicles explicitly blames the caliph for the death of his vizier, but most of them imply that he was responsible. In this respect, Fakhīmzādeh is again faithful to the spirit of the sources. Again, however, he goes beyond them for dramatic effect, in this case inventing a scene based on the premise that al-Faḍl knows he is being sent away to die. Though terrified, the vizier accepts the decision as the only course of action available to his master, whom he himself trained in the harsh necessities of *Realpolitik*. As in the chronicles, he is stabbed to death in a bathhouse, and the caliph's party continues its journey to Baghdad.

In the meantime, it has become increasingly clear that the caliph is also planning to rid himself of his heir apparent. In the closing scene of the series (Episode 10), Fakhīmzādeh allows al-Maʾmūn to explain his decision. Alone with al-Riḍā in a candlelit hall, the caliph accuses him of having acted in bad faith when he accepted the heir apparency. Why, for example, did he encourage the people to weep for him when he left Medina? Al-Riḍā replies that the weeping was justified, since he is indeed going to perish, just as the people feared. Undeterred, al-Maʾmūn continues to level accusations. Why, he asks, did al-Riḍā recite a hadith-report in which God says "Whoever enters my fortress [= the house of ʿAlī] will be spared Hell"? Such talk, he says, can only have been intended to stir up support for the Alids at the expense of the Abbasids. And why did he refuse to have anything to do with the business of government? Provoked, al-Riḍā replies that he never sought the heir apparency, adding that the caliph has no position to offer that would be worthy of him. Indeed, he says, he knew that al-Maʾmūn intended only to use him as a means to confer legitimacy upon himself. The caliph, grimly resolved to do away with al-Riḍā, remarks that he is through with making mistakes. "No, you're not," replies the Imam, evidently meaning that by murdering him, al-Maʾmūn will damn his own soul to Hell. Holding out a cup of poison, the agitated caliph commands the Imam to drink it. "Not by my own hand," says al-Riḍā. Ordering his guards to raise their weapons, al-Maʾmūn commands him again, adding that he does not wish to shed the blood of one of the Prophet's descendants. "Drink," he cries out, "I can bear no more!" Ignoring him, al-Riḍā gazes heavenward and addresses his own dead father, who, he says, "drank from the same cup" (referring to Mūsā al-Kāẓim, who was reportedly poisoned by al-Rashīd). "Now I will greet the Prophet," he says. "Father, take my hand!" He drinks and shortly thereafter dies.[51]

51. This description is based on the DVD acquired directly from the production company. The versions of the episode available on YouTube and AnwarNet cut almost immediately from al-Maʾmūn's offering of the cup to the Imam's death.

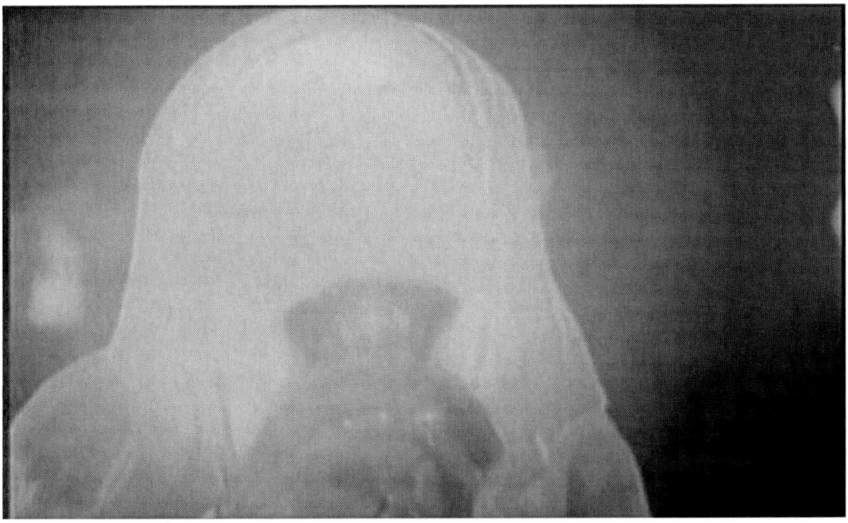

The imam 'Alī al-Riḍā, his face concealed by a halo, drinks the poison given him by al-Ma'mūn. From *Velāyat-e Eshgh*, dir. Mehdī Fakhīmzādeh (Soroush Multimedia Corporation, 1996–2000).

In this final scene, Fakhīmzādeh again remains within the broad guidelines drawn by tradition, which insists that the caliph, having been insincere all along, poisoned the Imam. Again, however, the filmmaker offers a more persuasive account of the event than any of the chroniclers. The caliph of the series appears to believe that the Imam has wronged him; his own bad faith notwithstanding, his sense of grievance appears to be genuine. Most cleverly, Fakhīmzādeh fills out this depiction of al-Ma'mūn with information that appears in other contexts in the classical sources. According to his biographers, al-Riḍā did predict that he would die in exile, he did recite Alid hadith while traveling through Nishapur, and he did accept the heir apparency only on condition that he play no part in government (Ibn Bābawayh 2:138–40; 154–78; 134 and 180–3). None of the sources, however, depicts al-Ma'mūn as resenting any one of these actions in particular, or using them to justify his murder of al-Riḍā. Using the information available to him, Fakhīmzādeh constructs a psychologically plausible account of the caliph's motives — at least as far as modern viewers are concerned.[52] Critical, too, is Ṣādeghī's interpretation of the role. In the final scene, al-Ma'mūn appears

52. As Prof. Afsaneh Najmabadi notes in her comments on a draft of this paper, making a character plausible to modern viewers may require manipulations that make the production less plausible as history.

grimly determined to do something he knows he will regret. The performance thus lends retrospective weight to the possibility that the caliph is, after all, fated to murder the Imam.[53]

For historians, of course, Fakhīmzādeh's account is no more believable as an account of the past than the Twelver hagiographies upon which it is based. But, like the hagiographies, it represents a creative manipulation of the available facts, and as such, is no less deserving of a critical reading than the work of Ibn Bābawayh. Of course, such a critical reading should do more than compare Fakhīmzādeh to his sources. Among other things, it should read the series in light of the history of the genre of which it forms a part, and in light of the historical moment at which it was produced. As I confessed at the outset, I am not qualified to embark on either of these inquiries. I can, nevertheless, offer a few remarks, again from the perspective of a classical Arabist interested in questions of historical representation.

In many respects, as I have tried to show, Fakhīmzādeh's retelling is true to the spirit of the sources. In other respects, however, the filmmaker strays quite far afield. For example, he introduces four characters, two men and two women, who play crucial roles in foiling the plots against al-Riḍā. These characters, as well as the plots they foil, are entirely invented. Here it seems that Fakhīmzādeh is faithful not to the sources but to a tradition of historical fiction that goes back to Sir Walter Scott (d. 1832). In Scott's historical novels, the great men of history are rarely seen; instead, the protagonists are invented characters whose adventures are meant to suggest the effects of historical change among ordinary people.[54] This approach to historical fiction may have come to Iran through the translations of the Arabic historical novels of Jurjī Zaydān (d. 1914), who was a great admirer of Scott.[55] As deployed by Fakhīmzādeh, the ordinary-people device serves the additional purpose of creating roles for women. Given, however, their skill in horseback riding and hand-to-hand combat, Fakhīmzādeh's two invented female characters would appear to be modeled not on the Arabic sources but on the television character Xena, the Warrior Princess (1995–2001).

Despite its many deviations from the sources, *Velāyat-e ʿEshgh* is also noteworthy for the mistakes it does not make. Notably, it avoids back-projecting the conflict between the Sunnah and the Shīʿah. In the third/ninth century, neither group existed in the modern sense of the term. The Shīʿah,

53. The Twelver accounts contain some precedent for seeing the caliph as a tragic victim (see, e.g., Ibn Bābawayh, *ʿUyūn*, 2: 249) although Twelver theologians denied predestination (see Cooperson 2000, 98).

54. Lukács 1962, 19–88; Grindon 1994, 5–8; and Davis 2000, 6.

55. For a humorous testament to Zaydān's popularity in Iran, see Pezeshkzād's *Māshāllāh Khān*, in which a bank guard obsessed with the Lebanese author's historical novels is transported back in time to the age of al-Rashīd (I thank Mahsa Maleki for this reference).

in the sense of "partisans of ʿAlī," were certainly a recognizable group, but they by no means agreed on the identity of their imams, much less on the complex of theological and legal notions that came to characterize the Twelver sect of later times. The Sunnah, meanwhile, were beginning to emerge in the form of a community of quietist, hadith-minded Muslims who rejected the notion of the imamate and in some cases hoped for the restoration of the Umayyad caliphate. Far from being a "Sunni caliph," al-Maʾmūn was a bitter enemy of the hadith-minded literalists. He was also notoriously sympathetic to many positions associated with the Shīʿah of ʿAlī. The series, of course, imagines Shiism as being largely the same then as it is today (with the important difference that the earthly imamate had not yet come to an end). Even so, it depicts al-Maʾmūn as sympathetic to ʿAlid causes, and says nothing at all about Sunnism.

The series also avoids a simpleminded equation between Shiism and Iranian ethnicity, not to mention the temptation to make all the villains Arabs. As it happens, recent scholarship has credibly revived the old Orientalist ideas that the recurrent conflict between Iraq and Khurasan was at least in part a conflict between Arabs and Persians, and that Shiism had a special appeal to non-Arab Muslims.[56] At the same time, the old-fashioned notion of Arabs vs. Persians has been considerably complicated by the increased attention being paid to those whose status was somewhere in between, as well as to those who belonged to other ethnic groups. I do not for a moment imagine that Fakhīmzādeh is aware of recent scholarship on these matters. Most likely, his avoidance of ethnic and sectarian terms arises from political considerations: for example, an unwillingness to offend the many Iranian citizens who are Sunnis or Arabs. But, whatever the reason, the series tends to replicate the effect of the original sources by mentioning ethnic origin only in passing, and by assuming no necessary relationship between ethnicity and sect.[57] Whether this egalitarian tone makes the series more plausible, or less so, to Iranian viewers is a matter that remains to be investigated.

Parallel Realities

Being a nitpicking classical Arabist, I could go on and on keeping score for and against the film. Pursued in moderation, such exercises do produce insights into the nature of historical representation. But, as I suggested in the introduction, an overly literal investigation of historical accuracy is doomed to incoherence. There are two reasons why. First, as we have seen, no historical film can be true to its sources, simply because written accounts cannot

56. Crone 2004, 84–6.

57. Cf. Davis 2000, 28–40, where we learn what Stanley Kubrick got right — accidentally or otherwise — in *Spartacus*.

be translated directly into a visual narrative medium. Second, this series, like almost all historical films that are specifically religious in character, was never intended to be historically accurate, if by "historically accurate" we mean faithful to all the available information on the period in which the events it depicts reportedly took place. In the case of *Velāyet-e ʿEshgh*, the reason for this deliberate inaccuracy seems to be the conviction that the historical sources cannot be trusted to tell the real story, at least not from a Twelver Shiite point of view.

As I confessed at the outset, I have not been able to find any statements about the series by Fakhīmzādeh himself. I have, however, learned of a document of related interest: a long interview with Shahreyār Boḥrānī, who has directed a historical series about Mary, the mother of Jesus, and was working on a series about the Imam Ḥusayn until that project was suspended. In an interview with *Kayhān* posted on the Soroush production company website, Boḥrānī states flatly that the historical sources on Jesus are largely worthless. The reason, he says, is that the chroniclers of the period were concerned with glorifying kings, not prophets. Asked whether the same is true of Muslim historiography, he replies that the sources are better, but nevertheless contain "ambiguities or distortions." As a result, he says, there is no point in trying to make historical films authentic in the conventional sense (*kollan aṣālat dādan be-tārīkh barāye mā maṭraḥ nīst*). Instead, he says, the only way to proceed is to depict the prophets and imams as we know them to have been: that is, in such a way as to highlight their exemplary character. The result may not agree with the history books, but it will be more faithful to reality.[58]

In the case of *Velāyat-e ʿEshgh*, which seems to have been produced with similar aims in mind, the result is something one might call a parallel reality. In this parallel reality, al-Maʾmūn's *wilāyatu l-ʿahd* (heir apparency) becomes al-Riḍā's *velāyato l-ʿeshgh* (reign of love). The world is conveniently divided into those who acknowledge his imamate and those who do not, and all of the latter eventually reveal themselves to be villains. This world is not the world of the historical sources, including the Shiite ones, which acknowledge in their own way the difficulty of correctly identifying the imam. Rather, the series presents a rewriting or translation of that world into the idiom of post-classical Twelver ideology.

Such a rewriting is of course nothing new: any historical film based on religiously significant events does the same thing. One element, nevertheless, seems unusual: namely, the visual signs that alert us to the fact that we are seeing a parallel reality, not a reconstruction of historical events. The most striking of these signs is the appearance of the Imam. Whenever he

58. http://www.soroush-media.com/en/?action=artists&c=06 (I thank Mahsa Maleki for this reference).

appears on the screen, his head is hidden behind a penumbra of light. I do not think that the filmmakers want us to believe that in the real world of the early ninth century, this halo was visible to al-Riḍā's contemporaries. If it had been, they would have had little trouble accepting him as imam. Therefore, we must conclude that the halo exists only in parallel reality, that is, in that version of the ninth century that has been constructed for us with the appropriate labels attached. This parallel reality is not meant to be mistaken for the real thing; rather, it is meant to be accepted as a more faithful representation of ultimate reality than the real thing could ever be, especially since the real thing has been distorted beyond recovery by the historians.

The kind of parallel reality presented in *Velāyat-e ʿEshgh* may not be unique, but it clearly represents a historical sensibility different from the one on display in Mel Gibson's *The Passion of the Christ* (2004). Unlike Fakhīmzādeh, Gibson begins with the premise that if past reality can be reconstructed in sufficient detail, the religious message will simply manifest itself. On this basis, it seems, he decided to have all of his actors speak in Latin or Aramaic, and to devote the bulk of the film to a hyperrealistic depiction of the bodily sufferings of Christ. In *Velāyat-e ʿEshgh*, by contrast, the actors speak modern literary Persian, not reconstructed facsimiles of third/ninth-century Arabic and Iranian dialects; and the Imam's death occupies only minutes of screen time. For Fakhīmzādeh, religious truth is more important than original languages. Similarly, the Imam's call to piety and justice is more significant than the physiological circumstances of his death.

At this point the reader may object that the halo around al-Riḍā's head is not the result of a directorial decision; rather, it appears in compliance with a regulation that forbids the depiction of the features of the imams. Yet it is precisely this irruption that permits a reading of the series in its own historical context. To the extent that it bears the visible trace of official intervention, Fakhīmzādeh's parallel reality may be understood as a correlate of the one that the state seeks to impose as the image of itself. In *Velāyat-e ʿEshgh*, the viewer is asked to overlook historical reality in favor of an idealized reality where the doctrines of Shiism are as plain as the halo that surrounds the imam. By implication, indeed, the doctrines of Shiism are perfectly plain *only* in such a world. In similar fashion, the Islamic Republic, which sponsors historical television productions such as *Velāyat-e ʿEshgh*, seeks to persuade its citizens that it and it alone enacts the ideals of piety and justice. To succeed in this task, it must ask its citizens to look beyond the historical reality of authoritarianism and corruption to an ultimate reality where *velāyatu l-faghīh* is revealed as *velāyat-e ʿeshgh*. Unfortunately, as the series demonstrates, such an equivalence can be asserted only within a carefully manipulated space of historical imagination.

References

Akbarpur, Ḥabībollāh (1383/2004–5), *Zeyāratgāhhā va-seyātgāhhā-ye Mashhad va-ḥome*. Ketābkhāneh-ye Mellī-ye Īrān.

Amīn, Ḥasan al- (1995), *Al-Riḍā wa-l-Maʾmūn wa-wilāyat al-ʿahd, wa-ṣafaḥāt min al-taʾrīkh al-ʿAbbāsī,* Beirut.

Amīn, Muḥsin al- (1380/1960), *Aʿyan al-Shīʿa*, 3rd. ed., 17 vols., Beirut.

Arazi, Albert and ʿAmikam El'ad (1987 and 1988), "'L'Epître à l'armée': al-Maʾmūn et la seconde daʿwa," *Studia Islamica* 66: 27–70 and 67: 29–73.

Bayhom-Daou, Tamima (2008), "Al-Maʾmūn's Alleged Apocalyptic Beliefs: A reconsideration of the evidence," *Bulletin of the School of Oriental and African Studies* 71 (1): 1–24.

Boḥrānī, Shahreyār (n.d.), interview at *http://www.soroush-media.com/en/?action=artists&c=06*

Cooperson, Michael (2000), *Classical Arabic Biography. The Heirs of the prophets in the age of al-Maʾmūn*, Cambridge.

—— (2005), *Al-Maʾmūn*, Oxford.

Crone, Patricia (1989), "On the Meaning of the ʿAbbasid Call to al-Riḍā," in: C. E. Bosworth, C. Issawi, R. Savory, & A. L. Udovitch (eds.), *The Islamic World from Classical to Modern Times. Essays in honor of Bernard Lewis*, Princeton, 95–111.

—— (2004), *God's Rule: Government and Islam. Six Centuries of Medieval Islamic Political Thought*, New York.

Crone, Patricia, and Martin Hinds (1986), *God's Caliph: Religious authority in the first centuries of Islam*, University of Cambridge Oriental Publications No. 37, Cambridge.

Davis, Natalie Zemon (2000), *Slaves on Screen: Film and Historical Vision*, Harvard.

El-Hibri, Tayeb (1992), "Hārūn Al-Rashīd and the Mecca Protocol of 802: A plan for division or succession?" *International Journal of Middle East Studies* 24: 461–80.

—— (1994), *The Reign of the Abbasid Caliph al-Maʾmūn (811–833): The quest for power and the crisis of legitimacy*, unpublished Columbia University dissertation.

—— (1999), *Reinterpreting Islamic Historiography. Hārūn al-Rashīd and the Narrative of the ʿAbbasid caliphate,* Cambridge.

Ess, Josef van (1991–97), *Theologie und Gesellschaft im 2. und 3. Jahrhundert Hidschra. Eine Geschichte des religiösen Denkens im frühen Islam,* 6 vols., Berlin and New York.

Fakhīmzādeh, Mehdī (writer and director, 1996–2000), *Velāyat-e ʿEshgh*, Tehran.

Gabrieli, Francesco (1929), *Al-Maʾmūn e gli ʿAlidi.* Leipzig.

Grindon, Leger (1994), *Shadows on the Past: Studies in the Historical Fiction Film*, Philadelphia.

Ibn Abī Ṭāhir Ṭayfūr (1388/1968), *Kitāb Baghdād*, published as *Baghdād fī taʾrīkh al-khilāfa al-ʿAbbasīya.* Baghdad.

Ibn Bābawayh al-Qummī (1377/1957–58), *'Uyūn akhbār al-Riḍā,* ed. Mahdī al-Ḥusaynī al-Lājavardī, Qum.

Ibn al-Jawzī (1412/1992), *al-Muntaẓam fī ta'rīkh al-mulūk wa-l-umam,* ed. Muḥammad 'Abd al-Qādir 'Aṭā, Muṣṭafā 'Abd al-Qādir 'Aṭā, and Nu'aym Zarzūr, 18 vols., Beirut.

al-Irbilī, 'Alī b. 'Īsā (1381/1962), *Kashf al-ghumma fī ma'rifat al-a'imma,* ed. I. al-Miyānjī, 3 vols., Tabriz.

al-Iṣfahānī, Abū al-Faraj (1385/1965), *Maqātil al-Ṭālibīyīn.* ed. Kāẓim al-Muẓaffar, 2nd. ed., Najaf.

Jafri, S. H. M. (1979), *The Origins and Development of Shi'i Islam,* London and New York.

al-Jahshiyarī (1401/1980), *al-Wuzarā' wa-l-kuttāb*, ed. Muṣṭafā al-Saqqā, Ibrāhīm al-Abyārī, and 'Abd al-Ḥāfiz Shalabī, 2nd. ed., Cairo.

Kennedy, Hugh (1981), *The Early Abbasid Caliphate: A political history,* London.

Kimber, R. A (1986), "Hārūn al-Rashīd's Meccan Settlement of AH 186/AD 802," *Occasional Papers of the School of Abbasid Studies* 1: 55–75.

Kohlberg, Etan (1979), "From Imāmīya to Ithnā 'Asharīya," *Bulletin of the School of Oriental and African Studies* 39: 521–34.

—— (1988), "Imam and Community in the Pre-*ghayba* Period," in: Said Amir Arjomand (ed.), *Authority and Political Culture in Shi'ism,* Albany, 25–53.

al-Kulaynī (1377–81/1957–61), *Uṣūl min al-Kāfī,* ed. 'Alī Akbar al-Ghaffārī, 8 vols., Tehran.

Lukács, Georg (1962), *The Historical Novel,* tr. Hannah and Stanley Mitchell, Lincoln.

Madelung, Wilferd (1965), *Der Imām al-Qāsim ibn Ibrāhīm und die Glaubenslehre der Zaiditen,* Studien zur Sprache, Geschichte, und Kultur des islamischen Orients, New Series 1, Berlin.

—— (1981), "New Documents Concerning al-Ma'mūn, al-Faḍl b. Sahl and 'Alī al-Riḍā," in: *Studia Arabica et Islamica. Festschrift for Iḥsān 'Abbās on his sixtieth birthday*, ed. Wadad al-Qadi, Beirut, 333–346.

al-Mas'udī (n.d), *Murūj al-dhahab wa-ma'ādin al-jawhar*, ed. Muḥyī al-Dīn 'Abd al-Ḥamīd, 4 vols., Beirut.

Modarressi, Hossein (1993), *Crisis and Consolidation in the Formative Period of Shiite Islam. Abū Ja'far ibn Qiba al-Razī and His Contribution to Imamite Shiite Thought,* Princeton.

Menard, M. C. Barbier de (1869), "Ibrahim fils de Mehdi," in *Journal Asiatique* 13: 201–342.

Momen, Moojan (1985), *An Introduction to Shi'i Islam,* New Haven.

al-Mufīd, al-Shaykh (1364/1945), *Sharḥ 'aqā'id al-Ṣadūq, aw taṣḥīḥ al-i'tiqād*, ed. al-Ḥājj 'Abbāsqulī, Tabriz (printed in one volume with Mufīd, *Awā'il*).

——(1364/1945), *Awā'il al-maqālāt fī l-madhāhib al-mukhtārāt,* ed. Faḍl al-Zanjānī, Tabriz.

Nagel, Tilman (1975), *Rechtleitung und Kalifat. Versuch über eine Grundfrage der islamischen Geschichte,* Studien zum Minderheitenproblem im Islam 2, Bonn.
Nawas, John A. (1996), "A Psychoanalytic View of Some Oddities in the Behavior of the ʿAbbasid Caliph al-Maʾmūn," *Sharqiyyat* 8: 1: 69–81.
Pezeshkzād, Īraj (n. d.), *Māshāllāh Khān dar bargāh-e Hārūn ul-Rashīd*, Tehran [?].
al-Qazwīnī (1998), *Āthār al-bilād wa-akhbār al-ʿibād*, Beirut.
Rosenstone, Robert (1995), *Visions of the Past. The Challenge of Film to Our Idea of History,* Harvard.
—— (2002), "Does a Filmic Writing of History Exist?" (review of Davis, *Slaves*), in *History and Theory, Theme Issue* 41: 134–44.
Saunders, J. J. (1965), *A History of Medieval Islam*, London.
Sourdel, Dominique (1959–60), *Le vizirat abbaside de 749 à 936 (132 à 324 de l'Hégire),* 2 vols., Damascus.
—— (1962), "La politique religieuse du caliph ʿabbaside al-Maʾmūn," *Revue des études islamiques* 20: 27–48.
Strothmann, R. (1911) "Die Literatur der Zaiditen (Schluß)," *Der Islam* 2: 49–78.
al-Ṭabarī (1979), *Taʾrīkh al-rusul wa-l-mulūk*, ed. Muḥammad Abū al-Faḍl Ibrāhīm, 3rd ed., 10 vols., Cairo.
Tor, D. G. (2001), "An Historiographical Re-examination of the Appointment and Death of ʿAlī al-Riḍā," *Der Islam* 78 (1): 103–28.
al-ʿUṭāridī, ʿAzīz Allāh (1413/1993), *Musnad al-Imām al-Riḍā*, 2 vols., Beirut.
al-Yaʿqūbī (1883), *Taʾrīkh al-Yaʿqūbī*, 2 vols., ed. M. Th. Houtsma, Leiden.
Yücesoy, Hayrettin (2009), *Messianic Beliefs and Imperial Politics in Medieval Islam: The ʿAbbāsid Caliphate in the Early Ninth Century*, Columbia, South Carolina.

Contributors

Michael Cooperson received his Ph.D. from Harvard in 1994, and has been Professor of Arabic Language and Literature at UCLA since 1995. He has also taught at Dartmouth College, the School of Arabic at Middlebury College, and Stanford University. He is the author of *Classical Arabic Biography: The Heirs of the Prophets in the Age of al-Maʾmūn* (Cambridge: Cambridge University Press, 2000); a co-author, with the RRAALL group, of *Interpreting the Self: Autobiography in the Arabic Literary Tradition* (Berkeley: University of California Press, 2001); co-editor, with Shawkat Toorawa, of *The Dictionary of Literary Biography: Arabic Literary Culture, 500–915* (Detroit: Thomson Gale, 2005); and author of *Al-Maʾmūn* (Oxford: Oneworld, 2005), a biography of the caliph. He is also the translator of Abdelfattah Kilito's *The Author and His Doubles: Essays on Classical Arabic Culture* (Syracuse: Syracuse University Press, 2001) and Khairy Shalaby's *Voyages of the Pickle and Sweet Vendor* (forthcoming). His interests include the cultural history of the early Abbasid caliphate and time travel as a literary device.

Stephen F. Dale, Professor of Islamic and South Asian History at the Ohio State University, received his Ph.D. from the University of California at Berkeley. His research interests lie in the fields of Indo-Muslim and Central Asian history. His publications include *Islamic Society on the South Asian Frontier: The Māppilas of Malabar 1498–1922* (Oxford: Clarendon, 1980); *Indian Merchants and Eurasian Trade, 1600–1750* (Cambridge: Cambridge University Press, 1994); *The Garden of the Eight Paradises: Bābur and the Culture of Empire in Central Asia, Afghanistan and India (1483–1530)* (Leiden and Boston: Brill, 2004); and *The Muslim Empires of the Ottomans, Safavids and Mughals* (Cambridge: Cambridge University Press, 2010).

Olga Merck Davidson received her Ph.D. from Princeton University and her B.A. from Boston University. She is Research Fellow in the Institute for the Study of Muslim Society and Civilizations at Boston University, as well as Founder and Chairman of the Board of Trustees of the Ilex Foundation. She is the author of *Poet and Hero in the Persian Book of Kings* (Ithaca: Cornell University Press, 1994, 2nd ed., 2004) and *Comparative Literature and Classical Persian Poetics: Seven Essays* (Costa Mesa: Mazda Press, 2000), both of which have been translated into Persian, as well as numerous articles, including "Genre and Occasion in the *Rubāʿiyyāt* of ʿUmar Khayyām," in: *Writers and Rulers: Perspectives on Their Relationship from Abbasid to Safavid Times*, ed. B. Gruendler and L. Marlow (Wiesbaden: Reichert Verlag, 2004), 133–47; "Women's Lamentations as Protest in the 'Shāhnāma'," in: *Women in the Medieval Islamic World*, ed. G. R. G. Hambly (New York: St. Martin's

Press, 1998), 131–46, and "The Dream as a Narrative Device in the *Shāhnāma*," in: *Dreaming across Boundaries: The Interpretation of Dreams in Islamic Lands*, ed. L. Marlow (Boston: Ilex Foundation and Washington, DC: Center for Hellenic Studies, 2008), 131–41.

Mohammad Jafar Mahallati is Presidential Scholar in Islamic Studies in the Department of Religion, Oberlin College. He received his Ph.D. in Islamic Studies from McGill University. He served as Ambassador to the United Nations from 1987–1989, a period that coincided with the peak of the eight-year long Iran-Iraq War, and he was instrumental in bringing peace between the two countries. Mahallati has also taught at Columbia, Princeton, Yale, and Georgetown since 1991. He was the recipient of the Harvard Fellowship for Persian Studies in 2005–2006. He has also served as senior scholar and affiliate with several think tanks, including the Middle East Institute, the Center for Strategic and International Affairs, Search for Common Ground, and the Annual University of Colorado Conference on World Affairs (since 2004). Recent publications include "The Significance of Dreams and Dream Interpretation in the Qurʾan: Two Sufi Commentaries on *Sūrat Yūsuf*," in: *Dreaming across Boundaries: The Interpretation of Dreams in Islamic Lands*, ed. L. Marlow (Boston: Ilex Foundation and Washington, DC: Center for Hellenic Studies, 2008), 153–78. In his research and writing, Mahallati draws on several classical and modern academic disciplines as well as his diplomatic experience. His current research interests include the ethics of war, and friendship in Muslim cultures.

Louise Marlow is Director of Middle Eastern Studies at Wellesley College and a specialist in the history of Muslim societies of the tenth-thirteenth centuries and classical Arabic and Persian prose literature of the same period. Her recent publications include "Surveying recent literature on the Arabic and Persian mirrors for princes genre," *History Compass* VII, Issue 2 (2009), 523–38, as well as two edited volumes: with Beatrice Gruendler, *Writers and Rulers: Perspectives on Their Relationship from Abbasid to Safavid Times* (Wiesbaden: Reichert Verlag, 2004), and *Dreaming across Boundaries: The Interpretation of Dreams in Islamic Lands* (Boston: Ilex Foundation and Washington, DC: Center for Hellenic Studies, 2008).

Devin J. Stewart received a B.A. in Near Eastern Studies from Princeton University in 1984 and earned a Ph.D. in Arabic and Islamic Studies from the University of Pennsylvania in 1991. He has been teaching at Emory in the Department of Middle Eastern and South Asian Studies since 1990. His research has focused on Shiite Islam, the Qur'an, Islamic law and legal education, the Moriscos of Spain, and Arabic dialectology. Recent publications include: "The Identity of 'the Mufti of Oran': Abū al-ʿAbbās Aḥmad b. Abī Jumʿah al-Maghrāwī al-Wahrānī (d. 917/1511)," *Al-Qantara: Revista de Estudios Árabes* 27.2 (2006): 265–

301; "The Structure of the *Fihrist*: Ibn al-Nadīm as a Historian of Islamic Law and Theology," *International Journal of Middle East Studies* 39 (2007): 369–87; "The Students' Representative in the Law Colleges of Fourteenth-Century Damascus," *Islamic Law and Society* 15.2 (2008): 185–218; "The Ottoman Execution of Zayn al-Dīn al-ʿĀmilī," *Die Welt des Islams* 48 (2008): 289–347; "The *Maqāmāt* of Aḥmad b. Abī Bakr al-Rāzī al-Ḥanafī and the Ideology of the Counter-Crusade in Twelfth-Century Syria," *Middle Eastern Literatures* 11.2 (2008): 211–32; "Ibn al-Nadīm's Ismāʿīlī Contacts," *Journal of the Royal Asiatic Society*, Series 3, 19.1 (2008): 21–40; "Polemics and Patronage in Safavid Iran: The Debate on Friday Prayer during the Reign of Shah Tahmasb," *Bulletin of the School of Oriental and African Studies* 72.3 (2009): 425–57; and "Poetic License in the Qurʾan: Ibn al-Ṣāʾigh al-Ḥanafī's *Iḥkām al-rāy fī aḥkām al-āy*," *Journal of Qurʾanic Studies* 11.1 (2009): 1–54.

Maria Szuppe (Ph.D. Sorbonne Nouvelle, 1991) is Research Fellow at the Centre National de la Recherche Scientifique (CNRS), Paris, with the "Mondes iranien et indien" research group. In 1997–8, she acted as Scientific Secretary at the Institut Français d'Études sur l'Asie Centrale, Tashkent (Uzbekistan). She was Visiting Scholar at the Oriental Faculty, University of Cambridge (1992–3), and at the Institute for Languages and Cultures of Asia and Africa, Tokyo University of Foreign Studies (2009). Her main field of research is the late medieval and early modern history and culture of Iranian societies, especially during the Timurid, Safavid, and Uzbek periods (15th–18th centuries). Her book *Entre Timourides, Uzbeks et Safavides: questions de l'histoire politique et sociale de Hérat dans la première moitié du XVIe siècle* (Cahiers de Studia Iranica, 12, Paris, 1992), was followed by a series of articles on women in the Safavid period, including "La participation des femmes de la famille royale à l'exercice du pouvoir en Iran safavide au XVIe siècle" (*Studia Iranica* 23/2, 1994, and 24/1, 1995), and "Status, Knowledge and Politics: Women in Sixteenth-Century Safavid Iran," in: *Women in Iran, I : From the Rise of Islam to 1800*, ed. L. Beck and G. Nashat (University of Illinois Press, 2003). Her recent publications include, with Bakhtyar Babajanov, *Les inscriptions persanes de Chār Bakr, nécropole familiale des* khwāja *Jūybārī près de Boukhara* (Corpus Inscriptionum Iranicarum IV, vol. XXXI. London: SOAS, 2002), and several articles on the history of written culture, such as "Circulation des lettrés et cercles littéraires: entre Asie centrale, Iran et Inde du nord" (*Annales. Histoire, Sciences sociales*, 59/5–6, 2004), and "Notes sur l'historiographie indo-persane: une 'chronique' en chronogrammes de 'Abdallâh Kâboli (*ca.* 990/1582)" (*Eurasian Studies* V/1–2, 2006). She edited the volume *L'héritage timouride: Iran, Asie centrale, Inde, XVe–XVIIIe siècles* (Cahiers d'Asie Centrale, 3–4, Tashkent - Aix-en-Provence, 1997) and, with Francis Richard, *Écrit et culture en Asie centrale et dans le monde turco-iranien, X^e^–XIXe s. / Writing and Culture in Central Asia and the Turko-Iranian World, 10th–19th c.* (Cahiers de Studia Iranica, 40, Paris, 2009).

Index